Jorge Iber, *series editor*

Also in the series

Becoming Iron Men: The Story of the 1963 Loyola Ramblers, by Lew Freedman

Our White Boy, by Jerry Craft, with Kathleen Sullivan

More Than Just Peloteros: Sport and U.S. Latino Communities, edited by Jorge Iber

Playing in Shadows: Texas and Negro League Baseball, by Rob Fink

Remembering Bulldog Turner: Unsung Monster of the Midway, by Michael Barr

Shooting for the Record: Adolph Toepperwein, Tom Frye, and Sharpshooting's Forgotten Controversy, by Tim Price

West Texas Middleweight: The Story of LaVern Roach, by Frank Sikes

Wil the Thrill: The Untold Story of Wilbert Montgomery, by Edward J. Robinson

BAUGH TO BRADY

THE EVOLUTION OF THE FORWARD PASS

Lew Freedman

Texas Tech University Press

This book is typeset in Amasis. The paper used in this book meets the minimum requirements of ANSI/NISO Z39.48-1992 (R1997). ♾

Designed by Kasey McBeath
Cover photograph courtesy the Texas Tech University Southwest Collections / Special Collections Library

Library of Congress Cataloging-in-Publication Data

Names: Freedman, Lew, author.
Title: Baugh to Brady : the evolution of the forward pass / Lew Freedman.
Description: Lubbock, Texas : Texas Tech University Press, 2018. | Series: Sport in the American West | Includes bibliographical references and index.
Identifiers: LCCN 2017038954 (print) | LCCN 2017054047 (ebook) | ISBN 9781682830222 (ebook) | ISBN 9781682830215 (hardcover : alk. paper)
Subjects: LCSH: Passing (Football)—History. | Quarterbacking—History. | Quarterbacks (Football players)—United States—Biography. | National Football League—History.
Classification: LCC GV951.5 (ebook) | LCC GV951.5 .F74 2018 (print) | DDC 796.332/25—dc23
LC record available at https://lccn.loc.gov/2017038954.

18 19 20 21 22 23 24 25 26 / 9 8 7 6 5 4 3 2 1

Texas Tech University Press
Box 41037 | Lubbock, Texas 79409-1037 USA
800.832.4042 | ttup@ttu.edu | www.ttupress.org

Contents

ILLUSTRATIONS

INTRODUCTION

For the young football fan who believes that the passing game began when Peyton Manning and Tom Brady entered the National Football League, it should be instructive to learn that trying to obtain first downs and touchdowns by throwing the ball forward beyond the line of scrimmage was flat-out illegal before 1906.

The term "forward pass," which is rarely used at all in the modern era, was coined to differentiate it from the lateral. Laterals are what are generally called "pitchouts" today, and the word describes a ball carrier heaving the ball either behind or sideways to a teammate.

When the colleges first began playing football in the nineteenth century, offensive football was all about running the ball—tucking it under an arm and plunging ahead. Once in a while someone would dream up a play that called for advancing the ball with a tricky lateral toss.

To a large extent early football play resembled trench warfare during World War I. While one was a sport and the other deadly earnest killing, football of the late nineteenth century and into the first several years of the twentieth century was a brutal activity.

Teams competed without helmets. The offensive and defensive lines were stacked against one another, each surging forward with all of their strength when a play began.

By 1904 college football was a far more dangerous game than either boxing or today's Ultimate Fighting Championship circuit. Compared to college football, those modern-day sports are often termed barbaric, but really they are Ping-Pong compared to college football back then.

The death rate—note, not the injury rate—was so high the sport faced a crisis, with pleas for banning college football reaching to the White House. Although

President Theodore Roosevelt is remembered and hailed for many achievements, including establishing the US Forest Service and greatly expanding the National Parks list, lesser publicized a century later is the role the sporting president played in rescuing college football.

During the 1904 season, 18 players had been killed on the gridiron and another 159 had been classified as seriously injured. On October 8, 1905, Roosevelt convened a White House summit involving the head coaches of Harvard, Princeton, and Yale, the Ivy League powers in the forefront of the sport at the time. The goal was to revamp the sport, make it safer, and prevent its elimination by saving it from itself.

Roosevelt's son, Teddy, Jr., was playing for the Harvard freshman team. The president was always a fan of the game, but he recognized it could not continue in the same vein, so overwhelmed by risk. The discussions were preliminary, but when things did not change during the 1905 season, with 19 additional players being killed on the field and 137 more serious injuries recorded, Roosevelt gathered a second influential college football group at the White House in December 1905 and ordered them to make changes in the sport.

The president had always enjoyed life in the outdoors—hunting, fishing, working on ranches, being in the wild. He believed that some rough experiences formed character. He liked football, but it was obvious that things had gone too far. Roosevelt made it clear the future of the sport was in jeopardy if young college men continued becoming casualties at such a high rate.

Making the forward pass legal was one of the rules approved to open up the game. One season later, in 1906, passing became legal in football. It took decades for coaches and players to truly realize the potency of the weapon, to perfect sophisticated formations that made it seem as if the best passers could not be stopped.

The evolution of the pass as we know it began in September 1906 in a game featuring St. Louis University, led by Coach Eddie Cochems. He was essentially the founding father of the forward pass, though he is certainly not as well-remembered today as a founding father of the nation.

But Cochems begat Knute Rockne, who begat Benny Friedman, who begat Arnie Herber, Cecil Isbell, Sammy Baugh, Sid Luckman, and onward, through Johnny Unitas and Joe Namath, to the modern era.

The football itself changed in shape from a roundish ball to a more streamlined, aerodynamic one, making it easier to wrap the hand around it, grasp control of it, and throw it farther.

As the twentieth century progressed, the pass on the football field made heroes and celebrities of quarterbacks. In the past, despite the respect that came with the leadership role, the quarterback was merely one of eleven men on the field for the offense.

The quarterback then morphed into a field general, the leader of the squad, just as a general was the leader of troops. He knew when to hold 'em and he knew when to fold 'em. He knew when to throw the bomb, the deep pass, and mix in the short passes and give running backs a turn lugging the ball through the line. It became a matter of simple acknowledgment that if a team did not feature a star at quarterback it could not win a championship.

Still, being a quarterback is not all glamour. Quarterbacks are in the crosshairs of defenses. Defensive players know if they hit the quarterback they might cause a fumble or an interception, or if they sack a quarterback he may be forced out of the game. Playing against a second-stringer might aid their cause and help their team win.

Bobby Layne, one of the brashest Texans who ever lived—meaning that he is near the top of any rating system—was inducted into the College Football Hall of Fame and the Pro Football Hall of Fame.

He did not possess the arm strength of the big guns in the sport today but he possessed an intense will to win, and the word "clutch" might as well have been his middle name. By the time Layne graduated from the University of Texas and began his fifteen-year NFL career with the Chicago Bears in 1948 (though he gained fame with the Detroit Lions), the era of the Big Man On Campus, in college and the pros, had arrived for the quarterback. Still, Layne recognized the hazards.

"I'm positive no professional fighter gets knocked out as many times in a year as a quarterback does in a season," Layne said. "Not to mention the elbowing, slugging, kneeing, clawing, scratching, gouging, and twisting he gets."[1]

Making the forward pass legal was supposed to eliminate much of that—not all of the contact, of course, but a sport that produced fatalities in the common course of events clearly had to be changed. Teddy Roosevelt was satisfied the roughness of the game survived the tweaking of the rules. He wanted it to remain a man's sport.

No one alive in 1906, however, would ever have imagined the manner in which the forward pass would forever change football. Meant to alter the nature of the sport, the forward pass gradually and incrementally developed into an offensive force that surpassed the running game.

Once legal, it took an innovative coach to introduce the passing game to his team's repertoire. Even when some of those creative coaches began wielding the pass as a weapon, it was used sparingly. Reliance on more forward passing began with the professionals in the early days of the National Football League in the late 1920s.

During the first decade of its existence, the NFL was on uncertain ground. Owners recognized after a time that fans wanted to see more scoring, more excitement. The old style of trench warfare seemed boring. Yet it took a coach—the caller of plays, the organizer of the offense—to institute change. And it took a capable thrower, one who had fine-tuned his game in college (as rare as that was), to make the transition to the pros and bring the more open game with him.

The first men who set records for touchdown passes, who threw the ball downfield more than their contemporaries, needed the support of their coaches and the freedom to make those choices. They became the true pioneers of the passing game.

Benny Friedman with the New York Giants and Arnie Herber with the Green Bay Packers set the tone for their clubs. They were important figures in the evolution of the passing game. But emphasis on the forward pass in the most committed of ways, with the most enthusiasm, was left to Sammy Baugh.

The Texan who joined the Washington Redskins as the number-one draft pick of the NFL in 1935 is the pivotal player in the development of the forward pass. Before Baugh, even the best practitioners were curiosities. After Baugh's emergence—which was immediate as a rookie—other teams began searching for how they could also acquire a player of such sublime skill in the passing game. At first, only the Chicago Bears were able to do so, with George Halas sweet-talking Sid Luckman into casting his lot with the pros.

Pretty much for a decade Baugh and Luckman were the stars of their respective teams and together uplifted the notion of a passing offense. It became clear that if a professional team harbored aspirations to win championships, it had better find a Baugh or Luckman of its own because a team could no longer rely solely on running backs.

Once Baugh and Luckman demonstrated their abilities—and the T-formation, an offense that opened up football for throwers like them, was embraced—it indeed became obvious the passing game was no passing fancy.

From there, gradually, steadily, even as Baugh and Luckman retired in the early 1950s, passing became more and more important. The quarterbacks who followed those historical figures took passing to the next level, throwing the ball more frequently and setting records by the year for most yards gained in a season and most touchdown passes thrown.

Passing represented more finesse, allowing offenses to swallow gulps of yardage in bigger bites than most running plays. The quarterback became the most critical component on a team, the fiery leader who was most admired and whom teammates counted on to carry them to victory, even when it seemed ridiculous to believe it could happen.

Men like Johnny Unitas, Joe Namath, and future generations of other quarterbacks made believers of the other players. Teams swooped in for wins when games seemed hopelessly lost because the quarterback could move a team the 100-yard length of the football field in less than two minutes in the fourth quarter.

The expansion of the role of the quarterback, the man who bore the weight of expectations and responsibility, came with an air of invincibility. This evolution from an afterthought portion of the offense to a full-speed-ahead role made it seem as if nothing was impossible if you had one of the all-time greats on your side. This attitude became more deeply ingrained as the years passed, reaching a point almost of one-upmanship between the two finest quarterbacks of the modern era. If Baugh and Luckman truly propelled the quarterback's image forward, it was left to Peyton Manning and Tom Brady, linear great-grandsons of the masters, if not their blood relatives, to raise the standard of the forward pass to seemingly unreal heights.

The present era of the National Football League displays more reliance on the forward pass than ever. More great quarterbacks have overlapped in their careers in the past three decades than came up in all the previous decades combined. More than ever, the forward pass is the weapon of choice, having risen in prominence over the running game.

Those at the top of the game are more efficient than quarterbacks of the past, with an uncanny skill to place a fired pass through a tiny available space with speed enough to break a receiver's finger. They place the ball precisely, within inches of where it must fly to be caught.

From Dan Marino to Brett Favre, from Aaron Rodgers and Drew Brees, to Manning and Brady, the statistical list of all-time greats is rewritten season by season by men with cannon arms who throw for the most yards in a season or a career, or who throw for the most touchdown passes in a season or career—and with the sharpest accuracy of all time. Whereas all-star quarterbacks once completed perhaps 48 percent of their pass attempts, now those listed at the top of the NFL passing ratings routinely complete two-thirds of their tosses.

As for their forebears, surely Eddie Cochems never would have imagined that someday a professional quarterback would throw for more than 5,000 yards in one season, would complete 50 passes for touchdowns in one year, and would complete about 70 percent of all attempts in a regular season.

In the minds of many, Baugh was the seminal figure, with Luckman soon chasing, sometimes equaling, and at times surpassing him. Their pioneering roles jump-started a revolution.

Lew Freedman

BAUGH TO BRADY

CHAPTER 1 • ST. LOUIS WHO?

Anyone still living who played college football for St. Louis University is a senior citizen. The Billikens, best known for soccer achievements in recent years and intermittent men's basketball success, last played a football game in 1949.

St. Louis U. first fielded a college football team in 1899 and did so for a half century before dropping the sport. The heyday of Billikens football goes way back. St. Louis recorded three undefeated seasons between 1901 and 1906 (the other came in 1904). This was the era of the sport's worst brutality, when President Theodore Roosevelt was summoning those Ivy League football coaches to his office and hitting them with the mandate to make the game safer.

After the consultation produced rules changes, the 1906 season began with the forward pass legalized for the first time. It so happened that St. Louis's schedule called for that team opening its season earlier than other schools. The Billikens met Carroll College on September 5 in Waukesha, Wisconsin.

While the forward pass was now legal, teams had limited experience thinking about how to use it to their advantage and had only practiced with it during the preseason. Also, a now-seemingly strange rule put in place in conjunction with the legalization of the play declared that an incomplete pass was a turnover: if a thrower heaved the ball and the receiver did not catch it, the ball went to the other team. This quirk put an inordinate amount of pressure on the throwing team to catch the pass and served as a governor on a coach's risk-taking tendencies.

In the early days of football, the ball itself was much rounder than it is today. It more resembled a rugby ball than the ball with narrower ends that invites comparisons to missiles. Players could not always get a solid grip on the old ball to pass it very accurately. Still in use today, the word "pigskin" was applied to early footballs because they were actually made out of pig bladders.

The first pass attempted in the St. Louis–Carroll game by Billikens quarterback Bradbury Robinson was sent in the direction of Jack Schneider. The pass fell incomplete and Carroll gained possession. At the time the score was 0-0, so losing the ball to the opposition had significance.

Coach Eddie Cochems was born February 4, 1877, in Sturgeon Bay, Wisconsin. He attended the University of Wisconsin, the big school in the university system located in Madison. One of eleven children, the dark-haired Cochems later took to wearing bow ties. An older Cochems brother was a star football player for Wisconsin who also excelled in throwing the discus. Eddie Cochems had a twin brother, Carl, who chose a nonathletic path in life; Carl became an opera singer.

Eddie Cochems was a three-sport athlete for the Badgers in college, competing for the football, baseball, and track teams between 1898 and 1901. He was captain of the baseball team in 1901.

Wisconsin's football team, one of the charter members of the Big Ten when it was formed in 1896, has a distinguished football history, and Cochems was part of those beginnings. During his seasons as a Badger, Wisconsin football clubs went 35-4-1. There was no passing allowed during Cochems's college career.

Cochems, who was enshrined in the Madison Sports Hall of Fame in 1968, fifteen years after his death, had some spectacular games for the Badger football team. In 1900 Cochems scored four touchdowns in a 54-0 rout of Notre Dame. In 1901 he scored three touchdowns against the University of Chicago. One of those came on a 100-yard kickoff return.

Cochems knew exactly what he wanted to do when he graduated from college: stick with football. He immediately began a college coaching career. In 1902, when Cochems was twenty-five, he obtained a head coaching job at North Dakota Agricultural College in Fargo. The Bison later saw the school change its name to North Dakota State.

An aptitude for coaching surfaced immediately. North Dakota "Ag" school outscored foes 168-0 that season. Cochems lost just one game during his second season at the helm. Two years at a smaller school proved Cochems's mettle, and in 1903 he returned to Madison as assistant football coach and assistant athletic director. Cochems hoped that this role would lead to his hiring as the head coach when the opportunity presented itself, but it did not. The chance came soon, but the job did not follow. Cochems lost out to another candidate in 1904.

Not being wanted at Wisconsin, Cochems accepted the head job at Clemson. The season produced mixed results. The team turned in some sterling defensive efforts, but finished 3-2-1.

Cochems kept moving, taking the top job at St. Louis. He was already familiar with Robinson. Before transferring to the Billikens, Robinson was a Badger during Cochems's lone season as an assistant coach.

As much as any coach then in the game, Cochems saw the potential of the forward pass as a weapon that could change the entire shape of offenses and also challenge defenses in new ways. While at Wisconsin, Robinson's interest in passing the football was piqued by a teammate who could throw the ball as deep as Robinson could punt it.

Robinson's fate, however, altered history, or at least transplanted it. Robinson was born in Ohio but grew up in St. Louis. He chose Wisconsin for school and likely would have gained the reputation as an innovator in Madison but for the fact that, after getting into a fight, Robinson was expelled from the university. He then enrolled at St. Louis University, where he studied to become a doctor. At one point, Phil King, the man who beat out Cochems for the Wisconsin coaching position, offered to take Robinson back, but Robinson stuck with St. Louis.

As Cochems prepared for his first season in charge of the Billikens football team, he received special permission from the administration to sequester the players at a Jesuit retreat in southern Wisconsin for two weeks. Cochems admitted his passion for secrecy would hopefully deflect any distractions from his commitment to creating a passing game. Cochems said he sought the out-of-the-way site for "the sole purpose of studying and developing the pass."[1] Once the season began, it seemed as if Cochems and the Billikens might have been the only team around that made the effort to concentrate on what the new rule could do for it.

Moments after Robinson's first-ever legal pass attempt in college football went for an incompletion, he tried again, seeking the same receiver. This time Robinson connected with Schneider, who caught the ball and ran into the end zone for a 20-yard touchdown. This represented the first touchdown pass in intercollegiate history.

St. Louis won the game, 22-0. In fact, it might be said that the Billikens won the season. Under Cochems's guidance, St. Louis finished 11-0 and outscored the other teams 407-11. The forward pass, often referred to as the "projectile pass" at the time, was one reason that St. Louis excelled. Even so long ago an expression came into vogue that has lasted: "air attack." Cochems used the words, and they stayed alive in the football lexicon.

Later in the season Robinson completed a 67-yard touchdown pass. His initial receiver, Schneider, also completed a 65-yard touchdown pass. During a 31-0 victory over Iowa, the Billikens scored four times on touchdown passes. In the game against the Hawkeyes, St. Louis completed eight passes in ten attempts.

Of course, completing 80 percent of passes in a game did not prove to be a regular thing, especially with a clunky round ball probably best suited to dodgeball.

If Cochems gave any thought to choosing seclusion for his passing seminar at the retreat because he felt someone would spy on his plays, there seemed little reason for fear. Cochems's biggest surprise during the season was that so few teams bothered to take advantage of the new rules. Many other teams were either ill-prepared or disinterested in throwing the ball.

After that Iowa triumph, Cochems said that one reason St. Louis prevailed so easily was that the Hawkeyes did not run a high-powered offense. Iowa not doing well, he said, "resulted from its use of the old style of play and its failure to effectively use the forward pass."[2] Iowa barely tried out forward passes, attempting just two of them.

By then, Robinson had become enamored with passing. His partner in workouts at Wisconsin was H. P. Savage. What began with Robinson kicking to Savage became a tutorial with Savage teaching Robinson how to throw. How Savage became so adept at passing the football when he really had no reason to master the skill is an unknown tale.

But once Robinson realized what passing could do for the offense, he was all in on Cochems's schemes to incorporate it into the St. Louis playbook. He worked hard at throwing and termed this devotion "my football hobby."[3]

Coaching is now regarded as a copycat profession. Once anyone introduces a fresh idea, other coaches learn how to adapt the plays to their own teams. It doesn't take long for imitators to pop up and adopt the same plays that for a short time were considered innovative. However, that habit was not yet ingrained in 1906. Cochems was surprised that more teams did not employ passing to any serious effect that season. He had pretty much cornered the market on how to integrate passing into an offense, but no one else seemed to care very much for some time.

Rather than hide what he learned, the next year Cochems shared his knowledge about passing. He authored a ten-page article in a 1907 football guide edited by Walter Camp. It was titled "The Forward Pass and On-Side Kick" (apparently a bonus topic). The piece was also illustrated with photographs of Robinson showing off his passing form.

Cochems was trying to help the world open up the game of football, but the world wasn't paying attention. Cochems even stressed that there were so many aspects to explore in the passing game he could not contain all of the information in his article: "Should I begin to explain the different plays in which the pass could figure I would invite myself to an endless task," he wrote.[4]

St. Louis was not as strong a team in 1907, Cochems's second year on the job, but the Billikens did finish 7-3-1. Cochems coached one more season in St. Louis, going 7-2-1, and then took some time off from the sidelines. He became director of the playground system in St. Louis, and sketchy reports indicate he coached some minor-league football in the area for a couple of years.

Cochems remained an adherent of the passing game and whenever asked, he was a booster for that aspect of the sport. In 1909 he was sought out by the *Washington Post* to discuss his views.

"The story in a nutshell is this," Cochems said. "The ball is too large and too light. Some of the best teams in the country find it impossible to use the pass owing to a lack of players who can make it. Since it is impossible to grow larger hands and it is possible to make the ball conform to human dimensions, why not the ball fit the needed conditions?" Cochems felt reshaping the ball would turn football into "one of the most beautiful and versatile sports the world ever saw."[5]

In 1911 Cochems went after the head coaching job at his alma mater, Wisconsin, for a second time, and again was not hired. In 1914 he surfaced as the football coach at the University of Maine, although for just one season, finishing 6-3.

Starting in 1911 and returning to that role after his one-off season in Maine, Cochems went into politics as a speechwriter and campaigner. His presidential political efforts backed Theodore Roosevelt, Calvin Coolidge, and Herbert Hoover, and he spent twenty years living in New York City before returning to Madison.

Married with five children, Cochems had fourteen grandchildren as well. In 1940, after decades away from the sport, when an opening came about for a football coach at St. Louis University, he applied. The school hired someone else.

While Cochems is credited as being a strong supporter of the forward pass, the lines blur when discussion occurs about his contributions to its development. St. Louis certainly emphasized the forward pass before other schools did. The first legal forward pass in a college game, unquestionably took place in St. Louis's contest against Carroll.

Later, Cochems's own quarterback, Bradbury Robinson, disputed any claims that Cochems "invented" the forward pass. No, Robinson said, he did. Cochems, Robinson, and St. Louis can lay solid claims to firsts in the sport, but "invention" may be too strong a word. The forward pass evolved from trial and error, the way Thomas Edison's incandescent lightbulb did. Many others were on the trail of such an invention. Edison created the product that was a hit.

A century after Robinson passed to Schneider with Cochems's approval, newspapers and other organizations took note of the anniversary. An article written by St. Louis University personnel left no wiggle room about the issue. A subhead on the story read, "The Play Was the Brainchild of SLU Football Coach Eddie Cochems." In part the story read, "Tuesday marks the 100th anniversary of the first documented forward pass in American football history, a play that would change the game forever."[6]

Periodically, Cochems was referred to as "the father of the forward pass." But sometimes, due to his own self-promotion for the title, Robinson was given that nickname. Clearly, Cochems and Robinson could not be separated in their commitment and involvement to the passing game, anymore than partners Fred Astaire and Ginger Rogers would be viewed as soloists in their dance acts.

"I think the forward pass is sensational," Cochems said in 1906. "My men never think of throwing the ball underhand. They throw it overhand as hard as they can."[7]

On still another occasion Cochems expressed his befuddlement about why other teams did not swiftly embrace the forward pass in their games, particularly the big powers in the East.

"It's really a puzzle to me why the other teams are not given new-style plays by their coaches," Cochems said. "Eastern elevens are using nothing but the old-style formations. It will be a matter of a season or two until the coaches around the country come around to my way of thinking or I will be badly mistaken."[8] Actually, Cochems was badly mistaken. It took several more years for passing to catch on.

Cochems died in 1953, after the passing game had become established as a significant part of football, but well before it actually began to shunt aside running plays as the predominant method of picking up yardage and marching down the field.

CHAPTER 2 • Knute Rockne and Notre Dame

Knute Rockne invented Notre Dame football, but he did not invent the forward pass, as many believe.

A brilliant coach who put the Fighting Irish on the college football map and spread awareness of the Catholic school located in South Bend, Indiana, Rockne is best remembered for his coaching savvy and marketing wisdom. But he also played the sport and did play a role in the evolution of the passing game.

Eddie Cochems was surprised when many college football teams did not follow St. Louis's lead and place more emphasis on the forward pass soon after his Billikens threw the first one in competition in September 1906. In the ensuing decades, debate would sometimes take place over whether a star quarterback or the system he was placed in by his coach produced passing success. Certainly, a coach who refused to pass could have the best thrower in the universe on the roster and nobody would know. The will to pass was critical; finding the best person to pass turned theory into reality.

Notre Dame and Rockne, neither of whom were then as famous as they would soon become, did demonstrate a highly publicized proclivity for the pass in 1913. Somehow, that became construed as being responsible for inventing it.

Later, Rockne disavowed a pioneering role, giving credit to Cochems and St. Louis. The coach "enrolled a few boys with hands like steam shovels who could toss a football just as easily and almost as far as they could throw a baseball."[1]

That was hyperbole on Rockne's part, but he did not try to steal St. Louis's thunder. In fact, he seemed to echo Cochems rather than try to overshadow him.

"One would have thought that so effective a play would have been instantly copied and become the vogue," Rockne said. "The East, however, had not learned much or cared much about Midwest and Western football. Indeed, the East scarcely realized that football existed beyond the Alleghenies."[2]

Despite his denials, the myth that Notre Dame and Rockne were in on the invention of the forward pass in 1913 persisted in some quarters. In December 1999, as the twentieth century was ending, ESPN produced a ranking of the Greatest Coaching Decisions. It labeled Notre Dame coach Jesse Harper's decision to pass against Army on November 1, 1913, as the sixth-best coaching choice in all sports during the one-hundred-year period.

The rating read, "Notre Dame 'Invents' the Forward Pass. While the forward pass had been legalized in 1906, it was a play rarely used in college football."[3]

That was true enough. Being in the right place at the right time in scoring a big enough win to garner special attention uplifted Notre Dame's notoriety in forward-passing history to an undeserved level. This was before the Fighting Irish were nearly as big in the sport as they would become. Rockne, who as coach led Notre Dame to singular prominence, was still a player in South Bend, Indiana.

Knute Rockne was born in Voss, Norway, in March 1888. His family immigrated to the United States when he was five, and the Rocknes, whose name was spelled Rokne when they crossed the ocean, settled in Chicago.

The Rock played football and competed in track in high school in Chicago, but when he graduated he did not immediately move on to college. He spent four years working for the US Postal Service before enrolling at Notre Dame at twenty-two. Rockne played for the Irish between 1910 and 1913 and as a senior was named an All-American end.

During that season, the Irish faced Army, which was becoming one of

Notre Dame's traditional rivals. Army was a powerhouse, and when the squads met at West Point, the hosts were favored.

The Notre Dame football program was nondescript and was looking for a new coach to jump-start the team when the administration hired Jesse Harper for the 1913 campaign. Harper was born in Paw Paw, Illinois, in 1883. He began coaching college football at little-known Alma College in Michigan in 1906 and held that job for two seasons. In 1909 he took over Wabash College in Indiana and ran that school's team through the 1912 season.

When Notre Dame tapped Harper for its job, the school hoped he could lead the Irish to a higher level. Notre Dame had been winning games but played a small-time schedule and was not viewed as a major player in college football.

Harper made an impact immediately. He scheduled tougher competition, also putting his team on display under brighter lights, and in his rookie coaching season for the Irish they finished 7-0. The keystone victory was the 35-13 thumping of Army when Harper ordered his quarterback Charley "Gus" Dorais to throw early and often. Dorais, who completed 14 out of 17 attempts for 243 yards that day, considered Rockne, the team captain, his favorite receiver.

Over the preceding summer the teammates had worked as lifeguards and busboys at the Cedar Point Resort on Lake Erie in Sandusky, Ohio. In their spare time they practiced throwing the ball back and forth on the sand. At least that was a more benign activity than their risqué on-campus passion for late-night poker after hours with candles swiped from the landmark Grotto. Candles were typically lighted for religious reasons, not to better see who held a pair of jacks.

The legend of the Army game was good publicity for the forward pass, and it was magnified because New York newspapers covered the game at West Point. However, Dorais and Rockne had long before established a passing partnership. The first time Dorais completed a pass to Rockne in a game was when they were both sophomores. This summer background of working out, though, did serve them in good stead and curried favor with their new coach. Harper had a sharp football mind and enthusiastically embraced new offensive plays. He once admitted that he could be laying in bed at night and instead of counting sheep or sleeping, his restless mind imagined fresh X's and O's. Harper said he would "hop out of bed in the wee hours with some nutty idea about a play. And gosh, honestly, some of 'em worked like charms. I always believed in a lot of deception in your offense. That, plus speed, good kicking, and solid fundamentals. I never cared a lot about beef."[4]

The *New York Times* covered the rout of Army, and its writer on the scene recognized the significance of Notre Dame's offense making a splash.

> The Notre Dame eleven swept the Army off its feet on the Plains this afternoon and buried the soldiers under a 35-to-13 score, ... The Westerners flashed the most sensational football that has been seen in the East this year, baffling the Cadets with a style of open play and a perfectly developed forward pass, which carried the victors down the field 30 yards at a clip. Football men marveled at this display of open football.
>
> Bill Roper, former head coach at Princeton, who was one of the officials of the game, said that he had always believed that such playing was possible under the new rules, but that he had never seen the forward pass developed to such perfection.[5]

What was also quite apparent to the writer, as well as to the five thousand witnesses in the stands, it must be assumed, was that Army had no plan to defend against a throwing game. No offense had ever employed it as a key part of the game plan against the team before.

"The Army players were hopelessly confused and chagrined before Notre Dame's great playing . . . ," the story concluded.[6]

That day's performance was a vivid illustration of how explosive a weapon passing the ball could be. Rockne scored one touchdown in the game. Dorais was named All-American that season. Dorais and Rockne clearly had the makings of a successful combination, but it took a new coach to exploit it.

While Army and Notre Dame would become great rivals, the November 1, 1913, contest was the first time the schools met on the gridiron. Harper was trying to raise Notre Dame's profile, and he had written to Army requesting a game. Army had an open date because it lost Yale from its schedule. The Cadets agreed to face the Irish, but there was one sticking point. Showing how little Notre Dame counted in the big scheme of things at the time, Harper informed the Army athletic administration that the school could not afford to travel from South Bend, Indiana, for less than a one-thousand-dollar guarantee. Army had offered four hundred dollars, but did up the ante.

With the benefit of hindsight, Notre Dame's 1913 schedule was otherwise laughable. It would be classified pretty much at the NCAA Division III level today. The Irish opened with Ohio Northern, producing an 87-0 victory. They next topped South Dakota, 20-7. In the third contest, Notre Dame crushed Harper's old school, Alma, 62-0. After the Army game, Notre Dame did face and defeat Penn State and Texas, although there was a showdown with Christian Brothers mixed in.

While Harper would lay the groundwork for Notre Dame's ascension into the national spotlight, the future could not be foreseen in 1913. Harper and Rockne met for the first time on the practice field. Instantly, Harper admired Rockne's tenacity. He could not know that the leader of his team would follow him as Irish coach and build a juggernaut that even today remains one of the most storied in the country.

"He was one of those natural fighting players that a coach finds once in a blue moon," Harper said of Rockne. "He was a little light and inexperienced, but my, how that boy would battle 'em. That everlasting fight of his was his dominating trait."[7]

Harper did trot out the passing game in the opening slaughter of Ohio Northern. Ironically, it did not work well against an outclassed opponent. Dorais's first three passes were intercepted. Decades later, Texas coach Darrell Royal and Ohio State coach Woody Hayes both were credited with the saying, "three things can happen when you throw the ball, and two of them are bad." Those two things were an incompletion or an interception, with the interception being more harmful.

But the Irish had drilled hard, unofficially over the summer, as well as when official practice convened under Harper.

"Perfection of the forward pass came to us only through daily, tedious practice," Rockne said. "I'd run along the beach. Dorais would throw from all angles. People who didn't know we were two college seniors making painstaking preparations for our final season probably thought we were crazy."[8]

Dorais recovered from his mishaps against Ohio Northern, and when the occasion demanded it against Army, he was on fire, his arm as accurate as a pitcher throwing a fastball over the plate.

On a cold, cloudy day, Rockne, representing his team, won the coin toss, enabling Notre Dame to receive the opening kickoff. One reason the time had arrived to unleash the throwing game was that the Irish did not match up well against the Cadets' line, making it harder to advance the ball on the ground. To a man up front, Army was bigger. The forward pass was employed as an equalizer.

The pivotal moment came when Harper saw how the Army defense was lining up. In this era, teams did not use the now typical 4-3-4 defensive style. There was no real need up until then for four defensive backs. When Harper realized Army was defending Notre Dame against the run, he recognized if all went smoothly the Irish could feast on the pass.

Dorais opened by completing three straight passes to halfback Joe Pliska. While this was going on, Rockne was imitating a wounded duck. He ran his routes downfield, but limped while doing so. Notre Dame only brought nineteen players to New York, so this ploy was plausible.

It was not long into the first quarter before Notre Dame led 7-0. Dorais flung a 40-yard strike to Rockne, who gathered the ball in on the 2-yard line and strode into the end zone.

"I started limping down the field," Rockne said of the payoff route, "and the Army halfback covering me almost yawned in my face, he was that bored. I put on full speed and left him standing there flat-footed." Army had never absorbed a touchdown like this one. "Everybody seemed astonished. There had been no hurdling, no tackling, no plunging, no crushing of fiber and sinew. Just a long-distance touchdown by rapid transit."[9]

Somewhere, Teddy Roosevelt was smiling.

Thus began a long afternoon for the Cadets, who were ill-prepared to stop the forward pass. This is the stuff of which legends are made, even if the attendant use of the word "invented" as applied to the forward pass was inaccurate.

If ever a team took advantage of circumstances to burnish its reputation, it was Notre Dame at West Point that day. What had shaped up as a mismatch for heavily favored Army turned into a lesson and prima facie evidence that the day of the forward pass was coming.

"Army had its usual great team," Harper said, "but the passes demoralized them completely. By the time it ended, we could do anything we pleased, running or passing. They didn't know what to expect, or what to do about it. We just kicked hell out of 'em. We played a helluva game."[10]

If the forward pass was in its infancy when St. Louis University employed it, it had reached toddler status by the time Notre Dame whipped it out against Army.

Harper coached Notre Dame for five seasons, 1913 to 1917, mounting a record of 34-5-1 at South Bend. Adding in his other college coaching stints, Harper's career total was 57-17-7. He was inducted into the College Football Hall of Fame in 1971, ten years after his death.

After his reign at Notre Dame ended, Harper left college football coaching to begin a new life as a rancher in Kansas, where his family had moved following the stay in Illinois when he was born. He stuck with that for a while, but between 1931 and 1933 Harper returned to Notre Dame as athletic director.

Although Harper moved on, he and Rockne had formed a tight bond and remained lifelong friends. Rockne's fame far exceeded Harper's in the ensuing years as he led the Fighting Irish to the pinnacle of the sport. Rockne was not known for his modesty, but he always gave credit to Harper as the coach who transformed Notre Dame's status on the gridiron.

"Jesse, not myself, was the reason for Notre Dame becoming famous in football," Rockne said. "Jesse put the school on a high plane. I have tried to carry out what he started."[11] That was a gracious spin on what had transpired with Notre Dame football following Harper's departure. Rockne served as an Irish assistant coach between 1914 and 1917 under Harper, further solidifying the friendship between the two men. Rockne then succeeded Harper in 1918. During his tenure running the football program between that year and 1930, Rockne's leadership made Notre Dame a household brand. From 1920 to 1930 Rockne was also the athletic director.

The Rock presided over national championship squads in 1919, 1924, 1929, and 1930. His career head coaching record was a remarkable 102-12-5. There is no telling what type of records Rockne might have amassed if his career continued on the same trajectory. But he died in a plane crash in Kansas in 1931, not very far from Harper's property. At Rockne's funeral, Harper was approached to return to the school as the new athletic director.

Lesser known, but no less important, Dorais, the quarterback, played a couple of seasons of semiprofessional football before the National Football League was founded in 1920. Dorais worked as an assistant to Rockne at Notre Dame for one season, coached Gonzaga, and then made his mark in the NFL as a coach. Dorais led the Detroit Lions for five seasons and tossed in a single season as an assistant with the Pittsburgh Steelers as a last fling.

In 1937 Dorais coached the college team in the annual College All-Star Game in Chicago. The quarterback for his team, which upset the Green Bay Packers, 6-0, was a strong-armed young man out of Texas named Sammy Baugh.

Nearly a quarter of a century after Dorais wrote his own little piece of history with Rockne in the milestone game versus Army, he played a role, albeit a brief one, in nurturing the newfangled quarterback of the time. With his own magnificence Sammy Baugh would emphatically usher in a new era in the passing game. Once again it took a certain kind of boldness to embrace the risks inherent in going all in with the forward pass. Baugh possessed that self-confident cheekiness to be The Man.

CHAPTER 3 • Sammy Baugh

Sammy Baugh was born on a farm in Temple, Texas, in March 1914, several months after Knute Rockne caught his famous pass from Gus Dorais. Baugh was one of three children (two boys and a girl). His father, James, worked on the Santa Fe Railroad. However, Baugh's parents broke up, and his mother raised the three kids.

The family moved to Sweetwater in West Texas in time for him to become the quarterback for the Sweetwater High football team, nicknamed the Mustangs. Baugh was sixteen at the time and already showed proof of having a strong arm.

The county seat of Nolan County, Sweetwater was founded in 1879 but never became a large city. In the 2010 census Sweetwater's population was just under eleven thousand. Known for its dusty, windy climate, later some of those breezes would be harnessed for wind power generation as the town became known as the "Wind Turbine Capital of Texas."

Throughout his athletic career, Baugh was called "Sammy," although he preferred "Sam." It is a hard habit to break, and just about everyone in the world who watched him play ball and who observed him from afar stuck with "Sammy"; only his closest friends and relatives actually called him "Sam." Part of the reason was that those who admired how Baugh threw a football (and a baseball before that) regularly employed his popular nickname, "Slingin' Sammy." Slingin' balls whatever their shape was something Baugh did very well. However, even before that, Sammy's first nickname within the family was "Buddy."

Baugh's youth was not an easy one. When his parents divorced, the kids often had to work to help out with the family finances. When he was a youngster, Baugh sometimes picked cotton, which is often backbreaking work. The weather of West Texas was harsh. The dry climate was very hot, and picking cotton could be brutally hard in the absence of any shade. Before the Baughs moved to Sweetwater, Baugh got enough of picking cotton to last a lifetime. He was a small boy when first sent out to work the fields.

"It would take me all day to pick a sack of cotton when I was little," Baugh said. "I would remember that dang sack full and how it hurt my shoulders. Later on, when I was playing football and practicing football, it was hot and we were tired, and you'd think, 'Dang this is tough.' And then you'd think about dragging that sack and you'd jump up and you're ready to go again. So I always promised myself that if I ever had an acre of land I'd never plant a stalk of cotton."[1]

West Texas had definite physical attributes, and also to some degree carried with it a state of mind. In *West Texas: A Portrait of Its People and Its Wondrous and Raw Land*, the location is identified as west of Interstate 35 and even west of the town of West, Texas. The definition chosen reads this way:

> Locate the western horizon, the treeless plain. Go where the land prefers mesquite and thistle rather than pine. Where there are no 24-hour traffic jams. Where there are no downtowns with dozens of soaring glass boxes that block the sun at dawn and dusk. Find a place that yields only to those who persevere.[2]

It is a spare country, spacious, possibly unforgiving if the engine overheats and you are driving across flatlands baked dry by scorching sun, or if you are caught in a hailstorm or threatened by a tornado. They all come with the territory.

There have been ranchers who led cattle drives and entrepreneurs who struck oil, famous folks like cattle baron Charles Goodnight and places like the quirky Cadillac Ranch near Amarillo, and a poker player named Amarillo Slim, all of whom have their roots in West Texas. West Texas, as much as anywhere, including all other parts of Texas, enjoyed its legends writ large.

Goodnight was born in Illinois but was living in Texas by 1846. After the Civil War he began driving cattle to railheads to ship beef to the East. He was the biggest name fella in the Texas Panhandle for some time. Author Larry McMurtry's best-selling novel *Lonesome Dove* fictionalized one of Goodnight's cattle drives, and the Pulitzer Prize–winning book publicized his name for future generations.

Amarillo Slim's real name was Thomas Austin Preston, Jr., but likely no one ever called him that again after he won the World Series of Poker in 1972. Preston was actually born in Arkansas, but his parents died when he was a baby and he moved to Turkey, Texas.

Goodnight died in 1929, a year after Amarillo Slim was born. Some would say being a cattle man in the nineteenth century and playing poker for a living in the late twentieth century made both men professional gamblers.

Another legend of the region was Judge Roy Bean, the self-proclaimed "Law West of the Pecos." The irresistible image of a saloon keeper dispensing justice as he saw fit captured the fancy of many. While the judge, often described as a hanging judge despite limited supporting evidence, seemed immune to any governing body and ruled on his judgments, something in his character appealed to future-generation denizens of the Old West. He was granted immortality in popular culture when actor Paul Newman played Bean in a wildly entertaining and apparently highly fictionalized account of his life released on film in 1972.

Texas's relationship to football is similar to Indiana's connection to basketball. While neither can claim ownership of inventing the respective sports, the residents wish they had. Texans likely think it sacrilege that the sport was an outgrowth of rugby (seen only on channel 527 at 3 a.m.) in Britain. Oh, the horror. But Texans consider themselves as foster parents, at least. They hold a grudge that neither Amos Alonzo Stagg nor Glenn "Pop" Warner had any Texas ties, and no doubt Texans have tried to make the link.

Stagg was born in 1862 in West Orange, New Jersey, and lived to be 102 without coaching in Texas. Perhaps he passed through on his way to California, where he coached and died. Stagg was the sport's greatest innovator. He introduced laterals, the man in motion, the place kick, the tackling dummy, the Statue of Liberty play, the huddle, and the quick kick, and made many other contributions.

Glenn "Pop" Warner was born in 1871 and died in 1954. He coached at

Georgia, Iowa State, Cornell, Pittsburgh, Stanford, and Temple. Organized youth play is named after him. Somehow Warner also became famous, even legendary in the game, without a Texas base.

Football started later in Texas than it did in the East. Texas football fans probably laugh at the notion that the first college game was played in 1869 between Princeton and Rutgers. To Texans that represents the last time either of those schools mattered in the sport.

Football became so beloved in Texas—including, of course, West Texas—that it was said there were only three college sports that mattered; fall football, spring football, and the recruiting season. That didn't really count high school football, yet the passionate followings of local teams may be even more loyal, vociferous, and demanding than the fans of Texas Tech and other schools out west.

When a writer sought to tell the story of the heart of football territory, he chose Permian High School in Odessa, Texas. That writer, Buzz Bissinger, produced the remarkably reported and well-received book *Friday Night Lights* in 1990.

Texas has its National Football League teams in Dallas and Houston. The pros rent Sundays. The colleges lease Saturdays. Fridays, Friday nights, with those tall light stanchions illuminating the fields, are the high schools' time to shine.

Nobody did rivalries the way the old Southwest Conference did when the entire league minus one team was based in Texas. The league existed from 1914, born the same year as Baugh, until 1996. Everyone around the country knew that football was more important to the SWC schools than it was just about anywhere else, certainly as an entity representing many schools, not simply a single team.

Texas, Texas A&M, Texas Christian, Texas Tech, Rice, Southern Methodist, and Baylor University periodically adopted one other school to fill out a schedule for an eight-team league, either Oklahoma or Arkansas. The Sooners and Razorbacks were both located close enough to the Texas border to almost count as Texas schools. And they were hated just as much as one Texas school despised another.

"I remember when every boy in Texas wanted to go to a Southwest Conference school," Sammy Baugh said in 1997 when he had outlived the league. "They wouldn't even think of going anywhere else."[3]

It was enough for any football player from Sweetwater to enroll at a four-year college. Baugh said contrary to public opinion, or revisionist history, he was not the star player for the Sweetwater Mustangs his senior year when the team went undefeated in the regular season but lost in the state championship game.

Even as late as the early 1930s, the passing game was of limited interest to many football teams. The single-wing or double-wing offense still predominated. It was the tailback in those formations who was the offensive star, and those formations were all about bulling the ball downfield with the running game.

Yes, Baugh had a strong arm at an early age, but it was not put to use on the gridiron much in high school. He was a blocking back as much as he was a ball-carrying back. He did play safety on defense quite well, though. During his years as a quarterback in college and the pros, Baugh also played safety, figuring out opposing quarterbacks.

Baugh had heard reports of him being the one who led the Mustangs to the playoffs when he was in high school. "But it just ain't true," he said. "Hell, I was a long way from being the guy who led us to the playoffs."[4]

Baugh almost did not follow the path of playing football in college and specifically not in Texas. His first sporting love was baseball, and his strong and accurate arm made him an infield prospect. At one point he was promised a baseball scholarship to Washington State University. Baugh planned to head to Pullman, Washington.

"I had played baseball all my life, and that's what I wanted to be in the beginning—a professional baseball player," Baugh said.[5]

But about a month before he was scheduled to leave for Washington he suffered an injured knee in a semipro game, and the scholarship offer was rescinded. He was sliding into second base and tore cartilage. Baugh's future in any sport was on hold.

Although he did not overlap with Baugh in high school, rather remarkably, little old Sweetwater High sent another player to the pros who would become a Pro Football Hall of Famer. Clyde Turner, later nicknamed "Bulldog," was five years younger than Baugh. Turner was born in Plains, Texas, in 1919.

In 1940, after attending Hardin-Simmons University in Abilene, Texas, Turner was the number-one draft choice of the Chicago Bears. During that era, the Bears and the Washington Redskins, Baugh's pro team, were the top clubs in the National Football League. Although younger, by then Turner was classifying Baugh as his best friend.

But they were not pals when the teams met on the field. That was contrary to Turner's nature. Turner, as all top players were at the time, was a two-way player. He excelled as an offensive center and a linebacker, and on defense his job was to disrupt Baugh's game.

"I hate everybody when I walk on the football field," Turner once said. "I wouldn't even speak to my best friend [Baugh] in a game and we graduated from the same high school in Sweetwater, Texas. Sammy'd wink at me when he was calling signals for the Washington Redskins, but I'd just glare and do my best to rack 'em up."[6]

Turner could well identify with Baugh's recounting the strain of picking cotton. When his family moved from Plains to Sweetwater, the Turner kids worked on a cotton farm. His recollection of the hardships and the hardscrabble life that accompanied cotton pickers' efforts had much in common with Baugh's.

"I hated to pick cotton worse than anything I've ever done," Turner said. "Rather be whipped with barbed wire."[7]

Turner was a junior when he began attending Sweetwater High. Growing up he had not played any football, but what attracted him to the team were the colorful red letter sweaters the players modeled with a big "S" on them. He also noticed the girls were attracted to the guys who wore them. Fashion got Turner onto the field, but hunger and desire kept him there.

"Man, I went through many a rough hour to get that sweater," he said. "The first day I went out on the field was the roughest day I ever spent on a football field. That includes college through pro."[8]

Life was not easy for Turner in Sweetwater. The transition between schools led to failure one year, and he was denied the chance to play football as a senior. He had been a backup as a junior and had no resume line in the sport at all his last year.

Turner missed football and wanted to keep playing. But nobody knew who he was when he literally knocked on doors at colleges around Texas. He was running out of time and money and feared one thing above all. He dreaded the idea of going home to pick cotton again.

Down to his last dime (plus a candy bar in his pocket), a virtually destitute Turner hitchhiked up and down highways to various schools. He even tried a few schools in Oklahoma, but he could not talk himself in the door of any school and onto a team.

However, ultimately, the coach at Hardin-Simmons, located about forty miles west of Turner's home, came looking for him and offered a tryout. That's all Turner ever wanted.

There would still be some rough sailing ahead for Turner, who at different times was going to be kicked out of school for disciplinary reasons and would also flee the campus on his own.

There were also close calls for the boy from Sweetwater on several occasions, and they might have derailed his future as he made his way through the outside world beyond the small town's West Texas boundaries.

The baseball injury and the loss of the scholarship kept Baugh around Sweetwater longer than he intended as well. He had a bit stronger football pedigree than Turner, but he wasn't being recruited heavily either. Texas Christian coach Dutch Meyer had seen Baugh play football and thought he could make it with the Horned Frogs. However, Meyer had no scholarship money to offer. Meyer sought to put together some kind of school package that would provide an education for Baugh if he played football, basketball, and baseball.

For the second time Baugh made the choice of a college. But at the last minute, as he was committing to Texas Christian, the University of Texas wooed him with a late baseball scholarship deal. Baugh shifted gears and headed to Austin for a look-see. Baugh was ready to bite—but he also wanted to play football, and the Longhorn officials said it had to be baseball only for him.

Baugh hesitated. When he thought things over, he decided he badly wanted to play football. He was not ready to walk away from that sport. It was a decision that would change Baugh's destiny, the future of pro football, and the passing game itself.

CHAPTER 4 • Benny Friedman

Benny and the Giants. Not quite like the song "Benny and the Jets," but close enough. Benny Friedman was born in 1905, the year before Eddie Cochems's St. Louis University team threw the first sanctioned college football pass.

Friedman, who was born in Cleveland, probably had not graduated from a high chair then, so he was not paying attention between shakes of his rattle. By the time he enrolled at the University of Michigan, however, Friedman knew as much about the passing game as any college quarterback in America. He then brought that knowledge with him into the National Football League when he began running the New York Giants' offense.

Friedman played for the Wolverines between 1924 and 1926. In 1926 Friedman threw for five touchdowns against Indiana University in a game in which the quarterback accounted for 44 points through his throwing and kicking. Many a game had passed during the preceding two decades where a quarterback had not attempted five passes in a game.

As Cochems had learned, the football world was slow to gravitate to the passing game, whether because of fear of the unknown, laziness, or lack of the proper personnel. At Michigan, Friedman was an All-American quarterback in both his junior and senior years.

At a time when quarterbacks who had mastered throwing the ball were a comparative rarity, Friedman came to Ann Arbor with a ready-made reputation based on his excellence on the gridiron in high school. His family had moved to the Chicago area, but Friedman's initial schoolboy coach didn't see the talent in him. Friedman did not inspire confidence in his first tryout, and the coach advised that if he wanted to play football he should transfer. Big mistake. That coach turned away a future College and Pro Football Hall of Famer, and Friedman became an accomplished thrower at Glenville High.

Friedman was athletically gifted. He could run and throw. Glenville went undefeated, won the city championship, and then faced Oak Park, Illinois, in what was billed as a national championship high school game. This was hyperbole since there had been no organized playoff leading up to a title game. Nonetheless, Friedman led his school to this mythical championship.

One other thing distinguished Friedman from many other stars of the time: he was Jewish. There was widespread prejudice in American society against Jews at the time, but Friedman persevered and succeeded. He became the leader of his college and professional teams, showing that religious affiliation was irrelevant.

The first time the University of Michigan fielded a football team was 1879. The Wolverines played one game and won it. The coach coming along a little bit later who established the tradition, elevating Michigan into a powerhouse, was Fielding Yost, who took command in 1901. Yost stepped down after the 1923 season, but after a year off he returned to the sidelines for 1925 and 1926. This was no coincidence. Essentially Yost took a gander at what he would have in Friedman and realized the young man could take the Wolverines places. As soon as Friedman graduated, Yost would retire a second time.

By Friedman's undergraduate years, Yost, Amos Alonzo Stagg, and Illinois's Bob Zuppke had adopted a little bit friendlier relationship with the forward pass, though it would be an exaggeration to suggest they were truly enamored of throwing. They were wary of passing and tiptoed carefully around its use. It was employed as a counterpoint to the running game to keep defenses loose, but it was not an integral weapon.

Of course, there had to be good reasons to dissuade Yost from doing what he had been doing. Between 1901 and 1905 the Wolverines did not lose a game. Over one stretch Michigan went fifty-six straight games without a loss and outscored opponents, 2,841-42, an insane proportion. That was Michigan's run-up to the legalization of the forward pass in 1906. So why change what the team was doing?

It wasn't as if Michigan went into a major slump immediately after the streak ended and legal passing began either. The Wolverines went 4-1 in 1906 and 5-1 in 1907, when they outscored foes, 107-6. For the most part Michigan cruised past opponents throughout the years under Yost's guidance. He became athletic director as well in 1921, a job he held until 1941, and the Wolverines' record under his leadership was 165-29-10.

Physically, Friedman was no giant. He stood 5-foot-10 but weighed a sturdy 183 pounds. His size did not make coaches drool, but in the 1920s—unlike the 2000s when every quarterback seems to be 6-foot-4—his size did not rule him out as a thrower.

Yost was not a likely candidate to fully embrace the risks inherent in adapting to a passing game. His teams were well-drilled, but they were not flashy. They were tough and opportunistic. Some even thought they were dull. But they won. Once in a while Yost's Wolverines lost more than one game in a season, but he mixed in unbeaten years as well.

"Cynics," he said, "call our method the 'punt, pass, and prayer system,' but we generally have the last laugh."[1]

Actually, Yost did not particularly want to move full-time to a desk job, but in 1923, after an 8-0 season, Yost's doctor told him that continuing to coach was dangerous to his health. So he retreated upstairs, at least for a bit. Friedman did not bond well with new Michigan coach George Little in 1924. Little and the quarterback had a tense relationship, and Friedman for the most part rode the bench or played right halfback—a perfect example of how a superior passer could be benched because his coach did not believe either in him or a passing system.

However, when called upon against Wisconsin, despite Little's misgivings, Friedman shined. He scored on a 26-yard touchdown run, and tellingly, he completed some big passes. Michigan prevailed, 21-0, and while Friedman began the game as an unknown, he emerged from it in some quarters proclaimed as a budding star.

Yost was back in charge for 1925, and the Wolverines went 7-1. Friedman was the quarterback and made All–Big Ten and was chosen an All-American. A week later Michigan topped Minnesota, 13-0, and Friedman performed well again. He followed that up by intercepting a pass and throwing a touchdown pass in a shutout of Northwestern.

Friedman had bristled when he had not been given what he felt was a true opportunity to show his talents: he had nearly transferred to Carnegie in Pittsburgh. Now all eyes were on him. The grudge-match game against Ohio State did not proceed quite as smoothly. Although Michigan won, 16-6, Friedman was victimized by receivers dropping catchable balls and being sacked regularly by the Buckeyes. Worse, he took it personally, threw a tantrum, and embarrassed himself with his reaction.

"To hell with you guys!" Friedman declared. "If you're not going to catch them, I'm not going to take this licking."[2]

Rather remarkably, Friedman, in his petulance, began to walk off the field in the middle of a Michigan possession. Throwing teammates under the bus in such a public way was poor behavior, and Friedman heard about that from Little. Although the coach was certainly within his rights and responsibilities to berate Friedman for his actions, there was too much bad feeling in the air for Friedman to accept his lecture graciously.

"You no-good son-of-a-bitch," Friedman retorted, fracturing the relationship even further. "You can take my suit and shove it. I don't want to play for you."[3]

Michigan lost, 9-2, to Iowa the next week to conclude the season at 6-2. That also terminated Little's tenure as boss. Little left Michigan to become athletic director and football coach at Wisconsin. Yost, who did appreciate Friedman's skills, returned to the sideline in 1925. Somehow, despite outscoring opponents 227-3, the Wolverines managed to lose one of their eight games, 3-2, to Northwestern.

Yost's old style of play was going out of vogue to some extent. As round as it had been before the forward pass was made legal in 1906, the ball's shape was beginning to change to something a bit more aerodynamic. There had been a reshaping in 1912 that made the ball easier to grasp, though it was still not yet the smooth-looking missile of the future. The ball was altered again in the 1920s, leading to quarterbacks being able to throw spirals, not merely heave passes in their guys' direction.

For a quarterback who knew what he was doing—Friedman being a prime example—there was more comfort in unleashing passes. The odds improved of making the connection with the receiver's hands.

Yost deserved credit for adapting and for recognizing Friedman's potential. Although then, as now, the biggest game on the schedule was against Ohio State, it so happened that in the third week of the season Michigan was scheduled to meet Wisconsin with its new coach, George Little. Yost and Little had never been best pals either, but if their relationship in Ann Arbor had been a trifle frosty, it in no way compared to how angry Friedman was at his old coach. Friedman was after revenge and was well-positioned as the starting quarterback to obtain it.

The game was played at Camp Randall Stadium in Madison before forty-four thousand fans, but being on the road did not faze the Wolverines. On their first possession the Wolverines let Friedman wind up and throw deep. He completed a 60-yard pass for a touchdown and the early lead. The rules being somewhat different at the time, Wisconsin chose to kick off rather than take the ball. Sure enough, Friedman fielded the boot and ran the kick back 85 yards for another touchdown and a 14-0 lead.

"In less than a minute we had 14 points up on the board and had scuttled Mr. Little," Friedman said.[4]

Friedman had become an established star. He was voted an All-American that season and also in 1926 when Michigan again finished 7-1, falling only to Navy, 10-0. Friedman was also captain of the team in '26. The partnership between Yost and Friedman was far more fulfilling than the one Friedman experienced under Little. Yost grasped Friedman's gifts and praised his cleverness in using them to help Michigan win. "In Benny Friedman I have one of the greatest passers and one of the smartest quarterbacks in history," Yost said.[5]

The National Football League was established in 1920 as the American Professional Football Association in Canton, Ohio. The still-standing NFL name was adopted in 1922 as a replacement. So when Benny Friedman was completing his college degree, he had the opportunity to continue in the sport as a pro and make a living at football.

As a shaky start-up, the NFL in very few ways resembled the smooth-running corporate giant of today. Teams came and went at a rapid rate, and nearly a century later only the Chicago Bears, Green Bay Packers, and Arizona Cardinals, who began life as the Chicago Cardinals, remain. Many other hopefuls lasted just a few seasons before they went bankrupt.

A new team for the 1925 season was the New York Giants. Even then, New York was viewed as the media hub of the nation, and it was believed that for any professional sports league to succeed it must have a strong foundation in New York City. The NFL dearly wanted to place a franchise in New York, and President Joe Carr approached a friend of his whom he thought would be a worthy leader. The friend declined, but referred Carr to one of his friends, Tim Mara. Mara plunked down five hundred dollars to establish the Giants.

Despite only minimal investment, at first, it did not look like a sound one. The Giants at times were on the verge of going the way of the Kenosha Maroons and the Muncie Flyers, both original league clubs. In retrospect, Mara's payout looks like the deal of the century, especially since the Mara family still owns the Giants.

When Friedman completed his eligibility at Michigan, his rights belonged to the Cleveland Bulldogs. They were founded in 1923 as the Cleveland Indians, hopeful that choosing the same nickname as the American League baseball franchise would rub off in fan attention. In 1924 the Cleveland team merged with the Canton Bulldogs and took the Bulldog moniker. Illustrating what a terrific deal Mara got, Sam Deutsch paid twenty-five hundred dollars to take over Canton.

Cleveland won the NFL title in 1924 with a 7-1-1 record. As an All-American with a prominent name and having his roots in Cleveland, Friedman was an attractive get for the team he joined in the fall of 1927. Cleveland did well, finishing 8-4-1. But new ownership wanted a change of scenery and transferred the team to Detroit, where it became the Wolverines. It was nice symmetry for Friedman, since his college team had had the same nickname. Naturally, playing for a team in Detroit was like a second homecoming for Friedman, since he was less than an hour away from Ann Arbor.

Friedman got some playing time in his rookie-year opener and threw a 50-yard pass, but he realized quite quickly that there was a vast gulf in ability between the professional and college defenders who were coming after him.

"Precision, exactness, hard-hitting—those young men knew their business better than any varsity team I had ever opposed," Friedman said. "When they tackled, it was at your shoestrings. When they blocked, you went down and you stayed down."[6]

Red Grange, the legendary "Galloping Ghost," was a rival of Friedman's when he played for Illinois against Michigan and when he played for the Chicago Bears in the NFL. He watched as Friedman sought to absorb the nuances of the pro game and adjust. As Friedman implied, when the bigger, faster players in the pros hit you, you stayed hit.

"I saw Benny take terrific beatings in professional football, yet I never heard him cry about it," Grange said. "The big ends and tackles always tried harder to discourage a great passer in pro football than in the college game, but they never discouraged Benny."[7]

Friedman took his hard knocks and learned. He became more creative as a passer. Allowed to throw, he took advantage of teams that did not have sophisticated plans to stop him. To show how slowly passing had advanced as a weapon, in 1927 with Cleveland, Friedman's 11 touchdown passes represented a new league record for a season. That was twenty-one years after St. Louis U.

NFL stats are sketchy from the 1920s, with marks for yardage not being totaled. Touchdowns were counted, however. Friedman led the league in TD passes in 1927, 1928, 1929, and 1930, even as he bumped around from team to team. Friedman only collected nine touchdown passes in 1928, but it was still more than anyone else in the NFL.

While Friedman was toiling elsewhere, the New York Giants won their first championship in 1927. Mara watched Friedman play for a while and, inspired by the drawing card that Red Grange had become, decided he wanted a first-rate star on his club. He attempted to purchase Friedman from the Wolverines but was turned down. Instead, he waved a check (variously reported as worth thirty-five hundred or ten thousand dollars) at the Detroit owners and obtained the entire franchise merely so that he could put Friedman in his lineup.

Mara needed a gate attraction. Pro football had yet to catch on in New York, and the Giants were going to fold if they couldn't put more fannies in the seats at the Polo Grounds. Mara had lost forty thousand dollars in 1928. Mara saw Friedman as a winner on the field and as a player who could make his team a box-office success. New York also had a large Jewish population, and Mara was sure his new man would gather fans from that community. Friedman did not come cheap. Mara paid him ten thousand dollars in 1929, a huge sum for a pro football player at the time. Many of Friedman's teammates were making only a hundred dollars a game.

Friedman did become quite popular in New York, and in 1929 he threw for 20 touchdowns, a startling number for the time and a new NFL record. Friedman was selected as a first-team all-star in the NFL during his first four seasons and was also chosen as a second-team and third-team performer once each later in his career, following a knee injury that diminished some of his effectiveness.

The 20-touchdown-pass total was so far out of the norm, so far beyond what other quarterbacks were doing, that it took fifteen years before any other *team* matched that number for touchdown passes in a season.

Acknowledged as the league's first great quarterback, although it took until 2005 for Friedman to be enshrined in the Pro Football Hall of Fame, he retired with 66 touchdown passes. At the time, that record seemed as out of sight for anyone to match as Babe Ruth's 60 home runs for the New York Yankees in 1927.

Wellington Mara, who was a ball boy for the Giants as a youth and lived to be eighty-nine years old before passing away in 2005, said Friedman was a marvel to watch as a passer who was stuck with an old-fashioned ball that was difficult to aim with much accuracy.

"I think the most amazing thing about him was the way he could throw the kind of football that was in use in his days," the younger Mara said. "Did you ever see that ball? It was like trying to throw a wet sock."[8]

Despite the nation tumbling into the Great Depression, with Friedman at the controls, Mara began making a profit each year. Ticket holders were thrilled by his performance. Friedman accomplished what he was hired to do and enhanced his own reputation.

Friedman played for the Giants between 1929 and 1931 and completed his NFL career playing for the Brooklyn (football) Dodgers from 1932 through 1934. A navy man during World War II, Friedman spent most of the rest of his career in athletic administration. The Hall of Fame opened in Canton, Ohio, in 1963 and in his later years Friedman expressed frustration and anger about being overlooked for enshrinement. On November 24, 1982, suffering from depression, heart disease, and diabetes, which necessitated the amputation of one leg, he committed suicide. Friedman was seventy-seven.

George Halas, one of the founders of the NFL in 1920 and the founding owner of the Chicago Bears, always raved about Friedman's capabilities, especially with the clunky old ball, which Halas said measured "a plump 23 inches around the middle. Benny Friedman was the first pro quarterback to exploit the strategic possibilities of the pass. Until Friedman came along, the pass had been used as a desperation weapon in long-yardage situations on third down, or when your team was hopelessly behind."[9]

Halas said the sight of Friedman heaving the balloon ball led the rules committee to trim the size of the ball twice, in 1931 and in 1934, to make it more aerodynamic.

Twenty-three years after his death, Friedman was chosen for the Hall of Fame. He was right all along on that count.

"Benny revolutionized football," said Halas. "He forced the defenses out of the dark ages."[10]

CHAPTER 5 • Sammy Goes to College

His arm strength was natural, but the development of Sammy Baugh into a quarterback took work. There may have been skill similarities in the throwing motions between chucking a football and throwing a man out running to first base, but football and baseball are different sports requiring different mindsets and routines.

When he was still living in Sweetwater, and before he was a football player of major significance, Baugh practiced hard throwing the oversized ball. Many times Baugh threw passes to his brother Bob or someone else in the area, but when he could not find someone to run downfield he called an audible.

On a tree in the family backyard, a swing hung, held up by a sturdy rope. Baugh may or may not have asked permission, but he took down the swing and hooked an old tire to the rope. He pushed the tire back and forth, making for a moving target, and he faded back as if retreating from the line of scrimmage. The he either planted his foot for traction or threw on the move, aiming the pigskin for the doughnut hole in the middle of the tire.

Baugh put hours into the workouts, seeking to make his throws sharper and more direct. He did a lot of throwing on the move, which was not always recommended in games, but sometimes required. He even practiced throwing across his body where he was running right and throwing left. Again, such moves were not always an advisable strategy and could lead to interceptions, but they were occasionally called for in a game.

Many years later, Baugh once engaged in a promotional contest where he was one of five quarterbacks who threw a football at a hoop hanging from the crossbar of a goalpost. The other four quarterbacks missed, but Baugh made the throw just right on his first try. A fan commented that it was pretty neat that he pulled it off but noted that it was not relevant to what goes on in games when the pass catcher is on the run. Thinking back to his days of firing the ball through the swinging target, Baugh almost laughed out loud. "Yeah, I know," Baugh said.[1] A little private joke there.

When his prospects fizzled on the baseball front at Washington State, and then the University of Texas refused to allow him to play football if he was going to compete for the baseball team, Baugh made the life-altering choice to enroll at Texas Christian University.

Leo "Dutch" Meyer was then the head baseball coach and freshman football coach. Soon enough he would become head football coach, and eventually he would coach the basketball team, too. Meyer had played end for TCU in 1916 and 1917 and returned after World War I to play in 1920 and 1921. Meyers saw something special in Baugh as an athlete and was well placed to coax it to the surface.

In 1933, when Baugh showed up on campus in Fort Worth, he was lanky and nowhere near as filled out as he would become as a professional when he weighed 182 pounds. The first thing new players do when they turn out for a team at a college is get outfitted. The sight of what to him seemed to be a veritable Ichabod Crane led trainer and equipment man Albert Smith to ridicule Meyer's recruiting efforts.

"Coach," Smith said, "you'll kill that boy. He ain't built rugged enough. He may survive the first scrimmage, but he'll never live through a whole season. Why don't you give him his fielder's glove and let him go out and play catch?"[2]

Meyer had promised a chance for Baugh to play football, but although he had heard of him he recalled him mostly as a good punter. He really wanted Baugh for the baseball team since that was his acknowledged best sport at the time.

Meyer and head football coach Francis Schmidt slowly gained an appreciation for Baugh's right arm and realized he was the best thrower the Horned Frogs had, freshman or not. But Baugh was still quite raw. He had been mostly overlooked in high school and needed tutoring in the art of passing.

Meyer was an early proponent of integrating passing more into offenses. He saw the potential in passing and in Baugh—an early case of a passing quarterback landing in the right spot, at the right school. If Baugh had hooked on with a different school for football, he might have been wasted as a signal-caller who ran half the time and handed off to others the other half of the possessions. Another possibility, of course, is emerging from practice as someone a coach could not ignore, even if that coach wasn't keen on passing.

"Everything I ever learned about football I learned from Dutch Meyer," Baugh said. "Back in those days, nobody knew anything about the passing game. Most teams—even in the pros—would try to pound at you with the running game and then, in desperation, throw on third and long. Then they would just try to throw it as far as they could."[3]

What TCU did under Meyer was meld passing into the mainstream offense. Rather than devolve into the flying-wedge days with scads of blockers leading out in front of the ball carrier, the Horned Frogs actually worked at moving the ball for first downs as part of the game plan.

"Dutch taught us the short passing game," Baugh said, "and it was a revolutionary thing for that day and time. We would just move the ball right down the field using short passes—with little risk of an interception—and nobody could figure out how to stop it."[4]

Baugh was not exaggerating in viewing Meyer as a coach ahead of his time. The passing game's ascension into an equal partner on offense was very slow in coming. Meyer, who was smart enough to recognize that in Baugh he had a remarkable talent, gave his young charge an early pep talk. Meyer put the ball in Baugh's hands, and that choice put the fate of the team on the quarterback's shoulders. That was a lot of trust.

This also meant that TCU, on demand from Baugh, could fool foes by passing when nobody thought the Horned Frogs would. The older thinkers reviewed situations and felt they were obvious running downs. TCU, Meyer, and Baugh did not play that way.

"Early on," Baugh said, "he told me, 'You can throw from our 1-yard line if you see an opening and I'll never question you.' In a lot of ways he was years ahead of his time. I watch the TV today and I see 'em doing things they think are new concepts. And they're doing the same damn things Dutch was doing in the '30s."[5]

During Baugh's three seasons as quarterback for Texas Christian, the Horned Frogs went 29-7-2, won two bowl games, and won the 1935 National Championship. While Baugh's career passing statistics seem pedestrian in comparison to the numbers that contemporary quarterbacks put up, in the mid-1930s, they were extraordinary.

In fact, a typical quarterback in the NFL in the current decade would record the kind of statistics in a single year that Baugh accumulated during his career. Baugh's college-career totals included 270 pass completions for 3,384 yards and 39 touchdowns. Those were unheard-of statistics for the era. Baugh also punted for a 41.3-yard average, and many football observers actually thought kicking was Baugh's true forte.

Meyer, who loved Baugh's versatility, was one of those believers.

"He was the greatest I ever saw," Meyer said of Baugh's quarterbacking. "But as good as he was throwing the ball he was an even better punter. There was no spot on a football field where he could not drop a punt on a dime if he wanted to."[6]

Meyer was not taking over a team that was weak. Predecessor Francis Schmidt had run the program for five seasons, starting in 1929, winning at least eight games each year, and in 1932 went 10-0-1 before departing to take over at Ohio State.

Schmidt was famous for uttering a statement that has long since become a cliché in sports when coaches tell players not to worry about the reputation of a foe: "those fellows put their pants on one leg at a time, the same as everyone else," Schmidt said. Although some say the remark was commonly made in Texas, Schmidt gained credit for it after he used it with the Buckeyes.[7]

In 1934, Meyer's first year as head man—and with Baugh, the sophomore, holding down the quarterback job—the Horned Frogs went 8-4. Baugh attempted 161 passes. TCU won a national championship in 1935 with a 12-1 record, including a victory in the Cotton Bowl. Baugh threw 219 passes that year. The next season TCU's record was 9-2, and again Baugh threw 219 times.

That should have been lesson enough to the football world that passing was a valuable tool. Teams had to learn the hard way and then go out and find a player who could run an offense built around passing. TCU already had one.

In his later years in life, Baugh would remember little about his freshman season, which played out at LaGrave Field, a place that through the years was used more often for minor league baseball. Baugh said he only remembered playing a few games as he idled away his time in anticipation of a shift to the varsity the next year.

Ed Pritchard, whose family moved to Fort Worth just in time for him to watch Baugh play for the frosh, and who was also a student, said, "He was our idol, our hero. But we were never in awe of him because he was also our good friend."[8]

Baugh did make friends at TCU who would in one way or another remain part of his life forever.

This was not a great time in the United States. Anyone like Baugh who was fortunate enough to be enrolled in a college and had his way paid with a scholarship was faring better than most of the rest of the country. The stock market collapse in October 1929 triggered the massive fall of the US economy. It took basically a decade for things to return to normal. Gearing up for the likelihood of a world war that began for the United States after Japan bombed Pearl Harbor on December 7, 1941, would be what it took for the country's employment rate and manufacturing efforts to rebound. Approximately 14 million Americans were out of work in 1933, Baugh's freshman year, and almost half of the nation's banks failed because of panicking savers and investors who wanted their money in their own hands. Being sheltered on a college campus was not the worst place to be, especially if you were guaranteed a roof over your head and meals.

Baugh did not start his first game with the varsity in 1934. Joe Coleman, a senior who was an established player, quaterbacked the Horned Frogs to a 10-0 lead over Daniel Baker College before Meyer inserted Baugh into the game to see what he could do. Meyer very much liked what he saw. Baugh scored one touchdown and threw for three more.

In the next game, Baugh and Coleman alternated in the job, but Sammy Baugh was not quite Sammy Baugh yet. He was more prone to errors: in the game against Arkansas, Baugh fumbled and threw two interceptions that all led to Razorback touchdowns and the loss of the game.

Baugh kept improving, including in his role on defense as a safety. Against Baylor, Baugh intercepted two passes in the fourth quarter. He threw for 206 yards and two touchdowns against Texas, although again TCU fell, 20-19.

At the end of Baugh's sophomore year he suited up for the Horned Frogs baseball team, and his wicked throws to first on grounders led a sportswriter for the *Fort Worth Star-Telegram* to bless Baugh with a new nickname. He was called "Slingin' Sammy Baugh" in print for the first time, and it had nothing to do with football.

The Horned Frogs showed enough during the 1934 football season—particularly newcomer Baugh—to give prognosticators ammunition to rate them very highly going into the 1935 season. They were expected to rule the Southwest Conference. TCU fooled the observers. They did not win the league title, but instead won the national title with just one defeat.

TCU's defense was superb, recording shutout after shutout against the likes of Howard Payne, Loyola of New Orleans, Baylor, and Texas. Baugh's punting astonished spectators. He booted one for 73 yards and one for 75 yards. The only loss came to Southern Methodist, 20-14, as time ran out while Baugh was trying to orchestrate a winning drive.

It was SMU's defense that did the job. Baugh attempted 44 passes, a stunning number for the time, but completed just 17 for 180 yards. TCU receivers had an off day, dropping eight passes. Baugh credited the Mustangs' play. Grantland Rice, the legendary sportswriter, who had taken an interest in what Baugh might accomplish, seemed as impressed as ever by Baugh's powerful arm and his ability to lay the ball on the money, just as he did when he was firing at that swinging tire.

"He could murder a fly on a fence with the snout of that missile at any distance from one yard to 50," Rice wrote.[9]

Losing to SMU cost Texas Christian an unbeaten year and a trip to the Rose Bowl. The Mustangs were 12-0 and took the trail to Pasadena to meet Stanford. TCU was invited to the Sugar Bowl. SMU fell 7-0. On New Year's Day, January 1, 1936, the Horned Frogs faced Louisiana State before thirty-five thousand fans in Tulane Stadium. In one of the most unusual final scores in major bowl history, Texas Christian triumphed, 3-2.

It began raining in New Orleans three days before the game. There was a brief respite, and then it poured throughout the contest. The grassy field grew soggy, then muddy, then almost impassable. Footing was awful—not much different than trying to gain traction in quicksand. The conditions, also chilly, were hardly ideal for football, for running, for throwing the ball, or for just about anything besides staying home by a fire.

"There was standing water over your shoe tops," Meyer said. "After every play, when they put the ball down, an official had to stand there with his foot on it to keep it from floating away."[10]

Baugh gave LSU a safety. The Tigers went ahead 2-0 when he stepped on the end line of the end zone while trying to pass, but TCU won on a field goal. Much like in Major League Baseball where the ball remained in play despite scuffs for as long as possible, footballs were not swapped out during games. That meant the ball Baugh had to throw was mud-encrusted and extra heavy from water weight.

Texas Christian escaped the miserable conditions with a victory, though if the clock had run just long enough for one more play it is possible the Horned Frogs would have put up a touchdown. Baugh registered a 43-yard run to the LSU 1-yard line just before time ran out.

TCU's perseverance, combined with SMU's defeat, resulted in the Horned Frogs being ranked number one in the country after the bowls. There were no playoffs at the time, only ratings, and the voters spoke, giving Texas Christian the National Championship.

In this modern age, such an achievement would have been honored with flowers strewn in the path of their muddy shoes as they walked off the field, a parade, and appearances by key players on national television shows.

"Back then we really didn't make a big deal out of it," Baugh said. "I don't remember even being aware of the fact there was a national ranking until we were told after the season we had been voted the No. 1 team. What excited us most was that it provided some recognition for TCU outside the state of Texas."[11]

Considerable talent graduated from the championship squad, but TCU still had Baugh back for a final season in 1936. He was better than ever, but it took some time to comfortably mix new players into the lineup. The Horned Frogs started slowly, but finished strong, being invited to the Cotton Bowl.

By then Baugh's reputation had expanded well beyond the Texas border. His university took pains to promote him and spread the word about the exceptional passer. One interested observer was George Halas, who became a Baugh supporter early and whose Chicago Bears might well have had a stake in selecting Baugh in the NFL player draft.

Leading up to the 1936 season, the first year the NFL instituted a draft of college players, a team of college all-stars, coached by Dutch Meyer, met the Bears, coached by Halas, and the younger players won, 7-6.

"Passes did the trick," Meyer said. "The game certainly proves a long-contended point. The Southwest Conference, and southern players are in a class by themselves at the aerial game. The pros are big, clever, and tough. But there's no amount of brawn that pass trickery can't overcome."[12]

The Horned Frogs completed the regular season with an 8-2-2 record but had their season extended by an invitation to the Cotton Bowl. This was the inaugural Cotton Bowl Classic, which remains a staple of the postseason college football bowl season even into the second decade of the twenty-first century. There was a clamor in some quarters for a Texas team to be one of the teams selected for participation, and TCU got the nod to face Marquette of Milwaukee. (Marquette is now known for its success on the basketball scene, long after dropping football.)

On January 1, 1937, Marquette was the twentieth-ranked team in the land. Then nicknamed the Golden Avalanche, Marquette brought a 7-1 record to Texas for Sammy Baugh's last college game.

Marquette had its own star quarterback in Ray Buivid, nicknamed "Buzz." The Heisman Trophy, the annual award emblematic of the best player in college football, was in only its second year of being handed out, and the winner had already been proclaimed. That year's honoree was Larry Kelley of Yale. Buivid was third in the voting and Baugh fourth, so fans were expecting a shootout between the quarterbacks.

Before the game, Marquette coach Frank Murphy said he had never seen Baugh play but was confident his quarterback, Buivid, could throw as well as any college player. He thought Buivid could throw deep better than Baugh. Murphy's outlook proved to be optimistic.

TCU and Baugh outdid Marquette and Buivid, but it was not a weather day conducive to much passing. The Horned Frogs won, 16-6, with all of their points coming from "Little Dutch" Meyer, the coach's nephew. Baugh gained 100 yards through the air.

And that's how Baugh's college career came to an end. He and Meyer had made a statement to the football world that a team could pass its way to glory.

CHAPTER 6 • NFL RULE CHANGES

By 1932 the National Football League was shaking out. Franchises from small cities that had been part of the creation of pro football as we know it in 1920 were flaking off, dropping out of the league because they found participation too costly to continue. The cities they were based in loved the game, but were not big-time.

There were sixteen teams in 1920. The Chicago Tigers were gone. The Decatur Staleys became the Chicago Bears. The Rochester Jeffersons and Rock Island Independents were gone; the Hammond Pros and the Akron Pros both were no longer pros.

Few small-town clubs remained by 1932. The Green Bay Packers survived and persevered against all odds. The Portsmouth Spartans were another squad hanging on in Ohio. Soon enough, Portsmouth would become the Detroit Lions.

However, in 1932 the Spartans were one of the finest teams in the league. In those days the NFL did not have a playoff system. It still awarded its annual championship to the team with the fewest losses. However, since the teams did not play uniform schedules, some peculiar final standings resulted. That season the Bears finished 7-1-6. The Packers finished 10-3-1. Portsmouth finished 6-1-4. A lot of tie games happened that season; indeed, the Bears and Spartans tied one another twice that season, so the first tiebreaker to determine a champ did not break the tie. None of the other five franchises finished above .500.

Since the Bears and Spartans each had just one defeat, it was decided to conduct a playoff for the championship for the first time. In theory this was a solid idea, and the Bears were awarded home field. In those days the Bears played their home games at Wrigley Field, home of baseball's Chicago Cubs.

However, the scheduled December 18 championship meeting was placed in jeopardy by vicious weather striking the Windy City. A blizzard howled in off Lake Michigan and it snowed for days. Streets became virtually impassable. The temperature was frigid. It seemed possible that football players at Wrigley would suffer frostbite. Fans were likely to stay away in droves.

After studying the nasty weather, the league made the call to play the contest indoors at Chicago Stadium, where the Chicago Blackhawks National Hockey League team competed. This was the first indoor game in NFL history, long before anyone envisioned teams playing in cavernous domed stadiums. Besides having a roof, Chicago Stadium in no way resembled those futuristic stadiums. In fact, it was too small to play the game on a field with the proper dimensions.

Given the snow drifts that were several feet deep and the intensive labor it took for city workers to dig out the elevated train lines, it was somewhat miraculous that attendance registered 11,198 fans.

Everyone had to adjust. Rather than measuring 100 yards, the field was 80 yards long, the same length field the smallest high schools in the country use to play six-man football. Similarly, the normal width of 53 yards across was reduced to 45 yards. Even though no one had heard of such a thing at the time, the field more resembled what is used for arena football. The contest came to be known as "The Tom Thumb Game" because of the smaller-than-regulation field.

It was widely predicted that the showdown between the Bears and Spartans would be high-scoring. Things did not turn out that way. Chicago won the championship, 9-0, but the game triggered some major changes in the NFL.

The idea of concluding the season with a championship game took hold. Beginning with the 1933 season, teams were split into an East Division and a West Division, and from then on a title game between the winners was played. Also, the 1932 championship game's most critical play led to a rule change that opened up the passing game for the future.

Only one touchdown was scored in that 1932 title game. The Bears got six points on a pass play that began with a hike to quarterback Carl Brumbaugh. Brumbaugh handed off to fullback Bronko Nagurski, the iron man of the era who doubled as a hard-hitting linebacker. Nagurski fired a pass over the middle to halfback Red Grange, the onetime University of Illinois scatback.

Nagurski and Grange were legendary figures. Both were inducted into the first class of the Pro Football Hall of Fame in 1963. Grange gained coast-to-coast fame in college with an astounding game that ripped apart the University of Michigan. On the day Illinois opened its new Memorial Stadium in 1924, the 6-foot, 180-pound Grange shredded the Wolverines by scoring four touchdowns in the first 12 minutes and five total in a 39-14 romp.

In 1925, wooed by agent C. C. Pyle, nicknamed "Cash and Carry," Grange turned pro. That year, he was the featured player in a barnstorming tour with the Bears and was showcased all around the country before large crowds. The performance not only made Grange a rich man, it also solidified pro football in the eyes of the sporting public.

Nagurski was 6-foot-2 and weighed about 230 pounds. Few linemen weighed that much at the time. He also had a powerful physique and was described as a human battering ram.

The Bears gained possession on an interception by Dick Nesbitt, who returned the ball to the Portsmouth 7-yard line. On the key play that gave Chicago the title, Nagurski was supposed to bull up the middle. He made the call to throw on his own. Grange had originally been knocked down near the goal line, but he scrambled to his feet and grabbed Nagurski's toss.

There was an immediate outcry from Portsmouth's coaches claiming that Nagurski violated a fundamental passing rule. Spartan coach Potsy Clark ran onto the field screaming at the refs. He declared he was playing the game under protest. Bears coach and owner George Halas shot Clark a middle-finger insult and said, "Protest this!"[1]

At that time no pass could be thrown in an NFL game from nearer than 5 yards to the line of scrimmage. The Spartans asserted that Nagurski had not dropped back far enough and therefore the pass was illegal. The officials let the throw stand, however. They had no instant replay to consult.

The controversy lingered. In the off-season, with Halas spearheading the move, the NFL revisited the rules on passing. It seemed clear to Halas and to other allies that a more wide-open throwing game would result in more scoring and would likely attract bigger crowds.

Halas was an influential member of the NFL almost from its inception. He was present at the creation in a Hupmobile showroom in Canton, Ohio, and as the original owners disappeared one by one, his stature grew. A dozen years after it all began, Halas's power was increasing, and when he proposed any kind of change, the other owners listened. They did not always agree, and Halas, by his gruff nature, made enemies as well. But he had clout, and even those who disliked him recognized that when Halas became involved backing a proposal, he believed it was for the benefit of the entire league, not only his Chicago Bears.

While Halas had his say on this matter, he could not have forced the issue without the important cooperation of George Preston Marshall. Marshall, who entered the league as a partner in the Boston Redskins, obtained full control of that team and shifted it to Washington.

Halas was grumpy about following the circus into Chicago Stadium for the 1932 title game, but Marshall was a showman at heart. He loved the fanfare, marching bands, and the colorful life of show business. He married an actress and introduced the Redskins Marching Band. In his view, the passing game represented the future.

Marshall was essentially a newcomer to the club, with his debut season as an owner coming in 1933. But he was not a shrinking violet. If he had a strong opinion, it was not closely held. At the owners meeting where discussions took place to liberalize passing rules, Marshall made a thought-provoking argument.

"Gentleman," Marshall said, "you know far more about the game of football than me. But, gentlemen, the game you are playing is not entertaining. It is dull, uninteresting, and boring. This is how I look at it. We are in show business. And when the show gets dull, you throw it out. You put another one in its place. I want to give the public what it wants. I want to change the show."[2]

Marshall did more than issue a sweeping statement. He proposed the goalposts be moved up to the goal line, that hash marks be placed on the field, the divisional system be adopted, and the ball be altered to make it more aerodynamic. Halas, who had more clout within the group, stifled the dissent somewhat when he stood to speak and agreed with Marshall.

"Men, we all know that Mr. Marshall is a little different than us," Halas said. "But these are some issues we need to address. It wouldn't hurt to change our game. I find all of these proposals pretty damn satisfactory. I am behind each and every one of them."[3]

Other rules that had been in effect for some time held back the appeal of the passing game, and coaches were loath to throw too often because of them. At that meeting the owners did away with a 5-yard penalty for an incomplete forward pass. They eliminated the change-of-possession rule if a team threw incomplete into the end zone.

Above all, the roundish ball became more streamlined. From a circumference of fifteen inches, which made it unwieldy to throw, the size was reduced to twelve inches. The NFL went from a fat ball to a skinnier ball, as if the ball had enrolled in Weight Watchers. Halas was remembering the figures incorrectly when he spoke years after about the dimensions. The new ball came into use for the 1934 season.

When the rule was put in place giving the quarterback, or any thrower, the freedom to roam behind the line of scrimmage, it was given the appellation "The Bronko Nagurski Rule" because of his touchdown pass versus Portsmouth.

That may have been the most significant change adopted that led to the prominence of the quarterback in the offense. Up until then, the quarterback was merely one of the backfield mates. Once permitted to run around and throw, even while approaching the line of scrimmage, the quarterback became a more important weapon.

It is instructive to realize that Benny Friedman accomplished what he did with the old-style football and under the restrictive nature of the old rules. By 1934 Friedman was in his final season in the NFL. However, the New York Giants, who had thrived under his leadership, had discovered a more-than-adequate replacement.

Harry Newman was the second coming of Friedman at the University of Michigan and with the Giants. An All-American for the Wolverines in 1932, Newman stepped right in as the quarterback for New York in 1933. He was named All-Pro that season and led the NFL with 53 pass completions for 973 yards and 11 touchdowns. Those were hardly pinball numbers, but the passing game was inching its way along.

The next year, Newman, who stood just 5-foot-8 and weighed under 180 pounds, was selected All-Pro again. But even though the Giants won their first world championship in 1934, Newman broke two bones in his back in the tenth game. Ironically, Newman, who apparently was just an old-fashioned guy, actually complained about the new football in use being more difficult for him to handle than the old one. Of all things, Newman said the slimmer ball was "harder to pass" than its predecessor.[4] That did not make much sense, but Newman was more of a shooting star as a pro player. Since Friedman had brought the Giants so much good fortune, and Newman had been the same order of All-American star at Michigan, they paid him ten thousand dollars per season.

That was much more than the average player earned. For Newman that represented about eight hundred dollars per game in Depression-era dollars to others' one hundred dollars per game. When Newman's results began to diminish after his solid start, the Giants lost interest. Newman was out of the NFL after three years.

While Newman failed to adjust to the new ball, another team took over NFL leadership in the passing game. The Green Bay Packers, under Coach Curly Lambeau, emerged from the alteration of the rules as the fondest embracers of the passing game—at least temporarily.

As for Marshall, his Redskins were far more popular in Washington than they had been in Boston and became a hotter ticket still when he made a shrewd personnel decision in 1937. When Marshall was advocating for the rules changes after the 1932 season on the basis of entertainment value, he could not have imagined that in five years he would obtain a young man who would do more to revolutionize the passing game on the field than Marshall did in a conference room.

In 1932 Sammy Baugh was still at Sweetwater High in Texas. He had yet to be recruited by Texas Christian, never mind to be viewed as a savior of a professional franchise. For Marshall, who had his share of flaws—particularly his reprehensible efforts to keep the Redskins an all-white team and hold back integration in the NFL in later years—it might be said that drafting the grand prize in the coming quarterback sweepstakes was justice for his role in boosting the status of the forward pass.

CHAPTER 7 • Green Bay Guys I

Earl "Curly" Lambeau was coach of the Green Bay Packers before there was a National Football League, taking over the fledgling organization in 1919.

He was boss of the Pack when the NFL started, remaining in charge of the team through the 1949 season. Lambeau led the Packers through the formative years of the league and helped keep them alive and in Green Bay when every other small-city team folded or moved, a development that in retrospect is somewhat miraculous. Almost twenty years into the twenty-first century, Green Bay is the only community represented in the four major team sports in the United States without a base of a million or millions of fans.

Under Lambeau, the Packers were extremely successful, winning six world championships. They developed one of the most storied rivalries in sport against the Chicago Bears, the intensity of which continues to this day. And Lambeau was ahead of his time, a pioneer of the professional throwing game when it came to recognizing the potential of the forward pass.

The curly haired Lambeau—hence the nickname—was a native son, born in Green Bay in 1898 and a star athlete at Green Bay East High. He was one of four children in a Catholic family, that dark black hair appealing to the girls, the attention of whom he did not shun. Lambeau was multitalented enough to play several sports in high school. He starred in track and field, but football was his favorite.

As a high school player, Lambeau was blessed with a powerful build. He stood 5-foot-10 and weighed 185 pounds. He was stocky and powerful and an exceptional runner and kicker. Also, despite the era and how little exposure the passing game had received, Lambeau fell in love with the forward pass, even as a teenager. Of course, Lambeau was saddled with the old round ball, which did not help his accuracy, but he kept trying to throw and was convinced that passing was going to become a major element in football.

Lambeau was captain of his high school team and was good enough to pique the interest of Knute Rockne at Notre Dame.

This fit in with Lambeau's master life plan. His senior class yearbook contained a brash prediction out of his mouth: "When I get through with athletics, I'm going out and conquer the rest of the world," Lambeau said.[1] The young man did not lack for confidence.

Completing his high school sports career, Lambeau had a bit of trouble getting started in college athletics. He enrolled at the University of Wisconsin, but with the advent of World War I, the Badgers dropped freshman football for the year. Instead of matriculating at a college in 1917, Lambeau worked for his father's construction company. The work only added more muscle to his already-strong frame.

A year later Notre Dame held appeal for Lambeau. Knute Rockne was not yet the legendary coach he would become. The 1918 season was his first. As a good Catholic, however, Lambeau was naturally attracted to Notre Dame. He signed on with the Fighting Irish and suited up as a freshman that year.

During Christmas break, however, Lambeau incurred a sore throat, which morphed into a severe case of tonsillitis. So sick that he missed six weeks of school, Lambeau had surgery, but he felt that he had fallen so far behind in his studies he would never be able to catch up. The tonsillitis forced Lambeau to drop out of school and return to Green Bay. Those close to Lambeau—his family and girlfriend's family—urged him to return and pick up his schooling at Notre Dame, but Lambeau did not do it. This choice altered Lambeau's life trajectory, and the twists that followed never did place him in position to conquer the world—except the world of professional football, which he did, with commitment, energy, aplomb, some would say arrogance, and focus, a man who seemed single-minded about his team and profession.

Lambeau was looking for a good job and found it with the Indian Packing Company, which had relocated to Green Bay from Rhode Island. Lambeau became manager of the manufacturing company at a time when the sports editor of the local newspaper began lobbying for the establishment of a local football team.

From the start, the squad's nickname was the Packers. Like many other such outfits sprinkled around the Midwest, when the call went out to band together and start up a professional football league, the Packers were intrigued. The Packers became a cornerstone franchise of the new league. Two seasons later, the Indian Packing Company was bought and became the Acme Packers. Lambeau was captain of the first Packer eleven. At the same time his old high school needed a coach, and he took over that team, too, running the program for three seasons while he operated the Packers.

Statistics were sketchy in the early days of the NFL. Major League Baseball, renowned as the sport most steeped in numbers, did not even keep track of runs batted in at first, so it should not be a surprise that official math was not one of the football league's strong suits in its early years.

Lambeau had already displayed his fondness for passing, but years later he claimed that during one game in the 1920 season he threw the ball 45 times. He told sportswriters that he completed 37 of those tosses. Lambeau said a teammate kept track of the passes that day and afterwards told him what those totals were. It was definitely an unofficial tally, but Lambeau believed it, even if he could not prove it.

"Forward passing had been permitted for fourteen years," Lambeau said, "and most of the original restrictions had been removed. But the passer still had to throw from at least five yards behind the line of scrimmage, which greatly reduced the possibility of deception."[2]

Lambeau and his boss, George Calhoun, the local sports editor who was co-running the team, credited Lambeau with attempting 17 passes per game in 1920 when the league-wide average was six tries. Those statistics may or may not have been precisely correct since official league data were not compiled that year. The numbers do demonstrate that Lambeau had a strong infatuation with the passing game early in his career, well ahead of many others.

In 1921, Charlie Mathys, who had attended Green Bay West High and played college ball for Indiana University, was signed by the Packers after playing two seasons in the NFL for the Hammond Pros. At times he was the Packers' top receiver, but then he became the starting quarterback. Mathys was 5-foot-7 and weighed 165 pounds, making him small even for a high school quarterback in the 2000s, but he was a solid player. He solidified his place in Packer lore in September 1925 when he was the quarterback who led Green Bay to its first victory over the Chicago Bears. Mathys threw a last-second touchdown pass in the 14-10 win.

Although Mathys was later inducted into the team Hall of Fame, the only statistics listed on the Green Bay Packers website for him are the number of games he played each season through 1926. No completions, yards gained, or touchdown passes are mentioned. Another source lists Mathys with 15 points scored in 1922, second on the team behind Lambeau's 24 points.

Lambeau played for the Packers in the NFL between 1921 and 1929, also coaching and continuing in that capacity in Green Bay for another twenty years, when he had a falling out with club administrators and left to coach the Chicago Cardinals for two seasons.

When the Pro Football Hall of Fame was established in Canton, Ohio, in 1963, Lambeau was a member of the first class. Cited as one reason for his induction into the Hall, the institution's officials wrote, "First coach to make forward pass an integral part of the offense."[3] There you have it. All those years later, Lambeau's affinity for the forward pass was noted.

Lambeau retired as a player after the 1929 season. He was thrilled that the Packers won the crown that year with a 12-0-1 record. Lambeau did have a ready-made replacement for himself as a passer, however. Arnie Herber grew up in Green Bay, played ball for Green Bay West, and was a Packers fan throughout his youth. When he was young, he even sold game programs at the stadium.

He was part Oneida. Coming out of high school, Herber signed up to play football for the University of Wisconsin but transferred to Regis College in Denver after one year. Then Regis dropped football, a move that sent Herber back to his home state wondering what to do.

Herber was in Green Bay working odd jobs before he approached Lambeau for a tryout. One job he accepted was doing chores for the Packers. But Lambeau remembered Herber as an all-around athlete in high school. Players did not warm up to Herber instantly, at first dismissing him with the derogatory label of "Dummy." But Lambeau knew best, signing Herber to a seventy-five-dollar-a-game contract. Once it was shown how well Herber could play, other nicknames attached to him. One was "Kid," and the other was "Flash."

He came along at just the right time, as Lambeau was stepping aside, and for a walk-on out of nowhere, with limited achievements in college ball, Herber was a find. Herber was plugged in on an extremely talented team that repeated as NFL champs with a 10-3-1 mark. Packer stars included Johnny "Blood" McNally; Verne Lewellen, who scored a team-high 54 points; and Lavvie Dilweg.

During this feel-your-way-with-the-pass era, the 5-foot-11, 203-pound Herber had a most unusual throwing style. The ball was still fatter than it was ever going to be after 1934, so all quarterbacks had some difficulty controlling it when they threw. Herber was larger than many of his backfield mates, but he had small hands, which made it especially challenging for him to pass.

Herber recognized this disadvantage and adapted his form. All football fans of today's era have seen so many quarterbacks fade back and throw that they know the appropriate throwing style. Herber's technique might make purists cringe: he could not wrap his fingers around the ball's laces for control. Rather, he let the ball slip back in his palm and, as one writer described his motion, "Instead of throwing, he actually heaved the ball. He was extremely accurate and could throw it a mile."[4]

While some teammates seemed to resent Herber's presence, Lambeau was always in Herber's corner and even traded away one player who insulted Herber. Lambeau, that early savant of the passing game, understood Herber's value. "Herber is the best long passer ever," Lambeau said.[5] Herber liked to engage in long toss, trying to see just how far he could throw a football. More than once he threw it 80 yards in the air.

In 1931, although Herber was barely involved, with just three game appearances, the Packers became the first team in NFL history to win three straight championships. Even though Herber became a key part of the offense, the lack of stat-keeping during his first few seasons left a blank slate next to his name in the all-time records. Once the NFL began official record-keeping in 1932, Herber's third season, the empirical evidence was out there to compare Herber to other quarterbacks.

Lambeau may have asserted he once threw 45 passes in a game, but it is clear that he began asking Herber to throw more often. In 1932, Herber led the NFL in passes attempted with 101 attempts, 37 completions, 639 yards, and nine touchdown passes. Those are puny totals by modern standards, but Herber was busier than other quarterbacks of the time.

The next year Herber completed 50 out of 124 attempts for 656 yards and three touchdowns. Compared to current-day quarterbacks' efforts Herber's completion percentage was nothing to brag about: 36.6 and 40.3, respectively, in those two seasons.

Herber was back to normal in 1934, again on top of the league in most categories. His 42 completions led the league, a number several quarterbacks might attain in a single game in the 2000s. He also was top-rated with 115 attempts, 799 yards, and eight touchdown tosses. "Arnie Herber was certainly the team's first great passer," the Packers' team website reported in highlighting Herber's career, "if not also the NFL's."[6]

One opposing coach who appreciated Herber's abilities was Clark Shaughnessy, regarded as the father of the T-formation. Shaughnessy coached Stanford and then masterminded the Bears' shift to that style.

"Herber's touchdown passes can be as demoralizing as a Ruthian home run," said Shaughnessy, comparing the impact of the six-pointers with a Babe Ruth blast for the New York Yankees. "He has the uncanny knack of arching a long pass so that the receiver simply races to the spot, makes the catch, and speeds on without breaking stride."[7]

Close examination of Shaughnessy's statement merely explains the most routine aspect of the link between the quarterback and receiver in the game today. But in the 1930s, that smooth working relationship was something new and worthy of comment. Very few quarterbacks were doing what Herber was capable of in the early 1930s. It was pretty much him and Benny Friedman before the next wave of passers joined the NFL.

"Arnie Herber was certainly one of the premier quarterbacks at the time he played," said Packers' team historian Lee Remmel. "He was one of the first great long passers in the NFL."[8]

One way that Herber earned that accolade occurred in the off-season. In 1931, as the Packers were emerging as the first great NFL dynasty, a Hollywood director wanted to make a movie about them. He got the fancy idea that a kicker should stand just so far away and kick toward the camera. Clark Hinkle came up short a couple of times, but then pulled off the trick. Next, it was decided that the quarterback, Herber, should stand

50 yards away from his camera and fire the ball at a pane of glass about three feet square, hanging from the goalposts, the toss being filmed as it neared.

After Herber limbered up his arm, he took aim at the glass and fired. *Bam*, the glass shattered. The director, however, who figured Herber would miss from that distance and they would all have to move closer, did not have the film rolling. A new pane of glass was hung, and Herber zipped another pass at it. *Bam*, the new glass broke, again on his first attempt.

"There was sort of a twist to that story that isn't generally known," Herber said. "After I had broken the pane twice from 50 yards out, they moved the camera into the end zone for a close-up of the football shattering the glass. I wasn't going to be in the picture, so I stood about 10 feet away—and missed."[9]

Herber had made a name for himself as a thrower in charge of the champion Green Bay Packers. What he did not realize as the 1935 season approached was that things were about to get better. The Packers were about to sign the pass catcher of the century.

CHAPTER 8 • Green Bay Guys II

The first time Curly Lambeau saw Don Hutson, the man who would help revolutionize the passing game with his extraordinary prowess as a receiver, Hutson was practicing for the Rose Bowl in Pasadena, California, during the closing days of 1934.

Hutson, a college teammate of Paul "Bear" Bryant, whom many regard as the greatest college football coach of all time, was a member of the University of Alabama team that faced Stanford on January 1, 1935.

Nine months later, Hutson was a member of the Green Bay Packers, a rookie end with dazzling moves, savvy, and hands. The combination of his talents made Hutson a brilliant wide receiver, widely considered one of the National Football League's all-time greats.

Hutson was born January 13, 1914, one of three brothers growing up in Pine Bluff, Arkansas. The most athletic of his siblings, Hustson competed in sports at the local high school before matriculating at Alabama. Initially, he was not terribly interested in scholastic sports, but his best friend in Pine Bluff talked him into going out for football.

Hutson and his pal Bob Seawell made a pitching-and-catching combo on the gridiron, but Seawell was the better player at the time. Hutson weighed just 145 pounds, and colleges weren't terribly interested in the skinny kid. Seawell was so good he received numerous scholarship offers. It was Seawell's intervention, making it a condition of his attendance at Alabama, that convinced the Crimson Tide to accept Hutson, too. That enabled the end to play football in Tuscaloosa. Once in, Hutson more than carried his weight, but getting the chance wasn't that easy.

Hutson blossomed in college, starring in football and baseball and running track as well. He played baseball professionally in the minors for a few years. Even then Alabama, under Coach Frank Thomas, was a national power (much like the school is today), and Hutson received All-American recognition at his position.

Alabama controlled Stanford in the Rose Bowl. Leading 22-13, Thomas wanted to run out the clock. He put Hutson back in the game for the sole purpose of ordering quarterback Millard Howell to call only running plays. Howell saw Hutson entering the game and figured he knew what that meant: Thomas wanted him to throw the bomb.

Hutson didn't even have time to deliver his coach's message before Howell called a deep pass and the ball was hiked. Hutson ran his route and sure enough Howell threw long for Hutson. The end gathered the ball in and romped for a 56-yard touchdown. In explanation, Hutson said, "I had to catch it, Coach. It was just too good a pass to drop."[1]

During that Rose Bowl, won by the Crimson Tide, Hutson scored on two touchdown passes. Lambeau and his wife vacationed in California, and Lambeau made a point of scouting top teams like Stanford and Alabama. Thomas made him welcome at practice, and Lambeau was impressed by Hutson's skills. He was completely taken with the 6-foot-1, 183-pound end when he watched him perform in the game. "I'd always dreamed of an end who could do the things Hutson did," Lambeau said.[2]

The NFL did not institute a player draft of college players until 1936, when it suffered the embarrassment of having its first-ever number-one overall selection refuse to play. Running back Jay Berwanger won the first Heisman Trophy in 1935 (which for that year only was called the Downtown Athletic Club Trophy, named for the organization awarding it). He was a star for the University of Chicago and was coveted by George Halas of the nearby Chicago Bears.

The Philadelphia Eagles actually selected Berwanger, but realizing his price was too high, they traded his rights to the Bears for a tackle named Art Bruss. Berwanger's heart did not burn for pro football, however. Halas negotiated as high as $13,500—which was generous for the times—but Berwanger said he would not play for less than $15,000.

Professional football seemed like such an iffy career path to Berwanger that he actually became a sportswriter for a little while rather than accept

Halas's deal. Then he went into the field of manufacturing plastic car parts, spurning Halas and never playing pro ball.

In the years leading up to the first draft, securing fresh talent was a free-for-all for NFL teams. Recommendations were passed on to teams or league coaches by word of mouth from trusted friends in various parts of the country. Many a player was signed sight unseen, although the pro clubs knew who had earned All-American mention, which was definitely a selling point to them.

As an enthusiastic believer in the passing game, Lambeau knew Hutson was a perfect fit for the Packers. He already had Arnie Herber in place at quarterback, but Lambeau knew that the addition of a player of Hutson's ability would only make Herber better. Just days after seeing Hutson tear up the Cardinals in the Rose Bowl, Lambeau approached the player with an offer to play for Green Bay.

While Lambeau's eye for talent was undeniable and he represented one of the best franchises in the league, there was an obstacle. Hutson had previously been approached by the Brooklyn Dodgers to play with that football club. The Dodgers' emissary was John "Shipwreck" Kelly, a colorful figure based on that nickname alone. Kelly gained his moniker not as a survivor of the *Titanic* or any such mishap, but because as a player for the University of Kentucky, he "shipwrecked" opposing defenses. Kelly played in the NFL and then became a banker, accumulating enough wealth to gain ownership of the Brooklyn football team. Later, he married beautiful women who gained fame of their own, and during World War II he worked overseas for the FBI pinpointing Nazi sympathizers.

Hutson was shrewd enough not to sign promptly with his first suitor, but he told Kelly that if the Dodgers matched other offers, he would join Brooklyn. Several teams went after Hutson, but whatever any team offered, Lambeau and Kelly matched them. The bidding became too rich for the other teams when Hutson's payday offer reached three hundred dollars per game. For some time it was a standoff, but eventually, when Lambeau hit that plateau, Hutson did not hear back from Kelly. Twice, Hutson sent him notice, but got no answer.

When Lambeau shipped Hutson a contract for that amount, he signed it and put it in the mail. Only one day later Kelly showed up on Hutson's doorstep in Tuscaloosa, Alabama, explaining that he had been out of touch in Florida on vacation and was willing to match Lambeau's package. Kelly talked Hutson into signing another contract—the end felt guilty because he had broken the spirit of the original agreement—and Kelly said he would resolve the matter.

Both contracts were forwarded to the league office, and Commissioner Joe Carr made the call that the Packer contract was legal because it arrived first. That paperwork actually arrived only seventeen minutes before the second contract crossed the transom. Lambeau said he mailed his contract special delivery. He probably would have carried it in the front door on his own if he had realized the risk involved in losing Hutson.

Looking back, Hutson said his ending up with the Packers was the best thing that could have happened to him. "It was probably the biggest break I ever got in football," Hutson said. "Green Bay had a real good passer in Arnie Herber, and Lambeau was a very pass-oriented coach."[3]

Hutson was correct. He did land in the right place for his career. Hutson's own pro days outlasted the existence of the Brooklyn franchise itself, which was founded in 1930, spent its last season as the Brooklyn Tigers, and went out of business in 1944. Hutson was employed as a player in the NFL through 1945.

For all of the effort put into procuring Hutson's signature on a contract, Lambeau did not quite get full value out of the player in his rookie year of 1935. Herber had been around since 1930, and he had made significant use of the passing alignments Lambeau drew up.

It took a little time for Herber and Hutson to completely mesh, but Hutson showed flashes of the kind of impact he could have on a game. In the second game of the 1935 season, Green Bay bested the Chicago Bears, 7-0. The game's only touchdown came on a 65-yard pass to Hutson. Score one for the rook.

One reason scouting wasn't completely reliable in the 1930s is that there were no TV highlights on sports shows, no game films passed around. Some people immediately acknowledged Hutson's talent. Others had to be shown in person. Even several years after Hutson was in the league and putting up numbers that were difficult to ignore, personnel for other teams who had not witnessed him do his thing live had difficulty believing his skill.

Jock Sutherland was a spectacular college coach at the University of Pittsburgh from 1924 to 1938. In 1940 he moved into the NFL with the

Dodgers, the team Hutson nearly played for, and he asked other coaches questions about players on various teams. The in-league scouting report on Hutson was too unbelievable for Sutherland to accept.

"You're telling me to put two or three men on Hutson?" Sutherland responded to the tips. "That's nonsense. No one man can be that good. We aren't worried about Hutson. We're worried about the Green Bay defense."[4]

Sutherland learned his lesson. Green Bay, on its way to a 10-1 season, dismantled Sutherland's eleven, 30-7. Hutson, who also played defense during a time when most players went both ways, scored twice on touchdown passes and also kicked the extra points for the Packers. "That man can run three ways at the same time," Sutherland said after the game. "He's incredible."[5]

Certainly, if any other coach contacted Sutherland for information about Hutson, that coach would be much better armed with details than Sutherland had been. It's not clear if Cleveland Rams coach Dutch Clark bothered making any advance calls about Hutson, but his team paid the Hutson toll a week later in a 17-14 loss.

Clark assigned defensive back Dante Magnani to stick with Hutson on his routes. "Don't you dare let that guy inside you," Clark ordered.[6]

But Hutson was not only speedy, he was tricky. He often did not turn on the afterburners until yards downfield. The defender would run with him and suddenly Hutson would turn up the speed and pull away, or make an abrupt cut and have the defender running past him instead of where the ball was headed.

Sneaky Don definitely pulled a fast one on Magnani. Striding into the end zone to the left of the goalpost, Hutson stopped short, wrapped an arm around the upright, and spun so that he was now facing the line of scrimmage. The ball arrived soon after for a touchdown with the post running interference for him.

Green Bay finished 8-4 that season, second in the Western Division, but Hutson got into only nine games. His season totals were 18 catches for 420 yards. He did have an eye-opening 83-yarder in there, but that was a warm-up for what was to come.

Herber had a so-so year in 1935 by his standards. He did not lead the NFL in any significant passing category, although that 83-yard play with Hutson was the longest completion of the season.

In 1936 the Packers overpowered just about all comers, finishing 10-1-1. They captured the Western Division and topped the Boston Redskins, 21-6, in the league championship game. That was George Preston Marshall's team. Marshall was so disgusted by the lack of hometown support in Boston that even though the Hub was supposed to host the game, he moved it to New York, a neutral site, and never returned, shifting the club to Washington for the next season of play.

That season, 1937, is the one where Lambeau turned his passing game loose and is remembered as the year the forward pass took a quantum leap forward as a weapon. Herber threw for a career-high 1,239 yards, becoming the National Football League's first 1,000-yard thrower. He led the league with 77 completions, 177 attempts, and 11 touchdowns. Although low by future standards, Herber's pass completion percentage of 44.3 was the second highest of his career.

Hutson, who would turn into a touchdown machine during his career, caught 34 passes that season for 536 yards, an average of 15.8 yards per catch. All of those stats led the league, as did his seven receiving touchdowns.

Lambeau was a no-nonsense coach who regularly lost his temper and screamed at players, sometimes for good cause, sometimes irrationally. But he developed a closer relationship with Hutson than with any of his other players, tolerating the periodic lack of obedience from his star. Hutson was the teacher's pet, and sometimes he exploited that on behalf of his teammates. It was not that he outright challenged Lambeau verbally as much as Hutson was capable of mixing in a little levity when the coach got too hot.

Guard John Biolo said Hutson could get away with stuff sometimes. "Lambeau treated Hutson with kid gloves," Biolo said. "He was the only one, though. Don would make practice sessions jovial. He would half-heartedly do the exercises and Lambeau would kind of look at him and smile."[7]

No one ever caught Hutson going half-heartedly in games, though. Some of Hutson's reputation came ready-made out of Alabama, but no matter how good a college player is, he must always prove himself with his deeds in the big leagues. The NFL's draft history is heavily pockmarked with disappointments who had holes in their game revealed when they moved up a level.

It did not take very long for Hutson to show he had the right stuff. The Packers–Bears rivalry was the most intense (and long-lasting) in the league. Lambeau and Chicago's George Halas went back a long way, but they were not buddies. There were no more important games on the schedule than the annual home-and-home series.

Like so many stars, Hutson got up for big games. The bright lights seemed to rev him up more than usual, and any Bears game classified as a big game. Hutson shone regularly against Chicago.

Once, Halas, who saw plenty of Hutson over the years, was asked if he developed any special way of defending the prolific end. Halas had a sharp tongue and sometimes used it on journalists whose questions he did not like. But he was at his charming best on this topic. "I never plan to stop him," Halas said. "I just concede Hutson two touchdowns a game. Then I hope we can score more."[8]

Hutson was on his way to greatness, but unlike many future duos renowned as famed pass-throwing-and-catching combinations, he would not be a one-quarterback man. Usually, quarterbacks are given the most credit for making receivers look good. In Green Bay's situation, although the quarterbacks Lambeau hired were impressive on their own, Don Hutson greatly enhanced their production.

CHAPTER 9 • Green Bay Guys III

Arnie Herber was just twenty years old when he joined the Green Bay Packers in 1930, but by 1938, Coach Curly Lambeau was searching for his replacement.

Well aware that the most potent weapon in football was on his roster in Don Hutson, Lambeau wanted to make sure he could take full advantage. As an end, Hutson needed someone to get him the ball. He always did his part in getting open, but Lambeau sensed that Herber, with his odd throwing style, might be wearing down.

In 1937, the year after Green Bay won the NFL title, the club finished 7-4. Herber's stats were down across the board. He went 47 for 104 for 684 yards and seven touchdowns. Just as tellingly, tailback Bob Monett wrested the starting job and went 37 for 73, with a completion percentage of 50.3 for 580 yards and eight touchdowns.

Neither man neglected Hutson, who caught 41 passes for 552 yards and seven touchdowns, so there was at least that.

Seeing Herber being challenged from within his own team, Lambeau went quarterback shopping in 1938. He claimed Cecil Isbell with the Packers' number-one draft choice, based on his body of work at Purdue.

Isbell was from Houston, Texas—not a likely candidate for the Indiana school at a time when players did not often travel a thousand or more miles for college. He was a fine acquisition for the Boilermakers and quarterbacked the College All-Stars in 1938 when they bested the NFL champs, the Washington Redskins, in the annual charity football game at Soldier Field in Chicago. The poise and talent Isbell showed there confirmed Lambeau's judgment that he had selected wisely.

At 6-foot-1 and 190 pounds, Isbell was sturdy enough for the pro game, and he beat out the incumbents to take over the quarterback job that season. Lambeau was right about Isbell's potential, although it took him a couple of years to exceed Herber's best efforts.

As a twenty-three-year-old rookie, Isbell completed 37 of 91 attempts for 659 yards and eight touchdowns. His numbers increased incrementally over the next couple of seasons, and by his third year Isbell had completed 68 out of 150 passes for 1,037 yards and eight touchdowns.

Lambeau felt that Isbell needed time to learn the offense. In those days, players were forced to be more versatile, playing more than one position and almost always playing offense and defense. In some games Herber did the bulk of the throwing, and sometimes Isbell did. When he wasn't filling the quarterback role, Isbell was in the backfield as a runner.

In 1938 the Packers advanced to the championship game and lost. The next year, with Isbell and Herber sharing the throwing responsibilities, the Packers captured another NFL title.

That was a last hurrah for Herber with the Pack. His 1,107 yards passing led the team, but they were supplemented by Isbell's 749 yards. Together the duo completed 110 passes that season in 242 tries. Times were changing: those stats made for a large number of pass plays executed in the formerly all-running league.

Lambeau's keen eye and tough decision making concluded that Herber was losing steam on his passes, and the tackles he took over the year were affecting his physical prowess. Isbell had a reputation for toughness dating to his college days in the Big Ten. In a game against Northwestern, Isbell suffered a separated shoulder but did not retreat to the sidelines. The trainer patched him up, and he resumed action.

"The trainer came out and popped it back in and I continued in the game," is how Isbell described the scenario. "On the next kickoff, I went down to make the tackle and it went out again. They put it back in place on the field and I finished the game."[1]

This was Isbell's throwing arm. The shoulder kept giving him trouble, but he and the trainer worked together to create a protective device that enabled him to stay in charge of the team. Injured or not, he kept playing. That player attitude had great appeal for football coaches. Eventually, when Lambeau felt Isbell was ready for the responsibility, he gave up on Herber and turned the reins of the offense over to Isbell full-time.

"When I was with the Packers, I called the plays," Isbell said. "Lambeau would call a play once in a while, but mostly he was too excited."[2]

No other quarterback had a Don Hutson–caliber receiver to throw to when he faded back. It was almost as if Hutson had taken a time machine back from the future, he was so far ahead of other pass catchers. Some seventy years after he retired, Hutson is still considered the great innovator of receiving, the prototype of the first modern receiver. He had the feints and other moves and the speed of a deer. Defenders were at a loss on how to stay with him when he wiggled and cut for the sidelines, and they could not keep up when he floored it and ran deep. At a time when track runners competed on dirt with inferior equipment and were clocked over yards, Hutson ran 9.7 seconds for the 100-yard dash.

As evidence of how Hutson brought his special talents to NFL pass catching during a time period when few teams threw the ball much at all, consider his a stunning resume between 1935 and 1945. Hutson was first in the league in total number of catches eight times. He led the league in receiving yards seven times. He was tops in touchdown catches nine times. Hutson led in yards per game receiving eight times. During the 1942 season, Hutson caught 17 touchdown passes: that remained the league record for forty-two years.

Besides playing defensive back for the Pack (while he was back there, Hutson intercepted 30 passes), he was also the team's kicker. Between touchdowns, extra points, and the occasional field goal, he led the NFL in scoring five times. In one game against the Detroit Lions, Hutson scored 29 points in a single quarter.

Herber and Isbell were obviously quality quarterbacks—Lambeau did his due diligence—but the reality was that Hutson could make anyone look good. Herber and Isbell were good, but partnering with Hutson produced greatness. It was the ultimate wake-up call for the potential of the passing game.

Isbell made it clear that Hutson was in a class of his own as a receiver and was impossible for defensive backs to stop.

"He'd charge off the line with his head down like a bull out of a chute," Isbell said. "But he had great eyes and fine judgment and could see what was going on around him all the time. Most teams would try to beat him up on the line, not letting him get out, but he was tough to box in. He would follow the ball all the way, right into his hands. I've studied the movies on him closely when the ball got to him, his hands would go absolutely limp, he'd be so relaxed. He never fought the ball. He just guided it into his hands with his eyes. With his great concentration, nothing else mattered."[3]

Hutson was so slick that some in football called him the "Alabama Antelope." If they had been really examining his roots it would have been the "Arkansas Antelope." Neither southern state is really known for its antelopes, but both can claim Hutson as a favorite son.

Actually, Isbell was telling Lambeau nothing he did not already know. Those same moves were likely what Lambeau thought about in the first place when he went to so much trouble to snag Hutson in that bidding war with the Brooklyn Dodgers.

"He's amazing," Lambeau said of Hutson when he recruited him. "He glides downfield, leaning close to the ground as if to steady himself. Then suddenly, in the time it takes to blink an eye, he fakes one way, goes the other way, and then reaches up and squeezes the ball."[4]

Isbell had so much confidence in Hutson's talent to get free against coverage that he called passing plays for the receiver, plays that he would not call for other personnel.

The All-Star Game made its debut in 1938, and the format pitted the NFL defending champion against a team of stars from the other nine clubs. In 1940 the Packers faced the All-Stars and won, 16-7. The key play featured Hutson and Isbell.

Their side was trapped at its own 2-yard line, risky territory in the face of an aggressive defense. As the western squad huddled to choose a play, Isbell turned to Hutson and said, "Let's move! Let's really move!" The play was for a deep pass to Hutson. Isbell faded back into his own end zone, the possibility of a safety imminent. When Hutson had outdistanced the defenders, as usual, Isbell threw the ball as far as he could. Observers believed it traveled about 70 yards in the air. Hutson collected the pass and kept on running, going all the way, as the phrase was popularly used. Officially, it was a 98-yard touchdown, though Isbell had retreated far enough backward that other calculations indicated it was really a 108-yard play.

The funniest part of the entire little adventure was Isbell being quizzed on the appropriateness of his call by a sportswriter after the game. "That wasn't very smart, was it?" the reporter said. "A running play would have been far less risky."[5]

Clearly, that was true. It would have been the pedestrian call, not the daring one. But Isbell had the perfect riposte: "I always feel more certain of scoring with Hutson than in any other way," Isbell said—even if 98 yards were needed to cover the rest of the field.[6]

Some weeks it seemed as if the Packers—Herber to Hutson, or Isbell to Hutson—were the only ones in the entire NFL throwing the ball regularly. It may have even been true in the early 1930s, but that began to change as a few other teams developed their own explosive passing prowess, even if they didn't have a Don Hutson handy.

Football remained a rugged game, still very much built around the clash of two formidable lines bashing into one another when the ball was snapped. Even though teams had extraordinary difficulties staying up with Hutson, he took his share of hard hits and the fatigue wore on him over the years.

Hutson was even better in the 1940s than he was as a young receiver in the 1930s. In 1941 he caught 58 passes. The next year he grabbed 74. In 1943 he caught 47. In 1944 he again caught 58. He was only thirty-one years old that season, but Hutson was feeling older. He began considering retirement. "If I ever play again, I'll jump off the Empire State Building," Hutson said in 1944.[7] But he did play again in 1945, his final season.

Some irony was attached to a commentary Hutson produced for a book later in life about early football greats. He was asked to recount his greatest day in the sport, and despite many remarkable games to choose from, he selected the September 1935 game from his rookie year against the Chicago Bears.

The Packers had opened the season with a 7-6 loss to the Chicago Cardinals on September 15. Hutson's memories refer to the first game he played: a 7-0 victory on September 22 over the Chicago Bears, the Packers' number-one rival. Lambeau kept Hutson on the bench for the opener, so this was his NFL debut. As good as Hutson was at Alabama, he was still nervous going up against the mighty Chicago Bears and their oversized personnel.

"Despite my six feet, plus one inch in height, I looked like a side of a goalpost standing beside the giant frames of the Cal Hubbards, the George Mussos, the Ernie Smiths, and the other bruising behemoths," Hutson said. "Maybe that's one reason Coach Curly Lambeau let me sit out the National League opener against the Chicago Cardinals the previous week. He kept me from the Cardinals to toss me to the Bears."[8]

The Bears had reached the NFL title game the year before, and the Packers had not defeated Chicago in their last seven tries. "I admit I was a little bit shaky as we lined up to receive the kickoff," Hutson said.[9]

What followed was the Herber-to-Hutson 83-yard touchdown pass that was not only Hutson's first play as a pro, but the winning play in a close, low-scoring game and the play that stood up as the longest pass play of the season.

Hutson also took note of a memorable pass play between him and Isbell against the Cleveland Rams in October 1942. Green Bay had a first down, technically on the 1-yard line, but the actual distance was really only four inches from the end zone. Any good team prides itself on being able to move the ball on the ground in such short yardage situations, whether for a first down or a touchdown. The opposition stacks the line, hoping for the best as a quarterback keeps the ball and runs a sneak or hands it to a battering-ram of a back.

Only Isbell fooled everyone. He took the hike and fired the ball to Hutson: touchdown, Green Bay, in a nontraditional way. The play may have gone into the books as a 1-yarder, but everyone there knew the distance covered was much shorter.

Hutson suggested that Lambeau nearly suffered a heart attack when he saw Isbell throw, and when the offense came to the bench, Lambeau said, "Cece, don't ever do that again. Don't ever do that again."[10] Many at the time enjoyed joking that the pass play represented the shortest touchdown pass in league history.

"Thrills? Plenty of them," Hutson said of his career as a whole. "But none like my first professional football game."[11]

Herber's days with the Packers ended in 1940. Isbell had taken over as the number-one guy at quarterback, so Herber retired at age thirty.

Isbell was the new passing king. In 1941 he led the league with 117 completions in 206 attempts, his completion percentage reaching an impressive (especially for the time) 56.8 percent, for 1,479 yards and 15 touchdown throws. All of those statistics were tops in the NFL that year.

Isbell was even better the next year with 146 completions, 2,021 yards gained, and 24 touchdown passes.

But then he shocked Lambeau by retiring at age twenty-seven and going into coaching. Isbell said he had watched closely as neither Lambeau, nor the Packers, seemed to value loyalty and ruthlessly cut players who had long been staples of the roster, leaving them adrift. He vowed to himself he would not get caught in such a circumstance and would switch careers when it best suited him.

Isbell played just five pro seasons before making the change. In future years he would coach at Purdue, his alma mater; the Baltimore Colts, when they were in the All-America Football Conference; and the Chicago Cardinals; and he would also serve as an assistant coach at Louisiana State.

Although Hutson retired after the 1945 season, he could well have played longer. When he quit, Hutson owned every major NFL receiving record—and he kept them for a long time. Hutson collected 488 catches for 7,991 yards and 99 touchdowns. He added six more touchdowns via other methods to give him a lifetime total of 105 touchdowns. When Cleveland Browns standout Jim Brown retired in 1965, he owned the new record of 126 touchdowns, though that mark has been surpassed several times since.

It also took roughly two decades for anyone to pass Hutson's number of catches, although with the proliferation of the passing game in recent years he is now far, far down the all-time list.

Hutson was an assistant coach for the Packers for two seasons after he retired, but mostly he turned businessman in retirement. When he passed away at age eighty-four in 1997, the testimonials to his playing skills were shouted long and loud.

"Here's a guy who devised all the moves, the down-and-outs, the stop-and-gos, the hooks, everything," said onetime Packer teammate Tony Canadeo. "And to me, I think he could judge the ball better than a lot of guys do today. His instinct was the greatest I've ever seen."[12] Lee Remmel, the Packers' team historian, observed that Hutson was second on the all-time list in interceptions when he retired, too, making him, in Remmel's mind, "the greatest player who ever played."[13]

The Packers' pioneering passing game ended with the departure of Herber, Isbell, and Hutson. But Herber had a surprising last act on the big stage remaining in his right arm.

After the bombing of Pearl Harbor by the Japanese on December 7, 1941, the United States became embroiled in World War II. Pro football players were not exempt from either a willingness to fight or the draft. The NFL was far less essential to the home front than were steel manufacturing plants, and pro teams suffered from a shortage of personnel. Retired players who were older, or who would otherwise be exempt from military service, were approached by teams and asked to put on football uniforms once more.

One of those former players was Arnie Herber. In 1944, when he was thirty-four years old, the New York Giants invited him to join the team. Herber played two seasons with New York before the war ended and other players came back to resume their careers. For the most part, particularly without a Don Hutson at his disposal, Herber did a solid job. His yardage totals over the two seasons were 651 and 641, with six and eight touchdown passes, respectively, numbers comparable to his early days with Green Bay.

Herber was so excited to be asked, and so excited to be playing again, that when requested to choose his greatest day in football, he picked a contest where he represented the Giants, not Green Bay. The occasion was in New York on December 2, 1945, for a game against the Philadelphia Eagles. The Eagles, led by star runner Steve Van Buren, took a 21-0 lead early in the second half. Van Buren scored twice on rushes and then on a 98-yard kickoff return in the third quarter.

This was far from the Giants' best year. They would finish the 1945 season 3-6-1, but the second half of the Philadelphia game was probably their finest hour of the campaign, and a memorable career wrap-up for Herber. Herber fired three touchdown passes in the third period, all to Frank Liebel, and a fourth touchdown pass to Sam Fox in the fourth quarter as New York rallied for a 28-21 victory.

"When you get old and past your prime, to have a good day—any kind of good day—is a memorable thing in a player's life," Herber said. "What you do in your prime you expect of yourself, but days that come at the end of the trail provide unexpected thrills when you think of them."[14]

Herber had actually been riding the bench with a bothersome injury of a week's duration and was surprised when Coach Steve Owen inserted him into the game. At the time, after Van Buren's demoralizing kickoff return, he said, "You wouldn't have given an old scorecard for the Giants' chances."[15] Owen sent Herber in with instructions to pass. Owen had spotted Philadelphia's defensive weaknesses, and Heber found the holes, too. Herber tossed the three touchdowns to Liebel within seven minutes to tie the game. Liebel played seven seasons in the NFL in the 1940s, and 1945 was his best season, with 22 catches, 10 going for touchdowns. Herber well knew the difference between the 6-foot-1, 211-pound Liebel and Don Hutson, for sure, but during that special game Liebel might as well have been Hutson.

"Having pitched to ends like Don Hutson, and with him you can't go any further for greatness, I can safely say that Liebel that day was as great an end that ever caught a pass," Herber said.[16]

Nor could that four-touchdown-pass outing for Arnie Herber represent a finer valedictory address to crown his NFL career.

CHAPTER 10 • Sammy Goes Pro

After his 1936 Texas Christian University football season ended, Sammy Baugh turned back to his first love: baseball. He played his last season of eligibility for the Horned Frogs.

Although Baugh did not pursue professional baseball immediately, in 1938 he was good enough to catch the attention of the St. Louis Cardinals, which at the time was the southernmost and westernmost team in the Major Leagues and which possessed the most exhaustive scouting system and most developed farm system. He was invited to spring training in St. Petersburg, Florida, where he roomed with pitcher Mort Cooper. Cooper had a fine, eleven-year big-league career, winning 128 games with a lifetime 2.97 earned run average.

Cooper progressed at a more rapid rate than did Baugh. St. Louis turned Baugh into a shortstop—the Cardinals loved his throwing arm—and sent him to their Rochester club in the International league for thirty-seven games and then to the American Association to suit up for the Columbus Red Birds. Baugh barely hit his weight—.183—with Rochester, and then .220 with Columbus. The Cards didn't start him at the bottom, but they didn't start him at the top. Baugh played only in double-A ball.

Baugh was a terrific fielder, with soft hands and that powerful throwing arm. But as so many hopefuls learned before and after him, hitting professional curveballs is an entirely different animal than swinging successfully at lower levels of the game. Baugh knew that was his Achilles heel right away, too.

"Mom, they're throwing curveballs," the phrase went. "I'll be home soon."[1] Baugh took his chance and discovered that he wasn't cut out for the majors.

This was no misguided attempt to prove he could cut it in the majors, however. Baugh apparently had the goods to field with the best. Eddie Dyer, who managed the Cardinals between 1946 and 1950, after an apprenticeship in the minors, handled Baugh for part of his brief pro baseball career, comparing Baugh's glove work to the esteemed Marty Marion.

"He had two of the best hands I ever saw," Dyer said of Baugh. "He could hold anything he got his hands onto, and he could throw it harder and more accurately and quicker than anybody I ever saw. You could hardly tell them [Baugh and Marion] apart. You would have thought they were twins."[2]

Years later Cooper suggested that Baugh could have made the majors if he stuck with baseball—maybe even as a pitcher. "There goes one of the greatest athletes of all time," Cooper said after the two men crossed paths nearly a decade later in a hotel. "I think if he had wanted to he could have stayed in the big show and made the big leagues in baseball."[3]

Sammy Baugh, a big-league pitcher? Well, actually, he did turn into one, although with a football. After that one-year flirtation with professional baseball, Baugh never again wavered in his commitment to professional football. He had already begun to make his mark in the National Football League in 1937 with the Washington Redskins, but he had to put baseball to rest once and for all. It was like running into an old flame at the store and wondering, *What if?*

It is no surprise that Baugh could impress as an all-around athlete. Most star athletes at the professional level, whether it is in baseball, football, or basketball, probably excelled at more than one of those sports, plus perhaps track and field, when they were in high school or college. With rare exceptions—a Gene Conley in basketball and baseball, Dick Groat in basketball and baseball, Bo Jackson in football and baseball, and Deion Sanders in football and baseball—even the best athletes focus on refining their skills in one sport and eventually give up a second one.

The second NFL draft was conducted for the 1937 season on December 12, 1936, at the Hotel Lincoln in New York City. The league had been snubbed by its first-ever pick in the first draft, and the second overall number-one choice did not end up being a better investment than had Jay Berwanger.

Sam Francis was a running back out of Nebraska and an Olympic shot-putter. The Philadelphia Eagles selected him but traded him to the Chicago Bears for end Bill Hewitt and four thousand dollars. Francis survived in the NFL for four years with three teams: the Bears, the Pittsburgh Pirates (before they changed their name to the Steelers), and the Brooklyn Dodgers before they went away. Francis was already out of football, wrapping up a master's degree at the University of Iowa, when World War II broke out. He became an officer and a career serviceman. Francis would fight for his country not only in World War II but also in Korea and Vietnam, and he retired from the army as a lieutenant colonel.

The Dodgers had the second pick and chose Ed Goddard, a back from Washington State. Then followed the third pick: Marquette quarterback Ray "Buzz" Buivid, who had faced Baugh in the Cotton Bowl. Buivid went to the Chicago Cardinals.

The fourth choice was Ed Widseth, a back from Minnesota who went to the New York Giants. The fifth player taken was Mike Basrak, a center from Duquesne, who went to the hometown Pirates.

Finally, someone at the draft table woke up and selected Sammy Baugh. He went to the Redskins as the sixth player taken. No other famous player was taken in the first round that year either, and mostly lesser-known players who are little remembered were taken in the entire draft.

The Sammy Baugh who would not turn twenty-three until the spring of 1937, months after the draft, was a much more seasoned football player than was the Sammy Baugh who, coming out of high school had told the world he had little to do with Sweetwater's first-class season. Baugh had had everything to do with how TCU fared. He had thrown 40 touchdown passes for the Horned Frogs in this three seasons, completing more than 50 percent of his throws as a senior.

If an NFL owner was a forward-passing believer and wanted to spice up his attack, Baugh was on the market with handsome credentials. Redskins owner George Preston Marshall was just such an owner. As one of the proponents of change to open up the pro game, it was natural that he would search for a quarterback who could fulfill his visionary outlook. Just as importantly, Marshall the show-biz man was ditching Boston as the Redskins' home and moving his franchise to Washington. There would be a new audience in the nation's capital, and he wanted to captivate it from the start.

Marshall, a theatrical producer, was creating a marching band and would do his best to provide entertainment, but he also knew that in the sports segment of the entertainment world, there was nothing more pleasing than to root for a winning team. Hiring an adroit passer with talent and spunk was like having the right leading man on Broadway.

As Berwanger had indicated by refusing to bother with pro football, it was not a terribly secure or glamorous career choice in the mid-1930s. The Redskins gained the negotiating rights to discuss business with Baugh, but Baugh wasn't yet sure what he wanted to do. He investigated a job with a lumber company and an offer that would have made him football coach at a high school in Phoenix, Arizona. Baugh was also offered a job as an assistant coach for football, basketball, and baseball at Texas Christian. The salary was about five thousand dollars, not bad at all during the Depression.

But Marshall was the type of owner who would outbid competitors if he had set his sights on a talent. He decided he not only wanted Baugh to lead his football team, he wanted to sell him to the fans in just the right manner to make him seem like a fresh face with a colorful background.

In the spring of 1937, Marshall got in touch with Baugh and told him to fly to DC from Texas, and, before he got on the plane, to make sure he put on some western clothing. That included a proper cowboy hat and boots and a suit or shirt that fit the bill of a Gene Autry or someone of that nature. Actually, when Marshall first instructed Baugh to do that shopping, Baugh thought that Marshall wanted his new quarterback to shop for him and deliver the clothes to him in DC. "What size do you wear?" Baugh asked.[4]

Marshall was playing to stereotype. Baugh may have been from Texas, but he didn't ordinarily dress for hoedowns.

Baugh had excelled at football in a football state, but in Texas that was mostly about high school and college ball. The pros had not yet engaged anyone in the Southwest. The NFL was on much firmer footing than it was in 1920, but it was still a struggling outfit feeling its way in the sporting world.

"Pro football was not something that was on a lot of people's minds," Baugh said later. "Hell, at that time I couldn't have named any of the pro teams for you, and I had no idea how many there were exactly."[5]

Baugh flew to Washington on American Airlines, and Marshall's show business nature took over when the lanky quarterback descended the stairs. He was decked out in full cowboy regalia, and Marshall had a press conference prepared right there. His new cowboy had arrived to lead his Indians, the Redskins, in their inaugural season in Washington.

Of course, Baugh, who had never flown before and had never been east, had no contract yet. This exercise in public relations unfolded on the tarmac. Marshall approached Baugh to shake hands and, to Marshall's polite offering of "How are you," Baugh replied, "Mah feet hurt."[6]

The Slingin' Sammy the sportswriters would get to know was a blunt, honest, straightforward man, and he began with them the same way, informing them he really didn't dress like that all of the time and he wasn't actually a for-real cowboy. But he said he would dress the cowboy way if his boss wanted him to do so. He pretty much put the writers on alert that they should be wary of what Marshall said about him—for good reason, since the owner had already told the world that Baugh was the Texas state lasso champion, whatever exactly that was supposed to mean.

The day Sammy Baugh stepped off that plane in Washington for Marshall to introduce him as his favored draft pick and future quarterback—months before their association would culminate with a contract—the future NFL star also met Shirley Povich. The man with the woman's name once mistakenly and humorously had his name included in the book *Who's Who of American Women.* (It would have been priceless to be in that publication's offices when the editors learned of their faux pas.)

Povich, born in 1905, was a legendary sportswriter who joined the *Washington Post* while still in college in 1923. Although he retired somewhere along the way after decades as sports editor and full-time sports columnist, he kept writing until he died in 1998 at age ninety-two.

Povich chronicled Baugh's entire Redskins career and the coaching one that would follow, making Povich the keenest of observers and one of Baugh's greatest-informed admirers.

Marshall took Baugh out for a fancy lunch and sounded him out about playing for the Redskins. Baugh had yet to graduate from TCU, however, so he could not sign a contract at that sitting. Marshall extracted a promise that if Baugh played pro football it would be for him.

Immediately after he graduated, Baugh joined a semipro baseball team for the summer. At the time the *Denver Post* Tournament was the biggest thing going for such teams, and any team that was any good entered. The tournament was a showcase for scouts as well. Baugh's team was pretty good and won its first two games. But then it came up against a squad of Negro Leagues All-Stars. Among those playing for that club were future Hall of Famers Satchel Paige, Josh Gibson, and Cool Papa Bell. Baugh was impressed by Paige's arm, Gibson's hitting ability, and Bell's speed. He batted a couple of times against Paige, who some believe may have been the best pitcher of all time, without any success except for getting wood on the ball.

As Marshall continued to woo Baugh, he was also engaged in discussions with St. Louis general manager Branch Rickey. Eventually, Baugh told the Cardinals he wanted to give pro football a try. That led Baugh to playing a rookie season in the NFL before he suited up for those minor-league clubs in the Cardinals' system.

Meanwhile, Baugh was also invited to play for the College All-Stars in the annual Chicago charity football game against the defending NFL champion. The NFL winner that year was Green Bay. Baugh was a key factor in an All-Star upset. The collegians won, 6-0. Baugh intercepted two passes and ran the offense part of the time. If anything, his showing made Marshall hunger even more for his signature on a dotted line.

The All-Star Game tradition had begun in 1934, and the 1937 contest was the fourth in the series. It also marked the first time the All-Stars won. More than eighty-four thousand fans witnessed the game at Chicago's Soldier Field on September 1. A Baugh touchdown pass was the game's only score.

As an intriguing aside, Gus Dorais, then the Detroit Lions' coach and the man who threw the milestone pass to Knute Rockne at Notre Dame, was the architect of the All-Stars' offense. Dorais was mighty impressed by Baugh and said so.

"He'll do until some supernatural passer comes along," Dorais said. "He showed me that he's all the Texas people claimed him to be. He's an exception, that Baugh. Usually when a coach picks up one of these passing babies and sticks him in there to throw, he sacrifices something in the running attack or the blocking or on the defense. But Baugh is no drawback in any way."[7]

Baugh was slow to sign with the Redskins. Marshall, who had been happy to show off the cowboy in Washington, began hemming and hawing about his potential, likely thinking he could drive down Baugh's price.

Marshall offered Baugh five thousand dollars to sign, which was only slightly higher than what he would have made as a TCU coach. Baugh conferred with his college coach Dutch Meyer, who informed the player that five thousand was more than any coach at his alma mater was making. While Baugh was pretty much ready to take the offer, he decided to shoot for the sky and see how Marshall reacted if he asked for much more. The figure he chose was eight thousand dollars, believing Marshall would compromise. Instead, Marshall said yes right away, as long as Baugh was prepared to sign.

Baugh did not hesitate any longer. "Hell, I got more money than I was thinking he'd give me," Baugh said. "To me that looked like a million bucks."[8] During the Depression, millions of Americans would have agreed.

CHAPTER 11 • Sammy's Rookie Year

In 1936 the Redskins finished 7-5, but that was good enough to win the Eastern Conference. Based in Boston, the team did not draw well, which had prompted irritated owner George Preston Marshall to yank the club out of town and moved his Redskins to Washington, DC, for the start of Sammy Baugh's career.

The Redskins had a future Hall of Famer in Ray Flaherty as a coach and added Baugh to a division champion roster. The tailback was twenty-seven-year-old Cliff Battles, who, despite a short career (this was his final season), also became a Hall of Famer. In 1937 Battles rushed for 874 yards, and the Redskins won the East again with an 8-3 mark.

Battles stood 6-foot-1 and weighed 195 pounds. He came out of tiny West Virginia Wesleyan, but he gained 576 yards on the ground as a rookie in 1932 despite playing in only eight games. That total led the league in rushing, as did his 874 yards in 1937.

What should have been a longtime pairing of Battles and Baugh lasted just that one season. Battles's salary had been frozen at three thousand dollars a year since he was a rookie. He repeatedly was named to the all-star team but received no increase from Marshall. When Marshall once again proposed a new contract for Battles without more money, Battles said enough was enough and walked away from pro football. Battles became an assistant coach for Columbia University in the Ivy League instead—for a raise of one thousand dollars.

It was great for Baugh and Battles for one season, though. Baugh led the NFL in passing. His 81 completions was a league record for one season at the time. He threw more passes (171), with a higher completion percentage (47.4), for more yards (1,127) than anybody in the game. He also led in interceptions with 14. Baugh only threw 8 touchdown passes.

By NFL standards in the 1930s Baugh was an exceptional thrower from the first minute he stepped on the field. Still, he was not quite the star he would become. But he demonstrated an exciting level of potential and showed even as a rookie that he was good enough to lead a pro team and take it far.

Marshall had chosen wisely, and he was impatient to see Baugh on the field. Baugh was not intimidated, even in training camp, when all anyone really knew about him was that he had been a pretty fair passer back in Texas.

Flaherty had seen Baugh play and knew he could fling it, but at training camp he challenged him to show others what he could do. One reason Flaherty was a bit testy was Baugh's absence from practice to perform with the College All-Stars. Flaherty wanted to maximize his time tutoring the newcomer, but instead Baugh had less practice time than the veterans because of that other commitment.

"They tell me you're quite a passer," Flaherty said, and he handed Baugh a football to throw. Baugh, a bit taken aback, smarted off a little. "I reckon I can throw," he said.[1] Wayne Millner, who came out of Notre Dame and also was en route to a Hall of Fame career, at that point ran onto the field to offer his services as his receiver.

Flaherty, coming on a little strong himself, said, "Let's see it. Hit that receiver in the eye." Baugh responded to his new coach with "Which eye?"[2]

That expressed Baugh's confidence, although years later, when confirming the story to Shirley Povich, with whom he had grown close during his career, Baugh admitted he shouldn't have put it quite that way. "First time in my life I was cocky," Baugh said.[3]

Nonetheless it was true. Baugh proved his accuracy, and he set about as a rookie establishing his reputation as the king of the quarterbacks.

As Marshall had hoped, Baugh became the new celebrity in town, a town more usually impressed by political power than athletic skill, although in later decades, when Jack Kent Cooke owned the Redskins, even the rich and politically muscled were thrilled to sit in his private box to watch home games.

In 1937 the Redskins played in Griffith Stadium, the baseball home of the Washington Senators that was named after team owner Clark Griffith, who ended up in the Baseball Hall of Fame. Griffith won 237 games as a pitcher and 1,491 as a manager, and he ran the franchise as a Washington institution for thirty-five years. Griffith Stadium was the Redskins' home from 1937, Baugh's rookie year, through 1960—and thus Baugh's home field for his entire NFL career.

Washington opened at home, on September 16, 1937, with Baugh at quarterback and the New York Giants on the other sideline. The Redskins and Baugh won, 13-3. Baugh may have had only a week of full practices with Washington before the opener, but he had stayed late and made sure to complete one hundred passes in a row per day before showering.

Baugh brought a big name to town, and it didn't take long for his presence on the field to jump-start fans' emotions. Some days as many as three thousand fans turned out for practice. That was almost too good to be true for Marshall, since the Redskins had drawn so poorly in Boston at times when three thousand didn't look like a bad game-day crowd.

They came to learn early on that Baugh's grip of the football did not conform to the style that most quarterbacks used. The common wisdom was to grasp the ball with fingers on the laces, but Baugh put his thumb on the laces instead. "All that matters is how it feels in your hand," Baugh said.[4]

If pro football had been televised as frequently as it is in the 2000s, no doubt Baugh would have spawned a generation of stylistic young imitators. But he was right: what worked was the best reason to choose a throwing method.

Actually, although Baugh is known as a quarterback great and he fulfilled the throwing role for the Redskins from the get-go, Flaherty was employing a single-wing offense. Technically, Baugh was a tailback, but for historical consistency and the way the offense changed later, calling him a quarterback was and is the easiest approach. Baugh did pass more than anyone else, no matter what position title was applied to him.

The single-wing was not a particularly friendly system for a quarterback, but it did not preclude the possibility of a throwing quarterback shining within its confines, and that's what Baugh did. This was no system designed for him. This was a system structured to possibly hinder him. However, Flaherty let Baugh loose within the limits, allowing an individual to push the boundaries of what had been done in an offense to the point that the position's name didn't matter.

Baugh ran the offense against the Giants soundly enough, but he did not account for any points. Washington took a 3-0 lead in the first quarter on a 19-yard field goal by Riley Smith. New York tied the game on a second-period 13-yard field goal by Tillie Manton. In the second half, Smith intercepted a pass and ran it back 58 yards for the game's only touchdown, and then he kicked the extra point. He added an 18-yard field goal to complete the scoring. So, the star of Sammy Baugh's first NFL game was . . . Riley Smith.

Smith, who played college ball for the University of Alabama, was the Redskins' number-one draft pick in 1936, taken as a quarterback, right behind Jay Berwanger. It can safely be said that Baugh eclipsed him at that position. The 6-foot-2, 200-pound Smith played three seasons with Washington and then went into college coaching. During World War II he served in the navy and then shifted to the real estate business after the war. The Sept 16, 1937, game was Smith's finest hour as a pro football player.

Still, Baugh completed 11 out of 16 passes against New York—a solid beginning.

The Redskins played their first five games at home. While all of the games were close, the team's record stood at just 3-2 after also beating the Brooklyn Dodgers and Pittsburgh Pirates. They fell to the Chicago Cardinals and the Philadelphia Eagles. The victory over the Pirates kicked off a three-game winning streak, and as Baugh improved and the team meshed, the Redskins won six of their last seven regular-season games, including a 49-14 thumping of the Giants in a season-ending rematch at the Polo Grounds in New York.

Baugh, the cowboy from Texas who spoke with an endearing drawl to the easterners' ears, was in short order, playing like a veteran. Also, his popularity rose with each win, and even though he was just a rookie, he was talked into writing what amounted to his life story by a national newspaper syndicate.

Since Baugh had not attended journalism school and had no literary credits to his name before that, it was likely that his bylined work had either been edited or ghostwritten. Only a month into his NFL career, Baugh was playing Shakespeare for a national audience and introducing himself to football fans outside of Texas and Washington. This was not Jim Bouton, tell-all stuff—jokes and anecdotes from inside the locker room—but more aw-shucks stuff about his background and football. Yet, given how little known Baugh really was beyond his statistics, the articles were revealing and even more so can serve as a window to his mind at a time he was beginning to make his mark in his chosen field.

Baugh explained that he obtained his nickname of “Slingin’ Sammy” from baseball and was certain he was surprising his readership with that news. In October 1937, Baugh was still twenty-three years old, and he said that when sportswriters asked him what his biggest thrill was, he had difficulty answering. He did not specifically say that he wasn’t yet old enough and had only just begun his pro career where hopefully his biggest thrill was still to come, but it was implied.

He chose the New Year’s Day 1936 Texas Christian victory over Louisiana State by that 3-2 score in the Sugar Bowl.

“The only claim to fame I had in the scoring of those three points was the fact I held the ball when [Tillie] Manton [ironically the Giants’ kicker in Baugh’s debut game against New York] booted it,” Baugh said. There was a bonus in the LSU win. The Tigers’ quarterback was Ernie Seago, who had once lived across the street from Baugh in Temple, Texas, and who in years past had a bigger reputation than he did. “Most of the boys in the neighborhood sort of looked up to Ernie and regarded him as something of a hero. How swell it was to me, riding back on the train, to think I had been playing quarterback on the team which defeated the team for which Seago was calling signals. Boys, that was the thrill of thrills.”[5]

Baugh subsequently tried to answer a question he said he was often asked: how to become a good football player. Sometimes those are tough questions for a natural athlete to answer because first on the list is talent. But every athlete who becomes great does more than get lucky with the right genes. Athletes have to put effort into development, too.

“Now, I do not think good football players are made,” Baugh said. “Of course, there have been exceptions, but as a rule, football players are born, not made. If I were asked when a boy should start his football career, I would say start as early as possible. Football is a funny game. I do not think there is any in-between about it. You either like it, or you don’t. Maybe that’s why football fans are the most rabid of them all.”[6]

Playing a semiparental role, Baugh proved a liberal, telling moms and dads to let the kid play the sport if he really wanted to do it. He did not sugarcoat how hard it would be to compete in the sport, however.

“If he likes it, he will stick to it,” Baugh said. “If he hasn’t the temperament to 'take it,' he'll quit of his own volition. And that will be that. No matter how strict a parent may try to be about keeping his or her son out of football, if the youngster likes the game he will sneak away and play it anyhow. If he doesn't like it, he'll quit, don't worry. One good thing about football is this. It will kill your timidity. If a boy is timid and afraid of getting hurt, he has no business playing. It seems only the timid ones get hurt seriously."[7]

That was a curious comment that surely medical professionals would take issue with, since plenty of tough guys get hurt in the NFL. Indeed, one of the complaints from observers is that players look at themselves as invulnerable and do not take good enough care of their hurts.

Baugh did spend a lot of words on the possibility of young players getting injured, and although he wasn't talking about himself, he surely was speaking from personal experience. "If the boy is a back he will learn how to take care of himself back there, especially if he is a passer or punter," Baugh said.[8]

Baugh, of course, was a passer and punter. His rookie year he also rushed for 240 yards, third best on the team.

"He will learn to rely on his other teammates for a certain length of time," Baugh said, "and then realize he is on his own. He will learn timing, both in getting the pass or the punt, and, in the case of the pass, he will learn to judge distance, the speed of his receiver going to left or right or straight down the field."[9]

Intriguingly, in this advice column, Baugh made a strong point without talking in strong language. While skirting insults, he made it clear that he believed passing is for quarterbacks, not for pretenders, regardless of athletic talent.

"I know for a fact that several All-American linemen have, in practice games, gone back to try to pass," Baugh said. "During practice they could throw a football well over 50 yards, but when they would get back during a scrimmage, with charging linemen in front of them they would, 90 percent of the time, throw the ball far wide of their target."[10]

Another thing Baugh commented on was whether he would let a son of his play this rugged game. Let? Why, yes he would, said the then-unmarried Baugh.

"If I had a son he would have a football on his first Christmas, maybe before," Baugh said. "If he wanted to play football that would be up to him. If he didn't, that would be OK, too."[11]

Although no one accused Sammy Baugh of being innocent, the football audience of the 1930s was much more innocent than it would become eighty years later. The topics of his first-person series seemed to dwell mostly on questions he had been asked by the public or perhaps some sportswriters. From the long distance of most of a century later, those questions sound innocent and overly simplistic.

Baugh said he had been asked how different it was being paid to play pro football compared to the true-blue nature of playing for his alma mater, TCU. Much to pro football luminaries' delight, he said that playing pro ball was much harder than competing in college. Chicago Bears founder George Halas had been trying to make that case for years. Also, yes, the so-called spirit to win was just as strong with the Redskins as it was with the Horned Frogs.

"Of course we want to win," Baugh said, addressing the bonus money that players received by playing for the championship and winning it. He referred to "juicy cuts" of the gate receipts players get. "Besides, it's our bread and butter to win and play well. And nobody is going to throw away his bread and butter without a struggle. Self-preservation is, after all, really the first law of nature."[12]

It used to drive Halas crazy after the Bears became one of the charter members of the NFL to hear skeptics belittle the pro game as not being of the same quality as the college game. Of course, any professional team would line up and regularly best any college team. Pro teams represented a culling of the herd, a narrowing of the talent funnel, with only the best being offered cash to keep playing. It took Baugh only days to realize the truism in that thesis.

"As to the caliber of the players, you can take it from me they are much better than in college," Baugh said. "Which isn't hard to explain, and, of course, logical, even to an ignoramus in logic. In the first place, professional players are the cream of the crop. They are the best players available in their positions or else the club would get the player or players better in each position. Thus, in every position a man is good. Blocking and tackling is better and harder. These blockers and tacklers are masters. They are the best or they wouldn't be playing with a big-league pro team. Most colleges would be tickled to death to have a punter who can average

50 yards and a passer of extraordinary caliber. In the pro game, every team has not one, but two, and sometimes three and four such performers."[13]

While Baugh's general argument was unassailable, he exaggerated somewhat. Baugh could boom the ball 50 yards regularly off of his foot and he was an extraordinary passer, but he was a rare species. Not every team had even one player capable of those feats, never mind two or three.

Maybe the rookie Baugh was still learning just how special a player he was compared to the other best football players in the land. He probably already suspected he was going right to the head of the class, but he wasn't going to brag about that after a month of games.

The amazing thing was that a national syndicate wanted to splash Baugh's story across the country when he was still such a callow player, not even close to completing his first season in the NFL. He was identified as a phenom, and as it proved out, that was true. Baugh was no flash in the pan by any definition. He was just beginning. And when the regular season ended with the Redskins holding an 8-3 record, they were champs of the East and slated to continue playing for an NFL crown.

CHAPTER 12 • Baugh Leads Redskins to Title

Knowing George Preston Marshall and his proclivity to think big, he probably expected rookie Sammy Baugh to step into the quarterback job and promptly lead the Washington Redskins to the National Football League title again. After all, the Redskins had gone to the championship game the year before, in 1936. There are no sure things in sport—great expectations, yes. But Baugh really was able to take the Redskins back to the title game in 1937.

In the earliest years of the NFL, the Decatur Staleys—then as the Chicago Bears—the prominent franchise led by George Halas, quickly established itself as a league powerhouse. Decatur finished as league runner-up in 1920, first in 1921, and then became the Chicago Bears. For the next three seasons, the Bears were the league's second-place finishers.

In 1932 Chicago won that indoor "Tom Thumb" championship game, the last of the informal titlists crowned before the NFL went to East-West division championship showdowns. The Bears beat the New York Giants in the 1933 title game and lost to the Giants in 1934.

If they were not winning a title, the Bears were contending for one. It was no different in 1937 when the Redskins' path was blocked by Halas and his crew. The Bears finished 9-1-1 and were regarded as the class of the league. They surrendered just 100 points all year, or 9.1 points per game. A few more years would pass before the Bears would become known as the "Monsters of the Midway," but the name fit already.

The Bears were deep at running back with fullback Bronko Nagurski still active and with Ray Nolting and Jack Manders also in the mix. So was Beattie Feathers, who in 1934 became the first player in NFL history to rush for 1,000 yards. However, Feathers was injured before that year was out and never again approached his season's accomplishments.

The starting quarterback was Bernie Masterson, not a masterful passer. He was not asked to throw much, but he did complete nine tosses for touchdowns. The backup was Ray Buivid, the Marquette player who kept crossing paths with Baugh one way or another. The Bears also possessed some fearsome linemen in future Hall of Famers George Musso, Danny Fortmann, and Joe Stydahar.

Besides Baugh, back Cliff Battles, and end Wayne Millner, another notable in Washington's lineup was future Hall of Famer Glen "Turk" Edwards, a rugged tackle.

The title game was scheduled for Wrigley Field, the Bears' home, borrowed each autumn from the Chicago Cubs. The weather that year was borrowed from Alaska, however. The days leading up to the game were frigid, and Bears management worked feverishly to thaw ice and make the grass playable. Although it was fifteen degrees for the December 12 contest, that was comparatively balmy compared to the preceding days. The official NFL summary cited that temperature, added that the wind was blowing at twelve miles per hour, and said, "Field is frozen."

It was cold enough that only 15,870 fans turned out. They were bundled in thick coats and hats, wore gloves, and wrapped blankets around their bodies. That crowd also included 3,000 Redskins fans making the trip west, borne over the railroad tracks by the spirit of optimism engendered by the team and Marshall's fanfare.

Turk Edwards kicked off to the Bears, but after advancing for one first down, Chicago was forced to punt. Nolting did the job, pinning the Redskins on their own 7-yard line for their first possession.

This kind of precarious field position kept coaches committed to the run. The ground game seemed much safer than throwing the ball up for grabs when the other team might intercept it and have only a short run back to the end zone for a tables-turning touchdown.

But those coaches didn't have Sammy Baugh working for them. Flaherty had seen enough magic from the young thrower's arm during the regular season to trust Baugh to do the right thing. On first down, with the Bears thinking "run," Baugh faded back into the end zone and flipped a short pass to Battles at the Washington 1-yard line. Battles gathered it in and darted downfield, eluding tacklers and chewing up yardage. He made it to the Redskin 49 and, voila, the 'Skins were out of trouble. "It was actually a fullback screen," Battles said. "I went from a blocking position. It worked so well, I thought I was going all the way."[1]

The original play had been called by Riley Smith, but Baugh overruled him and told the huddle he was going to back up as if to punt, fake it, and throw. Baugh actually instructed Battles to turn at the chunk of ice downfield he identified, as if it was street ball and the signal-caller was telling the other kid to cut sharply at the parked car.

That big gainer was the end of Washington's progress, but Baugh's daring completion in such iffy circumstances had to shake the Bears. He showed they must be aware of him and that he might pull a pass out of his trick bag at any time.

Baugh was also the Redskins' punter, an exceptional one. He boomed them high and deep and often trapped foes deep inside their own territory with his pinpoint kicks. Although Baugh five times led the NFL in punting and retired with a 45.1-yard-per-kick average, his contributions with his foot were often overlooked because of the singular contributions he made with his arm.

On one kick, Baugh's punt was downed at the Chicago 6-yard line. It was so far to the opposite end zone, it seemed the Bears might need to change trains to get there. Indeed, the Bears' offense went nowhere, and Chicago even punted *on third* down, figuring it was safer to get the ball farther away from their end zone than it was to try another offensive play. It was not much of a rescue operation. The Chicago kick gave Washington the ball on its own 47-yard line.

The new world of professional forward passing unveiled itself on Washington's possession. Baugh threw on the first five plays, on his way to 33 attempts on a day many believed was too cold to bother with the aerial game. Battles dropped the first one, and Charley Malone, who caught 28 passes during the regular season, couldn't come up with the second attempt. But on his third try Baugh found Smith, the man who had scored all of the points in the season opener against the Giants. Smith nabbed the ball and gained 14 yards. Going around the horn, Baugh went to Ernie Pinckert next for an 18-yard gain.

Masterson hit Pinckert hard with his tackle, and there was a lull while the receiver was treated on the field. Pinckert climbed to his feet and stayed in the game. Nothing Baugh had seen from the Bears' defense so far dissuaded him from throwing, so he did it again. This time Baugh threw another strike to Smith for a 6-yard gain before he was smacked down by Ray Nolting.

By this time the Bears had to wonder if Baugh was going to pass on every single offensive down. Taking advantage, Baugh faked a pass on the next play and ran off left tackle for a 3-yard gain.

Calling a little change-up, Baugh handed off to Battles, whose 2-yard run was good enough for a first down at the Bears' 10. By now it was apparent to the Bears that Baugh was liable to pass at any time—or not. How could they know when he might retreat to the tried-and-true running game? Baugh gave the ball back to Battles, and he battled for three more yards.

Baugh went back to the pass on the next play, but he also went back to Battles. He fired to Battles, but Jack Manders knocked it down. On third-and-7 from the 7-yard line, the tenth play of the drive, Baugh tricked Chicago by calling a reverse. Battles neither went out for a pass nor bucked up the middle. He dashed to the goal line and dove in. Six points for Washington at 6 minutes, 56 seconds of the first quarter. Smith kicked the extra point for the 7-0 lead.

Despite those repeated passes, Baugh said that was not necessarily by design—the plays were not mapped out in advance for the game plan during practice.

"I think we were improvising more than anything," Baugh said. "The defense tells a quarterback what he can do. I don't care what anybody says, the defense dictates. For instance, if they've got a linebacker and I find out I can throw to a back one-on-one against him, I'll wear the guy out."[2]

If the Bears were psyched out by the way Baugh marched the Redskins down the field, they didn't show it. Nolting took the kickoff at his own 8-yard line and returned the ball to the 28. He also ran on the first play for 2 yards. Masterson, whose quarterbacking credentials paled next to Baugh's, hit the estimable Eggs Manske with a pass at the Washington 40-yard line. Manske fell down on the catch, but when no defender touched him, he scrambled to his feet and ran to the Redskins' 19 before being tackled—by Baugh.

Masterson handed off to Bronko Nagurski on first down, and the plough horse rumbled through the Washington line to the 10. Baugh made the tackle, but he was the worse for it, being almost knocked cold and needing smelling salts on the field. "That sonofabitch ran plumb over me and he didn't even need no blocker in front of him," Baugh said.[3]

That big Bears line did its job then and followed up by creating a hole as gaping as an "L" tunnel. While it seemed a high-percentage move to give the ball right back to Bronko, Masterson instead gave it to Manders. Manders ran over from the 10 for a touchdown and then kicked the extra point himself for the 7-7 tie. The score was recorded slightly more than three minutes after Washington's touchdown.

On the next series, the Bears' growling defense showed why many remained unconvinced by the significance of the pass. After an incompletion, a 12-yard-run on a keeper, and two completions, Baugh goofed. He threw an interception to rookie defensive back George Wilson. It was a big play. Wilson would later coach the Detroit Lions and Miami Dolphins and win the 1957 title leading Detroit, thus being involved in more than his share of key plays in his football career, on the field and on the sideline.

At the time, Wilson's pickoff was the biggest play of his life. Wilson gave Chicago the ball at the Redskins' 49-yard line. Fired up by how easily they moved the ball on their last possession, the Bears mixed up their calls and saw them work just as smoothly. After Manders ran for 4 yards and 5 yards on a second try, Nolting gained three on the ground.

That put the ball on the 37. Masterson flung the ball to Manders at the 25. Wilson, who started it all, made a crucial block, and Manders slithered into the end zone with thirty-five seconds remaining in the eventful opening quarter. It was Bears 14, Redskins 7 after one. The game had all the makings of a classic.

Those in the know, or who learned details later, understood that George Halas was a no-mercy coach. He was irascible and lacked the tact gene. While Halas and Marshall teamed up to drive through new passing rules and other plans to boost the NFL's popularity, their alliance was a tenuous one, and it in no way lessened the competition between them. Perhaps only immediate family meant more to Halas than his other family, the Bears. It didn't faze Halas one bit to alienate Marshall.

During the 1936 season, the Bears were playing at Boston. Frustrated by how the action was going at Fenway Park with Chicago dominating en route to a 26-0 loss, Marshall paraded onto the field, not the place of an owner. In fact, his coach, Ray Flaherty, had it written into his contract that Marshall would stay off the field. It was difficult to determine who was angrier at the sight of Marshall coming out of the stands: Halas or Flaherty. "Get off the field, you sonofabitch," Halas yelled. "George," Marshall retorted, "this is my field and my town. I can do as I please." Flaherty jumped into the fray, reminding Marshall of the clause in his contract. "Yeah, but Halas needs to shut his damn mouth," Marshall said.[4]

Halas and Marshall sort of kissed and made up many times, but when either topped the other in a regular-season game and especially in a championship game, one was pleased to lord it over another. Halas was also known for looking for any tiny edge to help his Bears win games.

As someone who participated in writing rules, Halas certainly knew the NFL rulebook. Although some passing rules had been liberalized to aid the passing game, compared to modern play some rules were also restrictive or even dangerous to the quarterback's health. A key one that Halas reminded his defense about before the championship game was that it was legal to hit the quarterback, Baugh, even after he released the throw—up until the whistle blew the play dead.

Baugh was the player who posed the biggest threat to the Bears' chances, so Halas urged his defenders to clobber Baugh whenever they got the chance. It does not sound terribly sportsmanlike in retrospect, but the circumstances permitted what Halas urged. "I want you to hit that sonofabitch until blood is coming out of his ears," Halas ordered.[5]

Halas was also credited with once employing a particularly laughable angle of pregame pep talk. "You can have a session with your girlfriend, and how long does that last?" Halas said. "Twenty minutes? But a win in the National Football League is a thrill that lasts a whole week. And what a thrill!"[6] Halas was comparing an NFL victory favorably with sex, and that was only a regular-season win. Heck, a player could be thrilled for an entire year about a championship triumph.

Washington had the ball first to start the second quarter, but they didn't do much with the possession. On second down, Baugh was hit by Chicago's Dick Plasman, the last NFL player to compete without a helmet. Baugh fumbled in his own territory and the ball rolled and rolled, as if going downhill. Washington recovered the ball, but the line of scrimmage was now the 14-yard line after the 26-yard loss. On the next down, Baugh punted it away.

Halas gave backup Buivid a shot at quarterback for a couple of possessions, but nothing special came of it. There was much back-and-forth in the second quarter, but no scoring, so the Bears remained ahead, 14-7, at halftime.

The Redskins received the second-half kickoff, and after Don Irwin returned it 20 yards, Washington had a first down on its own 30. Irwin also carried on the first play from scrimmage but was stopped at the line. Baugh tried another pass, to Wayne Millner, and that completion gained 9 yards. Irwin's next run was more successful, scooting for 6 yards.

Washington had a first down on its own 45 when Baugh spotted an open Millner. He hit him with his throw, but Millner dropped it. Slightly altering the call, one play later Baugh threw to Millner cutting across the middle. This time Millner hung on at full speed and dashed all the way for the touchdown, a 55-yard scamper. Smith kicked the extra point, and less than a minute-and-a-half into the second half it was 14-14.

The deadlock did not last long. After the kickoff, Chicago began its drive on the 23. It was Bronko Nagurski time. Several players—teammates and foes alike—called Nagurski the greatest player who ever lived. There were myriad stories about his strength. Some of them were likely apocryphal, and others no doubt true. It was said that the University of Minnesota coach recruited Nagurski when he asked him for directions in International Falls, Minnesota, and the farming kid picked up his plow and pointed. Nagurski once put his head down and blew through the opponents' line for a touchdown and kept right on running until he smashed his noggin into the Wrigley Field wall beyond the end zone. He said something along the lines about how hard that last man hit.

On this 77-yard march downfield, Nagurski ran for 6 yards, ran for 20, ran for 1, attempted a pass, attempted a lateral, and it all ended up with a jump pass from Masterson to Manske for a 4-yard touchdown. After Manders's kick it was 21-14, with the Bears ahead again.

Chicago worked long and hard for that score. It is impossible to know if the defense took a relaxing breath, but Baugh fooled the heck out of them after Smith returned the kickoff to the Washington 22. Thirty seconds after the Bears took the lead, Washington was on the board again. Millner broke into the clear and Baugh found him again prancing through the Bears' secondary at midfield. Millner outran defenders, including Nagurski, going all the way for a 78-yard score. The kick was good, which made the score 21-21.

In the attempt to go ahead once more, the Bears fizzled. They advanced just 12 yards on the next possession before punting. Washington had the ball at its 20-yard line. This was the game's pivotal possession as the third quarter wound down.

Don Irwin, who played college ball at Colgate, had a four-year NFL career, and his best season was this 1937 campaign. He stayed in the title game in place of Battles, and Baugh worked him early on this drive. Irwin gained 9, 6, and 2 yards before Baugh returned to the air as a strategy.

Baugh nearly erred with a poor pass to Malone that was almost picked off. The next try, the throw was complete to Malone for 11 yards. A 7-yarder to Millner was good. On fourth-and-3, Irwin obtained a first down on a 3-yard run to keep things alive. Baugh rewarded him with a 7-yard pass.

The ball was on the 35: Baugh teased the Bears with a fake throw to Malone, then he switched sides and fired to Ed Justice for the touchdown. There were fifty-four seconds left in the quarter when Smith kicked the extra point for a seven-point lead, 28–21.

That set up a frantic fourth quarter that saw such notable activity as a partially blocked Baugh quick kick; Buivid steering the Bears to the Redskins' 23 before losing the ball on downs; the Redskins pushing to the Bears' 19, only to see Millner fumble the ball away; and a fight.

Bears' defenders had followed Halas's exhortations to batter Baugh when they could, and by this point in the game he was limping on a twisted knee and his nose was gushing blood all over his number 33 jersey. On the fourth series of the fourth quarter, Bears backup thrower Keith Molesworth completed a 35-yard pass to Plasman. Baugh was the defender, and he shoved the receiver out of bounds on the Bears' 49.

Plasman—who, it should be recalled, did not wear a helmet—landed on his head. Cuts on his lip and his eye bled, and more blood streamed from his nose. Furious, Plasman jumped up and punched Baugh in the face. Both teams' benches emptied, and fans came pouring out of the stands. Police, ushers, and some players prevented the confrontation from escalating.

One of those who sought to break up the melee was Nagurski. That was a good thing, since no one wanted to face off with an enraged Bronko and his 230 pounds of iron muscle.

At the sight of such a mob action today, officials would have thrown players out of the game left and right, and they would have been fined and suspended by the NFL office. In 1937, no penalties were assessed by the officials, and play resumed. The Bears reached the Redskins' 7-yard line, but couldn't score. That was really Chicago's last gasp. The Bears got the ball back once more, but with Masterson throwing for a big gainer, Riley Smith intercepted him, and the Redskins ran the clock out with a final play.

Marshall's Redskins were champions of the world. Sammy Baugh completed 18 of his 33 passes for 335 yards and three touchdowns. This was a milestone accomplishment for a quarterback and in the progression of the forward pass. Spotlighted under the bright lights with a title at stake, Baugh showed that an exceptional passer could be a difference maker.

Someone had to catch all of those passes, and Millner stood out. He grabbed seven balls and gained 172 yards through the air. Outside of a Don Hutson with Green Bay, who was in a class of his own, most receivers could only fantasize about having days like that.

During the Depression, it was hard to get rich in the NFL. Each player's winning share for capturing the championship was $225. The Bears' losing share was $127 apiece.

A few hundred of those three thousand visitors from Washington barreled past the protectors of the Redskins' locker room to celebrate with their heroes. They barged into the dressing room and feted Baugh and others. Baugh's reaction was as self-deprecating as could be, considering his role.

"What the heck?" he said. "Anyone can do the pitching. But it takes real ball players to do the catching."[7] A major oversimplification, to say the least.

Bernie Harter of the *Washington Herald* wrote in his postgame column more lavishly about Baugh's contributions. "Sammy Baugh, of course, stood out head and shoulders above the field," Harter wrote while trying to sum up a number of standout Redskin plays. "Never has there been such an exhibition. And he was given almost perfect support."[8]

Halas had recognized going into the game that Baugh was the key to a Washington victory. Rarely did Halas game-plan so specifically for an individual. Baugh's counterpart was Masterson, who came out of the University of Nebraska and spent 1934 to 1940 with the Bears. Of all the experts, Masterson as a quarterback comprehended what he was seeing as Baugh turned in the finest single game to date by an NFL passer. "I can't think of anything that describes Sammy Baugh," Masterson said. "You can use all your superlatives and you only have a mediocre description of that boy."[9]

Everyone who watched that game gushed about Baugh. That included Shirley Povich, the *Washington Post* columnist who observed the Texas transplant for his entire career in DC. "Lift a paean of praise to Sammy Baugh," Povich wrote as the Redskins secured their first title with young Sammy at the controls. "Pay him your tributes, sound your huzzahs. And shout his name loudly. For it was Slingin' Sammy Baugh, sweet Sammy from Sweetwater, Texas, who stood out there on a brutally frozen Wrigley Field this afternoon and almost with each rise and fall of his long right arm brought to Washington the National Football League championship."[10]

Povich had more to say, commenting, "All season the fellow was uncanny, and his Texas admirers were guilty of vast understatement all these years when they were saying that Slingin' Sammy could bloody your nostrils with a football at 50 yards."[11] Never mind taking someone's specific eye out with it if requested.

Coach Ray Flaherty, who had been taken aback by Baugh's cheekiness when he asked "Which eye?" in the preseason, called Sammy's championship game effort "the greatest one-man show ever put on in pro football."[12]

It was just the beginning, really. Baugh was only a rookie, but he had elevated the quarterback position and the throwing game to new heights on a national stage. The Baugh game yardage was nothing like anything anyone had ever seen from a quarterback, and the performance stood up for years as the standard for championship games.

CHAPTER 13 • Sammy, The New Star

After 1937, it was clear how valuable Sammy Baugh could be to the Redskins, but Baugh had not yet cleared his palate of baseball. Baseball was his first love, and he still heard whispers in his head telling him he might well be able to make it to the major leagues. Somewhere a voice kept repeating that perhaps Baugh was a better baseball player than football player. He couldn't—or didn't want to—shake that feeling. Besides, look what he had just done at the top level of football. He had to know.

So that became Baugh's off-season in the Cardinals' organization, the 1938 summer in the minor leagues, under Branch Rickey's supervision, not George Preston Marshall's. Marshall was not at all pleased, but Baugh had just completed a one-year contract. He remained under the control of Washington in the NFL, but Marshall could no more prevent Baugh from trying out for the Cardinals than he could stop him from running for governor of Texas.

Some might suggest that Baugh was foolish to risk his newfound reputation as a sterling pro passer and an NFL champion for baseball at that point in his life. The cynical might suggest that he hooked up with the Cardinals to increase his financial leverage for a richer contract from Marshall. Maybe there was something to that in the back of Baugh's mind, but evidence points to his sincerity and true infatuation with baseball. Marshall indulged Baugh. There was nothing else he could do. But he didn't have to like Baugh's minor-league AA tour. He hoped and believed Baugh would come around, back to the Redskins.

Baugh played out that summer in the Cardinals organization, making an impression as a fielder, but not a hitter. Clearly, he would need some seasoning if he stuck with baseball.

When Baugh's sojourn ended, Marshall made him an offer he couldn't refuse. Marshall came up with a three-year contract in an age when long-term contracts were virtually unheard of and many of Baugh's teammates were earning one hundred dollars per game. Remember that this was when all-star and eventual Hall of Famer Cliff Battles retired at age twenty-seven because Marshall stranded him at a salary of three thousand dollars a year for pretty much his entire career.

Marshall was as generous to Baugh as any owner in the NFL was to any player, but he included a clause in the deal. If Baugh signed, he would be forbidden from playing any other sport. The three-year package called for twenty-five thousand dollars. Interestingly, Marshall did not pluck that number out of thin air.

A few months after the Redskins won the title, turning Baugh into an overnight hero in Washington, and before he met the St. Louis Cardinals for spring training, Baugh was invited to the University of North Carolina by the football coach to provide passing pointers to his team. While there, a student working for the school news bureau interviewed Baugh. One question Baugh was asked was if he had a contract for the 1938 season, and he answered the young man honestly.

"I haven't signed a contract," Baugh said in an incident recounted by the no-longer-youthful man forty-six years later. "And I intend to quit professional football if Mr. Marshall doesn't give me a three-year contract for twenty-five thousand dollars."[1]

The young reporter was not only on a tight deadline, but he faced competition from others trying to get stories printed, as well as the challenge from at least one superior who predicted that no news agency would use his item. Not only did the story make it out the door—by mail—but the writer was stunned to see his story emblazoned across the front page of the *Washington Post*, albeit without his byline. "I couldn't believe my eyes, but there it was," Jim Kluttz said many years later.[2]

The Washington Times-Herald, another subscriber, also used the story.

That paper gave it less prominent play but did use Kluttz's name on it. Later, the Associated Press reported Baugh had signed a three-year contract with the Redskins for twenty-five thousand dollars. "I like to think that my story, and the way the *Post* played it up, gave Marshall a little push," Kluttz said.[3]

Baugh had quickly evolved into the celebrity Marshall had envisioned when he drafted him. As a showman who believed in glitz, and who understood box office name value, Marshall recognized that Baugh had exceeded his expectations far more quickly than anticipated. He was a miner who struck gold, a thoroughbred owner whose three-year-old won the Kentucky Derby. He didn't want to hear any more foolishness about Baugh leaving pro football for baseball. Once Baugh got what he wanted, he did terminate any future involvement in the national pastime.

Sportswriters noted that Baugh was the toast of the town in DC, even if he didn't spend much of his free time there—not then or ever. Baugh was a Texas boy born and remained one despite the artificiality of the wardrobe demanded by Marshall for that coming-out press conference.

One thing Baugh was not during the 1937–38 off-season in Washington was overexposed. The sportswriters had turned him into a demigod with their words after the deliverance of the NFL title, and he could coast on that for a little while.

It was not merely local adulation that trailed his name either. The day after Washington prevailed over the Chicago Bears, a prominent Chicago sportswriter wrote, "Sammy Baugh is the greatest forward passer football has ever seen." That was the lead on a story in the *Chicago Tribune* under a headline reading, "Bears Find Out Why They Call Baugh the Best." Below that was a subhead reading, "Washington Wizard Just Too Clever." There was no mystery why that guy believed Washington won.[4]

The story continued with an intriguing observation for so early in Baugh's pro career. This was a veteran writer who had been watching pro football for some time: "Benny Friedman and Harry Newman (both of the New York Giants), great forward passers, were expert," the story went. "But Baugh—and this was the consensus of yesterday's thousand—is superior to either of those men."[5]

This really was the opinion of one man, since he certainly did not conduct a poll of those 15,870 fans one by one. He may well have spoken for them based on what he saw, but he was definitely seeking to inform his readers about what they missed on that cold day in Chicago. After all, they needed such an interpreter because there was no television broadcast of the title game back then. The first televised NFL Championship Game was not until 1948, and it was 1951 before a game was shown nationwide. Except for radio broadcasts, the big-city newspapermen were the eyes and ears of the fan.

"Baugh not only threw accurately," the report said, "but he had the ability to hold his [throw] until the last possible second, regardless of the charging Bear linemen, who frequently sent him to the frozen ground as viciously as possible. Baugh could not be stopped. . . . Baugh was the deciding factor."[6] That analysis made it sound as if the Redskins were the equivalent of the only nation with long-range cannons while all the others were fighting with swords and shields.

In April 1938, after spring training and before Baugh played for the Cardinals and signed a fresh deal with the Redskins, he flew back to Texas to get married to his high school girlfriend, Edmonia Smith, who was called Mona. Before heading back to Sweetwater to get hitched, Baugh was waylaid by a Dallas newspaperman. He uttered what was, in retrospect, given what was soon to happen, a rather remarkable statement.

"Football pays me well," Baugh said, "although I think baseball beats football because you can play it longer. But I'll probably be on the gridiron again next season. After that I'll decide whether I want to play it any longer or not. I may and I may not."[7]

Perhaps Baugh really was ambivalent about pro football and did not truly convince himself the sport was the way to go until after his hitting in the minors informed him where he really belonged.

The wedding took place without much fanfare at the Smith home, officiated by Mona's father, a minister. Whether it was nerves, or simple carelessness, or distraction, Baugh forgot to bring the marriage license with him. Dad let Sammy slide for the moment, and the paperwork was completed later.

Although Baugh invested in a 750-acre ranch that came with a house, a horse, and cattle, the newlyweds left West Texas behind temporarily while Sammy chased his baseball dream. On a stop in Fort Worth, Baugh was recognized everywhere, and fans figured out who Mona was because the wire services had written about the wedding, even though it had been a small affair. College football had set Baugh up as a local hero, and his star never waned in the Lone Star State.

In later years Baugh admitted he was never going to be in Marty Marion's class as a shortstop, as kind as some players' comparisons were, and that, like so many hopefuls coming along before and after him, as a batter his weakness was hitting the curve.

Naturally enough Baugh's occasional comments to sportswriters about baseball versus football and how much money he could make drifted back to Marshall. The Redskins owner was not easily intimidated in a contract negotiation, even if it was long-distance repartee. But he was cognizant of Baugh's importance to his football team as well. Still, Marshall was always going to bluster a bit, too.

"We will pay Baugh his price," Marshall said. "But it will be my price, too. I will not have any trouble with Sammy Baugh. He can't keep away from football. If it came right down to it, he'd probably pay us to let him play."[8]

That was hyperbole. Baugh may have been a born football player, even if he was slow to admit it. But football had given him the wherewithal to buy land in Texas, and he was now a married man. He was a shrewd man with a buck, and in this Depression era—especially coming out of West Texas, which had seen its share of hard luck—Baugh was not going to throw away a solid-paying career.

Sammy and Edmonia's union eventually produced five children: Gary, David, Bruce, and Stephen in the 1940s, and Frances, the only girl, when Baugh was approaching retirement.

Baugh would have a tremendous career. It lasted for sixteen seasons and he set many records, but when he was asked about his most memorable single game, he returned to the rookie-year championship showing when the Redskins outlasted the Bears for the crown.

Not only did Baugh have a splendid day when he was given so much credit for the Washington victory, but it came early in his career when he wasn't quite so famous and when it was not quite so clear to the rest of the NFL just what he could do. More than a decade after the performance, Baugh was approached by two writers and asked to choose and recount his greatest day in football. Baugh still chose the big win over Chicago.

"For the one game that gave me my greatest day in football, I'll have to stick with the National League Championship game in which the Redskins beat the mighty Chicago Bears, 28 to 21," he said. "I've had many thrills and what one might call 'great days,' but that one turned out to be something special. . . . That year happened to be my first in the professional ranks."[9]

Another thing that stuck in Baugh's memory was the harshness of the weather that day. Even players with long careers only rarely have to compose themselves to fight against extreme winter weather, and this was one of those games, and a game with so much at stake.

"I'll never forget that setting for that ball game in Wrigley Field," Baugh said. "Three days before the game it snowed, leaving the ground like a skating rink and certainly in no shape for a football game. The field had been covered with a tarpaulin and straw to protect it from the snow, but the bitter cold, a wild northwest wind, and other tricks of the elements revealed a solid sheet of ice when the covering was removed at game time."[10]

Baugh noted that both teams wore sneakers so that the players could cope with the ice. This was a lesson learned in the 1934 championship game when the New York Giants employed that type of footwear to take advantage of the Bears and their cleats, which would not dig into the frozen surface. Baugh said the players still skidded around on the ice, with the sneakers providing only minimal assistance.

Baugh came off modestly in his report of what transpired in the game. "This must have been my day," he said. "I couldn't do anything wrong. But this was definitely the toughest game of football I ever played in."[11]

Rather than give George Halas the satisfaction of admitting he might have been bothered by the Bears' coach's orders to his men to do anything short of dismembering him, Baugh focused more on the tough Bears runners, who seemed particularly suited to taking advantage of the weather in the ground game. "Fingers numb in this zero weather that held even Chicago's rabid fans down to 15,000, we had to rub them continually to keep the circulation going," Baugh said. "The Bears, however, seemed unbothered either by the cold or our opening touchdown."[12]

For some strange reason, even though it seemed obvious to sportswriters covering the game and it became generally known that Halas did everything short of putting a bounty on Baugh, Sam remained skeptical of such a notion.

"I was limping badly from a bruise I'd received in the second period," Baugh said. "They said the Bears were out to get me, but that can't be true. I was a key man and they were doing their utmost to throttle my passes and bottle me up. That they didn't is a fine tribute not to me, but to ends like Wayne Millner and Ed Justice, who caught passes almost blindfolded, and to a line led by mighty Turk Edwards, Jim Barber, and the rest. That's football."[13]

Baugh revealed that his leg was so weak, the Redskins' coaches almost refused to allow him back onto the field after halftime. But he soldiered on. "As the game progressed, the Bears were swarming over me in ever-rougher hordes," Baugh said. "We played alert, hard football that day, too. Perhaps I played a little too hard."[14]

That reference was to the play where he knocked Dick Plasman out of bounds and became embroiled in a fight with him. "It was all the way, a bitter, battering game, my greatest day in football," Baugh said.[15]

As prized as the championship trophy was for the Redskins at the time—the title being the first in franchise history, and the renowned Sammy Baugh leading them to the crown—sometime over the years following, the symbol of that victory was shunted aside, lost and forgotten. The Redskins brought the trophy home to Washington, DC, and housed it at Griffith Stadium. However, in 1961 the Redskins moved to a new stadium. The new facility was named D.C. Stadium, and its name was changed to Robert F. Kennedy Stadium after the US senator from New York was assassinated while campaigning for the presidency in 1968.

Somewhere along the way, the trophy was misplaced. In 1996, when the Major League Soccer team D.C. United was preparing to move in and begin play at RFK, the Redskins had to move to new offices in the stadium. Public relations man Mike McCall was cleaning up and came upon a neglected trophy in a closet. He initially thought it was a replica, but it turned out to be the genuine article. The trophy was about to be disposed of when McCall decided it should be saved. He checked in with officials from the Pro Football Hall of Fame in Canton, Ohio, and only then determined it was the real-deal trophy.

An intrepid reporter tracked down a then-eighty-two-year-old Baugh in Texas and asked him what he thought about the treasure coming so close to a disgraced end. "To be honest," Baugh said, "I don't know that I ever heard about us getting a trophy."[16] So much for the romance of the loving cup called the Ed Thorp Memorial Trophy.

Even though almost nobody realized the 1937 trophy had gone missing, everyone was happy to have it back. The Redskins were also glad to have Sammy Baugh back in 1938, with baseball in his rearview mirror for good.

Baugh had distinguished himself during the 1937 season and shown the potential of the forward pass as a weapon. But he now had to prove he was not a one-hit wonder like a pop singer who zoomed to the top of the charts just once. History is littered with such ballplayers and crooners. No one thought Baugh was a fluke, but he still had to prove his consistency.

Unfortunately for Baugh, things did not go smoothly at all in 1938 and 1939. Injuries, one thing that he did fear in the context of football longevity compared to baseball, did interfere with his playing time and efficiency. The Sammy of those two seasons did not compare to the rookie Baugh.

Baugh appeared in just nine games during the 1938 season and did not lead the NFL in any passing category. His numbers declined across the board, and he threw just five touchdown passes while hurling eleven interceptions.

In 1939, while also appearing in nine games, Baugh threw even less, although he did complete 55.2 percent of his passes that year with six TD tosses against nine interceptions. Overall, despite Baugh's limitations, Washington fared surprisingly well. The Redskins finished 6-3-2 in 1938 and 8-2-1 in 1939.

The main quarterback for the Redskins in 1939 because of Baugh's woes was Frank Filchock. Filchock, who came out of Indiana University, had a superb 1939 season. He led the NFL with eleven touchdown passes, threw for 1,094 yards, and completed 61.8 percent of his throws.

Filchock was a talent. In 1939, when both he and Baugh played, they were known as Slingin' Sammy and Flingin' Frank. The signature play of Filchock's season was a 99-yard touchdown pass to Andy Farkas in a game against Pittsburgh. Because of the dimensions of the field and the way yardage gained is measured, that distance is the longest a touchdown pass can travel. This was the first 99-yarder in NFL history.

Filchock provided a devastating one-two punch at quarterback, akin to the Green Bay Packers' Arnie Herber–Cecil Isbell combo. Filchock and Baugh were teammates through 1941, when Filchock went into the navy during World War II. Filchock returned to Washington for the 1944 and 1945 seasons and was with the New York Giants in 1946.

That year with New York, Filchock passed for 1,262 yards and twelve touchdowns, but he became enmeshed in a gambling scandal on the eve of the championship game against the Bears. Filchock, recognized as a key man as quarterback by gamblers, was asked to fix the point spread. Although he declined and played hard, well, and through injury that day, he lied about being approached.

Filchock, who had been a two-time all-star, was suspended from the NFL for three years by Commissioner Bert Bell. He later returned to play in the All-America Football Conference and the Canadian Football League before becoming a coach.

Baugh's physical ailments began in 1938 only weeks after he signed his three-year deal with the Redskins in August. On the first play of the game against the College All-Stars, led by Isbell, in the annual charity game, Baugh was leveled, knocked out of the game, and carried off the field. He spent the sixty minutes of action being treated by doctors.

Two weeks later, in the September 11 opener against the Philadelphia Eagles, Baugh started out by completing twelve of his first thirteen passes. But a gang of Eagles clobbered him, and his left, nonthrowing shoulder was separated and suffered torn muscles and ligaments.

A doctor told Bell that Baugh was finished, that he would "never play again. He may never be able to use that arm again."[17] It was, however, Baugh's non-throwing arm. Baugh proved the gloomy prognosis incorrect and even returned to play the same season, but he was like an eight-cylinder automobile operating on only two cylinders.

The Chicago Bears, never known for their mercy, smashed the Redskins, 31-7, during this period. George Preston Marshall was furious during the game, climbing onto the field and confronting officials with pleas that they slap the Bears with penalties for unnecessary roughness. Needless to say, that was a pointless exercise.

Afterward, George Halas, he of the long memory, was hardly apologetic about the result of this rematch of the 1937 championship game, making fun of the Redskins and Marshall. "That's too bad, girlies," Halas said. "I'm awfully sorry my boys were a little rough. What say we all go down to the corner for a double banana split and a fistful of chocolate éclairs? And get this, Gertrude, one more squeak out of you pantywaists and I'll lick the lot of you myself, and that goes for your boss, too."[18]

Baugh spent the off-season recuperating and reported in good mettle for the 1939 season, but once again in the early going he was belted out of a game by defenders, carried off the field, and missed the better part of four games. This is when Filchock stepped into the lineup in top form and helped rescue the season.

It took some tender care, glue, baling wire, and rest, but Baugh did come back from his batterings to resume his rookie-year form in the 1940 season.

CHAPTER 14 • SID LUCKMAN: A CHALLENGER

A new first-class thrower burst on the National Football League scene in 1939.

It would not have been out of character for the wily George Halas to observe Sammy Baugh's success at quarterback with the Washington Redskins and think, *I need to get me one of those for the Bears.* After all, Halas had played a part in loosening league rules to aid the passing game, so he could anticipate a bit of the future. He had helped make it happen. Halas was always good at recognizing talent as well, so when he put his eye on Sid Luckman, a quarterback from Columbia, he could not imagine a finer future for the Ivy Leaguer than as the field leader of the Chicago Bears.

Luckman stood 6-foot-2 and weighed nearly 200 pounds. He grew up in Brooklyn and was a star athlete at Erasmus High. Halas realized Luckman owned one of the best arms he had ever seen, but Luckman had no intention of playing pro football. He planned to put his college education to work in the business field, and his wife, Estelle, was in favor of that idea, too.

The Bears did not have one of the highest picks in the 1939 draft, so Halas persuaded Pittsburgh to select Luckman in the first round of that draft with the number-two overall choice and then trade him to the Bears. Halas gave up end Eggs Manske for the right to talk contract with

Luckman, then went to work wooing him. Halas pursued Luckman almost as if it were a romantic courtship. He was ready to send him flowers, show him the bright lights of the big city, and make big promises.

Halas had become enamored of Luckman's talent while watching him play a game for Columbia University at Baker Field. It was a miserable day, rain pouring down, but Halas was impressed with how Luckman handled himself in the adverse conditions.

"I saw him play a game in the rain in Baker Field," Halas said, "and he did so many tricks with the ball I said, 'We have to have this man.'"[1]

Luckman said he spent an entire winter making up his mind whether to try pro football or go into business and that he wanted to play with a New York team if he went pro. That wasn't going to happen. Halas kept up the pressure. Halas wangled an invitation to Luckman's New York apartment for dinner and turned up the heat on his sales pitch. It was not easy to corral Luckman's signature on a contract. When Halas reached fifty-five hundred dollars on his offer, Luckman signed. Although Luckman had never played quarterback in the T-formation, a friendly passing style, that's what Halas envisioned for him.

"At that time, the T-formation was used almost exclusively by the Bears," Luckman said. "Since I had always played left halfback under the adept guidance of Lou Little, my great college coach at Columbia, that's where I started for the Chicago team. The normal position for the passer in the single-wing formation—which was the most popular formation employed at that time—was the left halfback spot in the backfield."[2]

Those days were very swiftly coming to an end. Soon, a premium would be placed on pocket passers who faded back and unleashed bullets with their strong arms. The T-formation was the offense for them and was the coming thing, as old-style, bludgeon-out-the-yards formations were becoming passé. Luckman, like Baugh, was a man of the moment, a quarterback with the skills to exploit all of the opportunities presented by fresh emphasis on the forward pass. Baugh may have been a brilliant quarterback, but he was not one of a kind. Rather, he was a prototype of a different kind of quarterback, one that would soon take over the sport.

Halas understood Luckman's background, but he was thinking ahead from the moment he had Luckman in the Bears' training camp.

"When I reported for the first practice session with the Bears, George

Halas handed me the assignments both for the left halfback and quarterback in the T-formation," Luckman said, "and told me to learn every detail of both. I took my first look at the T-formation. Frankly, I was unimpressed. The formation seemed like an invitation for the backs to commit hara-kiri. There you went, darting off into the line, with no more blocking or protection than a stray peanut vendor cutting across the field."[3]

Luckman was wrong. His first impression did not do that offense true justice. The T-formation was the coming thing, and he was the one who was going to make it special.

But it was going to take some studying. For a while Luckman must have thought he was back in a college classroom doing homework. But he did reach an aha moment as the possibilities unveiled themselves to him.

"But when I grasped the mechanics of the plan, and the quick-opening plays which developed from it, I was amazed," Luckman said. "The more it impressed me, the deeper I delved into its principles, attempting to solve every maneuver involved. I was determined to know what made it tick."[4]

The T-formation involves an offensive lineup with a seven-man front line, the quarterback behind the center and three running backs behind the QB. They form the "T".

Walter Camp, one of the originators of modern-day football, claimed he invented the T-formation in 1892. Camp actually obtained the nickname of "Father of American Football" and invented the line of scrimmage and the system of four downs. The T-formation's popularity waxed and waned, but fell out of favor by the 1920s and 1930s with few exceptions. Clark Shaughnessy, as head coach of Stanford, and then serving as an assistant coach for Halas with the Bears, helped restore its prominence for a period in the 1940s. The Bears ruled with the T.

"Formations may come and go through the years," Luckman said, "but to me the T will always stand out as the greatest of them all."[5]

Luckman was not an instant starter with the Bears. Halas did not trust him with the keys to the car just yet. Bernie Masterson held onto the top spot, but Luckman saw action in seven games. He completed 23 passes in 51 attempts for a 45.1 percent mark, with five touchdown passes, four interceptions, and 636 yards gained.

Luckman saw action in New York, his hometown, when the Bears trailed the Giants, 16-0. Halas was disappointed with his offense and inserted

Luckman, who threw for a couple of touchdown passes. "My folks and my relations, as well as my buddies, were in the stands," Luckman said. "They tell me a tremendous cheer went up when I trotted out on the field. Believe me, I never heard it. In fact, I don't remember if my feet were even touching the ground."[6]

Up until Luckman began scrutinizing the T-formation and got into some game action with the Bears as a rookie, he did not realize how scientific and complicated running an offense could be in the NFL. For the most part, things had come easily enough for Luckman before that. Even his name described his good fortune in his youth. Luckman said his father gave him his first football for his eleventh birthday. Maybe that was a hint, or maybe it was a routine gift for a boy of that age. The ball cost six dollars, and it was a luxury item in the Luckman household where no wealth was to be spared.

The Luckmans were middle class; there was food to eat, employment was constant, and as a treat Luckman's dad took Sid and his brother, Leo, to Giants football games at the Polo Grounds. In that way, Luckman gained an early peek at pro passing because the Giants quarterback was Benny Friedman.

Friedman made an impression on Luckman. He stood out as a player with touch, who could do intriguing things with the ball while all of the others surrounding him seemed to be involved in a different kind of game.

"The pro game was still comparatively undeveloped," Luckman said, "and the boys played a pile-up game, except when a fellow like Benny Friedman got hold of the ball for the Giants. He appeared mighty tricky in the eyes of a youngster, throwing forward passes high over the heads of burly tacklers who would have loved to tear him apart."[7]

This was no passing fancy for Luckman, no idle curiosity mentioned during games and then forgotten. It should be remembered that during Friedman's heyday the football was rounder, more difficult to hold and aim, and more like a soccer ball than a projectile. Luckman would watch the Giants and be fascinated at how Friedman made the ball behave. At home, when Luckman and his friends took to the cobblestone streets for their games, when Luckman was playing with his own football, it seemed to be fighting back at him. They did not play on lush, green fields, and artificial turf lay decades in the future. Once, Luckman caught his leg on the spike of a grated iron fence and needed twelve stitches to fix the wound. The scar stuck around for a lifetime. Other times Luckman hid bruises because his mother was not particularly enthusiastic about him playing such a rough game anyway.

Luckman devoted long hours to playing football and to throwing a football, but his little-boy hands and his devotion did not produce the kind of results that were visually pleasing. When Friedman threw the ball, it went where he wanted it to go and looked good getting there. When Luckman threw the ball, it wobbled like a wounded bird, an aesthetically unsatisfying delivery system.

"All of this I watched intently," Luckman said of Friedman's smoothness, "while pestering Dad with a thousand questions on football. 'How does Friedman hold that ball to pass? How does he make it spiral? All day long I keep trying, but the darned thing only flip-flops for me. Anybody who can make it spiral like that sure must be big-time.'"[8]

Luckman had no perspective on that belief, but, of course, he was right. Friedman was a big-time passer, the preeminent thrower in the NFL at the time and an eventual Hall of Famer.

It was Luckman's brother, Leo, either amused by his younger sibling's passion or tired of hearing all of the questions, who prevailed upon their father to somehow arrange a way for Sid to get his questions answered by Friedman. In those days, postgame situations were rather informal. People did not need a press pass to hover around the team locker room, and there were not hordes of people around wishing to do so. So after one game the Luckman family gathered outside the Giants' dressing room and waited for Friedman to appear.

When he stepped outside, the elder Luckman approached Friedman and told him he had brought along a prospective pro football player who needed some advice. The men winked, as Luckman remembered it, as if sharing a private joke. But Friedman retreated to the locker room and returned carrying a ball. Friedman showed Luckman how he handled the ball, the way he gripped it and made it fly. Luckman couldn't help but notice that he was already doing it the so-called right way, but with differing results.

"His fingers were strong and hard," Luckman said. "I stood there gawking at them with all the adulation a punk could muster. When I got home I wondered seriously about it. He didn't seem to have a better hold on the ball than I did, and yet Friedman could peg it 80 yards. Why? I had tried to squeeze the truth out of him, but he couldn't answer the question, not in the way a kid could understand. He had shrugged his shoulders and grinned."[9]

One thing Luckman did not wonder about was the possibility that Friedman was simply a better passer than he was. That would be one explanation for why Friedman's tosses looked more impressive. Also, not every great player can verbally translate what he does to a pupil. Some baseball hitters are natural hitters with a good eye. They know what works for them, but that doesn't mean they can transfer the skill solely by explanation.

Not everyone is cut out to be a coach, and many coaches are not necessarily superstars in their sport. They are more like teachers who can impart the subject matter.

Some eight years later, when Luckman was playing football and Friedman was coaching a high school team in New York, they crossed paths again. Luckman reminded Friedman of that long-ago meeting, which Friedman did not recall, and once again asked him why one ball looked better flying through the air than another. Once again Friedman had no answer for Luckman. Unlike the quarterbacks of today Luckman had few role models to measure himself against. That's why he figured Friedman must have been throwing the right way and he the wrong way.

Luckman did develop into a first-class player and thrower, and he was also interested in playing college football. He gave consideration to New York University, Princeton, the University of Pennsylvania, and the Naval Academy before ending up at Columbia. He might have preferred Notre Dame if it was an option.

When he was a teenager Luckman became a Notre Dame fan, and he cried when coach Knute Rockne, one of his predecessors in advancing the cause of the pass, died in a plane crash in 1931. Much later, another legendary Notre Dame coach, Frank Leahy, would ask Luckman to provide instruction for the Fighting Irish about the T-formation.

Luckman's brother, Leo, kept pressuring him to choose Columbia, and Luckman was very impressed by Coach Lou Little. Little coached the Lions from 1930 to 1956 and had played a few years of pro football, too, with the Frankford Yellowjackets. Frankford was one of those early NFL teams that faded away in 1931, although not before winning the 1926 title. "I'm out to make men first, and then football players," Little told Luckman.[10]

The breadth of the body of passing knowledge is so much deeper now, and there are many, many examples of different ways of throwing. For the most part a coach doesn't care how his quarterback throws as long as he gets the ball into the receiver's hands in a timely fashion. However, scouts do care how a quarterback's ball looks while it is traveling, and not having a pretty throw can harm a quarterback's draft prospects. Not throwing a bullet is often interpreted as not having a strong enough arm.

For all of his greatness, Luckman apparently never mastered the style-points aspect of the pitch-and-catch equation. Clyde "Bulldog" Turner —center from the same West Texas town as Sammy Baugh—became a future Hall of Fame lineman who centered the ball to Luckman when they both played for the Chicago Bears.

"He kept money in my pocket," Turner said of his shared championship triumphs with Luckman. "I thought he was the greatest. He didn't throw the ball as well as Baugh. In fact, lots of times his passes didn't look very good. But they always got there. You thought he was lucky at first. But when it kept happenin' year after year, you knew it wasn't luck."[11]

Luckman wore number 42 for the Bears, a number that would eventually be retired. He thrived in the T-formation after all, but occasionally one of his old coaches recalled his initial skepticism. When Luckman made his remark about not seeing how the backs could survive in this formation, then–assistant coach Luke Johnsos told him not to worry. "Sid, as fast as each halfback is murdered, we'll send another one out on the field."[12]

Halas was the professor demanding the study time from Luckman. He had a broad vision, and in his mind getting Luckman to buy into it was critical for the Bears' success.

"In Sid, we created a new type of football player, the T-formation quarterback," Halas said. "Newspapers switched their attention from the star runners to the quarterbacks. It marked a new era for the game." He wanted Luckman from the get-go not only because of his athletic skills, but his sharp mind. "We coaches would work until 11 p.m. on our plays for the next game. Then I'd call Sid at home and tell him the plays. The next morning I'd ask him to repeat the plays and have to say, 'Wait a minute. . . .

Go a little slower.' Luckman was a coach on the field because he studied so constantly."[13]

Luckman had been fascinated by the quarterback role and throwing the ball as a youth, and that was always his primary position. He was settled into the role by high school, and although during his pro career everyone played both ways, Luckman was a quarterback first and always. Unlike Baugh, Luckman was not so super-skilled that he would be an exceptional punter or defensive back.

By nature, as Lou Little told Luckman, he was a flat-footed passer. He was not inclined to throw on the run, but to settle back and fire. Gradually, Luckman realized he had to become more mobile or else get sacked constantly. The quarterback recognized the pressure from defenders and the frequent need to abandon the pocket, noting, "If half a dozen linemen from Brown or Cornell or Dartmouth weren't constantly charging in to smother the Columbia bright boy. I was dumped on my pants so often that many a game remained hazy in my mind for days afterward."[14]

One game Luckman instinctively moved up in the pocket to elude rushers, and he safely unleashed his throw. Little stressed that he had to do more of that to save himself a beating, and he adapted.

By the time Luckman completed his Columbia eligibility he was a more desirable product for the pros. While he was waffling over those months on whether to accept offers to begin in business at twenty-three or accept the Bears' offer, Luckman received a surprise visit from someone from his past: Benny Friedman.

Friedman offered an intriguing pep talk. He predicted the T-formation was the coming thing in pro football and that Luckman would excel at his role in that style of ball. "The scheming is so effective that you'll have more time than ever to get the ball away," Friedman told Luckman. "You'll find plays in which your receiver appears from out of nowhere to nab a ball. The players are arranged so that opponents aren't quite sure what to expect next."[15]

Once Luckman became a Bear and arrived at training camp, Halas made sure he was given all of the tools and information necessary to succeed. Clark Shaughnessy was virtually his private tutor. They spent long hours together discussing the T-formation, sometimes going for half the night. By the time the 1939 season was ready to start, Luckman had crammed an enormous amount of detail about the T into his head. But he had yet to live it in real, count-in-the-standings action.

For the most part, the rookie year was going to be a learning experience for Sid Luckman, both breaking into the pros and seeking to master a new offense that would set both he and the Bears up for one of the greatest stretches in National Football League history.

The new personnel, and the new offense, with so much emphasis on passing, also positioned Luckman as the potential foil to Baugh and hinted at making the Bears and Redskins, freshly minted, even more serious rivals than they had been before.

The birth of the forward pass in football can be traced to St. Louis University in the early twentieth century. After the rules of college football were altered, the Billikens, pictured here during their 1906 season, were the first team to employ the forward pass in a game. (Photo courtesy St. Louis University Archives).

Eddie Cochems was the coach of the St. Louis University Billikens football team that tossed the first pass in a college game. (Photo courtesy St. Louis University Archives).

On November 1, 1913, Notre Dame quarterback Gus Dorais threw for 243 yards in a contest against Army, partnering mostly with end Knute Rockne. Their connection was highly publicized in the 35–13 victory and was said to represent the propulsion of the pass into comparatively widespread recognition. (Photo courtesy Notre Dame University).

A five-time All-Pro who led the NFL in passing four times, Benny Friedman became a star at the University of Michigan, and, during his eight seasons in the pro game, he was regarded as the first genuine throwing quarterback. Friedman played for the Cleveland Bulldogs, the Detroit Wolverines, and the Brooklyn Dodgers, but the lights were brighter performing for the New York Giants between 1929 and 1931. (Photo courtesy AP Images).

Harry Newman followed Benny Friedman, both at the University of Michigan and with the New York Giants. He was the NFL's top passer in 1933 despite not throwing as frequently as Friedman, but he kept the passing game evolving until it truly blossomed. (Photo courtesy AP Images).

Green Bay's Arnie Herber led the Packers to four championships in the 1930s, seasons that were sparked by the addition of a passing game. Herber was inducted into the Pro Football Hall of Fame in 1966. (Photo courtesy AP Images).

Although his career was short, Cecil Isbell directly followed Arnie Herber as the Green Bay field leader and twice led the National Football League in touchdown passes and yards gained passing. (Photo courtesy AP Images).

Earl "Curly" Lambeau was a founder of the Green Bay Packers in 1919 and then coached the early powerhouse team through 1949. Lambeau was one of the first professional coaches to recognize the significance of the forward pass as a weapon, and he worked passing into his offense in the 1930s. (Photo courtesy the Library of Congress).

F

Young Sammy Baugh poses with right hand drawn back to demonstrate his passing style. The Texan, who starred for the Washington Redskins in the 1930s and 1940s, was the first great NFL quarterback. His frequent throws, his ability to change the momentum of a game, and his toughness all contributed to Baugh revolutionizing the passing game's role. (Photo courtesy the Texas Tech University Southwest Collections/Special Collections Library).

The helmets were leather and the pads were flimsy when No. 33 Sammy Baugh was dodging tacklers for the Washington Redskins between 1937 and 1952. One of the greatest pro football players of all time, Baugh was an all-star at quarterback, defensive back and punter, the only player to be recognized at three positions. (Photo courtesy the Texas Tech University Southwest Collections/Special Collections Library).

Joking around in practice, Sammy Baugh holds up his hands as if to catch a pass instead of throwing one for a change. He is pictured here wearing an old-style Washington Redskins shirt with the team logo on the front. (Photo courtesy Washington Redskins).

Although not technically true in a philosophical sense, it might be said that Sammy Baugh invented the forward pass in pro football. During his fifteen-year career with the Washington Redskins, Baugh led the team to two league championships. He was twice the NFL player of the year and a six-time All-Pro. (Photo courtesy Washington Redskins).

Sid Luckman's throwing style made him one of the most prolific quarterbacks of his era. He was the first quarterback to toss seven touchdown passes in a 1943 National Football League game. (Photo courtesy Chicago History Museum).

George Halas (left) and Sid Luckman (right) were partners from 1939 to 1950 with the Chicago Bears. Coach and owner Halas talked Luckman into playing football rather than to go into private business: neither man regretted it. The Bears won four championships with Luckman's leadership, who remains the greatest quarterback in club history. (Photo courtesy Chicago History Museum).

(Following page:) Johnny Unitas, who played for the Baltimore Colts from 1956 throug 1972, was a direct descendant of the quarterback pioneers. He bridges the gap between th early throwers and the modern-day passer. After Unitas demonstrated leadership and th ability to uplift and carry a team to victory (usually with his arm), the quarterback began t be acknowledged as the most important position on the field. (Photo courtesy AP Images

Hall-of-Fame coach Sid Gillman, a passionate believer in the lethal nature of a down-field passing game, showed the 1950s and 1960s football world new offensive formations and how throwing the ball could produce victories. (Photo courtesy San Diego Chargers).

Long before Jack Kemp became known as an influential Congressman, he was one of the premier quarterbacks in the American Football League. Tutored by Sid Gillman, Kemp thrived in an all-out passing attack and in 1960 became one of two quarterbacks to breach the 3,000-yards-passing milestone in the AFL. (Photo courtesy San Diego Chargers).

Brett Favre played in the National Football League between 1991 and 2010, primarily with the Green Bay Packers, but also with other teams. Favre was the embodiment of the quarterback as gunslinger, even more daring than Johnny Unitas. When Favre retired, he owned most career league passing records, although some have since been broken. (Photo courtesy AP Images).

Recently retired, Peyton Manning is widely acclaimed as one of the finest quarterbacks of all time. He was a Super Bowl leader for the Indianapolis Colts and Denver Broncos; Manning holds NFL career records for most yards passing (71,940), along with 539 touchdown passes. (Photo courtesy Eric Lars Bakke, Denver Broncos).

P

Tom Brady has led the New England Patriots to five Super Bowl championships since 2000, including leading the team to a remarkable comeback win over the Atlanta Falcons in the 2017 Super Bowl. This performance led many to proclaim Brady the greatest quarterback ever. (Photo courtesy of the New England Patriots/ David Silverman).

With just a flick of his right wrist, Tom Brady can create havoc for opponents of the New England Patriots. Brady is approaching the top listings of most all-important NFL career passing categories. (Photo courtesy of the New England Patriots/David Silverman).

CHAPTER 15 • Baugh vs. Luckman

After struggling with injuries for two seasons, Sammy Baugh was back in top form for the 1940 season. By that time Sid Luckman was a new quarterback on the block, a player with potential who was not yet in Baugh's class in terms of achievement, but who was projected to become the next great NFL quarterback.

You couldn't tell right off by Luckman's individual statistics, but he was coming into his own. Game by game he was getting better at mastering the T-formation.

Luckman threw for 941 yards and completed 45.7 percent of his passes during the regular season. It was more of a vamp-til-ready season for Luckman, but George Halas brought him to Chicago to win championships, not to show off statistics, and had trained him for two full seasons.

Meanwhile, Baugh excelled as a rookie and then had been slowed by two additional seasons that kept him hobbling around and missing games. But Baugh was outstanding all of 1940. He completed 62.7 percent of his passes for 1,367 yards. Overall, nobody around the league was in that class. But Baugh and the Washington Redskins, who had bested the Bears for their 1937 title, were about to meet the future on December 8, 1940. The Bears won the West Division with an 8-3 record, and the Redskins won the East with a 9-2 mark.

Tucked into those overall records was a November 17 Washington victory, 7-3, a low-scoring, defensive contest that particularly thrilled Redskins owner George Preston Marshall. Not only was Marshall pleased, as he always was during his ownership period when he was able to walk away triumphant over Halas, he didn't stop gloating from the time of the final gun until the next kickoff a few weeks later.

That regular-season mark left Marshall feeling overconfident. He was overjoyed when the season ended and it became clear that the path to a title ran through the Bears. Marshall could not contain himself. When Bears players complained about the lack of a pass interference call by the officials at the end of that 7-3 game, Marshall dismissed the Bears as "crybabies."[1]

That was just Marshall's tune-up. He kept right on going, making more inflammatory comments the longer he talked. "They are a bunch of quitters," Marshall said. "They fold up when the going gets tough. They are a first-half club. They don't know how to win a close game."[2]

You didn't catch Washington players talking like that. They knew how good the Bears were. They were not afraid of them, but they respected their talent. The last thing they wanted was an extra-fired-up Bears team on the field. Marshall's blathering may have resulted in the invention of bulletin board material, because in the days leading up to the championship game Halas did pin newspaper articles on the locker room bulletin board as Marshall ran his mouth. He didn't talk at all about Marshall's ill-advised statements, but he made sure his players saw what the other team's boss said. Halas was the middleman delivering the insults for perusal.

Marshall, who had no governor on his thoughts, also sent a telegram to Halas days before the championship game. It wasn't anything like what he was saying to his local reporters, but it wasn't clear what the point was or just how serious he was either. "Congratulations," it read. "You got me in this thing and I hope I have the pleasure of beating your ears off next Sunday and every year to come. Justice is triumphant. We should play for the championship every year. Game will be sold out by Thursday. Right Regards, George."[3]

The game was set for Griffith Stadium and it did sell out, with attendance put at 36,034. That was pretty much the only prediction that Marshall made about the contest that came true.

Halas had brought in Clark Shaughnessy to tune up the T-formation and make a few tweaks to add potency to the offense. Halas, for one, did not underestimate the Redskins, but he didn't put much stock in that low-scoring regular-season game either.

Luckman remembered how Halas played Marshall's remarks. It was not as if Halas was above saying nasty things about an opponent, but this time he took the quieter road.

"He never said a word about it the whole week before the game," Luckman said. "But everyone was grim. We all had our playbooks out and pored over them." But shortly before kickoff Halas whipped out those newspaper stories that had adorned the locker room wall and addressed them. "Gentlemen, this is what George Preston Marshall and the Redskins think of you. I think you're a great football team, the greatest ever assembled. Go out on the field and prove it."[4]

They did. The Bears–Redskins match turned into the biggest massacre in pro football history. Chicago won the championship that day by the unbelievable score of 73-0. In future years, although Halas was around the NFL from 1920 until his death in 1983, he always said this was his most satisfying victory.

The University of Chicago Maroons played college football between 1892 and 1939. One of their coaches, their most famous, was innovator Amos Alonzo Stagg. In the early days the school was a power. However, in 1939 the school dropped football. Up until then, mostly because of the school's location on the Midway where the 1893 Chicago World's Fair took place, the team was known as the "Monsters of the Midway." As soon as the university discontinued football, the Bears adopted the nickname, which became their signature calling card during their 1940s championship era and is still commonly applied to the team. (The University of Chicago did eventually reintroduce football, albeit on a much lower-key scale than it was in the early days when the Maroons were part of the Big Ten.)

The Bears were indeed monsters for this encounter with the Redskins. Washington had a brief drive down near the Bears' goal line in the first quarter. Baugh faded back and fired a pass to Charley Malone. The ball hit Malone on the numbers, but the receiver dropped it and Washington failed to score. That was as close as the Redskins would come to the end zone all day.

By halftime the Bears led 28-0. After three quarters the score was 54-0. It was craziness. The Bears could not be stopped, and the Redskins could not advance the ball. In the postgame interviews, when Baugh was asked if things might have been different if Malone had held onto that pass, he managed to remain polite and issued a brutal and blunt reply.

"If Charley had caught the ball, the final score would have been 73-7," Baugh said.[5]

None of the players could even believe what was going on when it was happening. The Bears' first score came on a 68-yard run by fullback Bill Osmanski. Luckman scored the second touchdown on a 1-yard run. Joe Maniaci scored on a 42-yard run. Luckman threw a 30-yard pass to Ken Kavanaugh for the last touchdown of the half.

Hampton Pool's 35-yard interception return brought the first touchdown of the third period. Ray Nolting scored on a 23-yard run. George McAfee ran a second interception back for a touchdown. Even Bulldog Turner got in on the scoring with a third interception touchdown runback. Harry Clarke added two running touchdowns, on bursts of 44 yards and 1 yard, and in-between Gary Famiglietti scored on a 2-yard run.

The touchdowns just kept on coming. Actually, so did the extra points. There was only one problem with that. The home team was running out of footballs because the Bears kept kicking them into the crowd. Late in the game, officials ran over to the Chicago sideline to consult with Halas and asked him not to kick anymore.

The Redskins were dizzy and dazed when the clock ran out. It was hardly Baugh's finest game. He was hurt early on and was in and out of the lineup the rest of the day, yielding to Frank Filchock at times. Baugh finished with 10 completions in 17 attempts for 102 yards and two interceptions. Filchock threw five interceptions.

The dominance of the defense made it easy on Luckman. While this huge victory is often referred to as a shining moment for Luckman, he was really a bit player except for field generalship. He only threw four passes, completing three, because the Bears didn't need him to throw.

However, from a historic perspective the game has long been remembered for many reasons: It was one in a series of Bears–Redskins championship games. It remains the most lopsided game in NFL history. And it is regarded as Luckman's coming-out party, the game that stamped him as a burgeoning star. Also, to that point in NFL history there had never been two such esteemed quarterbacks facing off in a championship gunslinger showdown. Ten different Chicago players scored 11 touchdowns that day. The Bears were the ultimate equal-opportunity scorers. It was a landmark game, never-to-be-forgotten in the careers of Luckman and Baugh, their first critical meeting, but neither of them was the star of the day.

"We were an angry bunch of Bears," said McAfee years later, recalling Marshall's insults.[6]

Periodically, especially on select anniversaries, the 73-0 game was trotted out for consumption by a new generation of football fans, although less frequently now that all of the participants have passed away. But what a group of participants were involved. On the Bears' side, Halas, Luckman, George McAfee, plus linemen Danny Fortmann, George Musso, Joe Stydahar, and Turner, were all elected to the Hall of Fame. On the Redskins' side, Marshall, Baugh, Turk Edwards, Coach Ray Flaherty, and Wayne Millner were likewise enshrined in Canton, Ohio.

"I guess we were the perfect football team that day," Luckman said. "I can't imagine any club having a better day." More or less officially, none has. "Redskins . . . Redskins . . . Redskins . . . that's all we heard for almost three weeks, day in and day out. Halas did a fantastic psychological job building us up for the playoff game. And George Marshall helped, too."[7]

Lesser known is what transpired in the Bears' locker room at halftime. Chicago was ahead, 28-0. While the Bears seemed to have things well in hand, it was not impossible to imagine a Washington comeback. Halas once again pulled out the clippings where Marshall demeaned the Bears. He didn't want his guys to forget. He believed there was nothing he could say that would motivate the Bears more than what Marshall had said.

It should be recalled that in Marshall's foolish litany, he had labeled the Bears a first-half team. That was the logical reason why Halas reminded his players what Marshall said during the intermission. The first half was in the bank, and the results were fantastic. Halas felt it appropriate to suggest to his men that they bear down just as hard in the second half.

"It was like lighting a new fire on us," Luckman said. "I remember in the third quarter when we were in front, 49-0, or something like that, one of our substitutes suggested we let up awhile. He was almost lynched in the huddle."[8] There was no letting up that day.

From the moment that massacre played out it was portrayed as the game that sent the single-wing to the scrap heap and promoted the wisdom of using the T-formation. That was true, but somewhat overlooked was the Bears' defense. The Bears did pitch a shutout that day, intercepting seven passes, and Filchock was Washington's leader on the ground with 20 yards rushing. The net rushing stats read 382 for Chicago and 22 for Washington.

"We controlled them at the line of scrimmage," Luckman said. "We knew what they were going to do, and we were able to attack them from every angle we could. They were unable to stem the power we generated. Whatever we did, we did right, and whatever they did, they did wrong. That was the start of the T-formation in sports because after that game every team in the United States watched the Bears."[9]

About that game and that day, Luckman said the Bears' real most valuable player against the Redskins was not even a player. To him it was Halas. "When I think of that game I think of one man," Luckman said. "I think of George Halas. He had the secret. The man in motion, the wide spread ends, the counter play—he was the pioneer, the man who made pro football what it is today. They should call it the Halas formation instead of the T-formation."[10]

While Baugh was definitely not at his best and was hurting physically, another reason the Bears did not feel quite safe with their big halftime lead was his presence running the Redskins' offense. They had tremendous respect for the man considered to be the finest quarterback in the league, and many of the same players were eyewitnesses when Baugh led his club to a victory in the 1937 championship game.

"We were only ahead 28-0 at the half, and they had Sammy Baugh," said Bears backup quarterback Solly Sherman.[11] Baugh was plenty good, but he was not Superman, although at other times some might have argued the point.

Baugh and other Redskins had held their tongue leading up to the game, but afterward they let loose a bit about their owner belittling the Bears. Baugh was foremost among them.

"He just kept making fun of them every chance he got," Baugh said of Marshall's poorly chosen words. "It was ridiculous for anyone to say stuff like that about a team that was as powerful as they were back then. Year in and year out they were the strongest team in pro football, and everyone knew it. Every time Marshall opened his mouth, they got madder and madder and our morale got lower and lower. He basically destroyed his own team."[12]

It was not as if Marshall perceived that. In the moments after the game ended and he was trying to digest how such a disaster visited itself on his club, Marshall could have been gracious or even remained silent. A more prudent man might have. Instead, Marshall opened his yap again and alienated his own players. “Those guys out there quit today,” Marshall told reporters. His only hint of backtracking came when Marshall added, “Maybe they didn’t lack courage, but they lost their heads.”[13]

Marshall did have the presence of mind not to insult Baugh at the time. He knew he was still going to need Sammy Baugh, even if he planned to clean house, cut salaries, and bring in some new players. Baugh did not utter the words until later, but he apparently did not consider himself a pal of Marshall’s. He said nobody really liked the guy.

This was a game like no other, and it has endured in NFL lore. But it also was very much a step along the path of football changes establishing the quarterback as the new man of the moment when the title was on the line. For Sid Luckman, the result burnished his reputation when he was young and just starting out. For Sammy Baugh, who achieved so much, no one game could diminish his accomplishments.

But Luckman and Baugh were trendsetters, important figures in the evolution of the passing game who would continue to influence changes throughout the next decade—and beyond.

CHAPTER 16 • Luckman and Baugh

The Bears' 1940 wipeout of the Redskins elevated Sid Luckman's stature. Although this was the most one-sided game in the history of the National Football League, it was really just part of a continuum in the rivalry between Chicago and Washington.

Washington won, 28-21, in 1937. Chicago won, 73-0, in 1940. But the two teams were not finished with one another. Blessed with considerable talent, the clubs regularly battled to their division titles and often found the other standing there in wait, trying to prevent ascension to another championship.

Concurrent with this was the elevation of the passing game. As the two best teams (most of the time), the big games showcased the two premier quarterbacks. Sammy Baugh and Sid Luckman would both end up in the Pro Football Hall of Fame, although even its creation lay in the distant future.

In his third season, 1941, Luckman was a far superior quarterback than he had been during his first two seasons, when he was learning the T-formation as he played. In the season after his first title at the helm of the Bears, Luckman completed 68 out of 119 pass attempts for a 57.1 percentage, 1,181 yards, and nine touchdown passes.

In 1941, the Bears, who had just displayed the mightiest single-game effort in league history, were even better than they had been during the 1940 season. They finished the regular season 10-1, with only a loss to the Green Bay Packers. The 16-14 defeat meant that Chicago and Green Bay tied for the West Division crown and met in a playoff. Chicago won that game, 33-14, and advanced to meet the New York Giants for the league championship.

Although Luckman was emerging, the Packers still had Cecil Isbell in charge in the backfield, and Isbell had a better season as the quarterback. He threw for 15 touchdowns and completed 56.8 percent of his passes for 1,479 yards. More dramatically, Isbell threw the ball 206 times. The passing game was a big part of Green Bay's offensive plan.

Whether it was a hangover from the 73-0 thrashing, personnel changes, or a growing sense of discomfort with Marshall, the Redskins were only a so-so 6-5 that season. Baugh rebounded from his injury years to complete 54.9 percent of his passes for 1,236 yards and 10 touchdowns. He did, however, toss 19 interceptions in his 193 attempts.

What this all demonstrated, however, was that the forward pass was growing in importance. More teams were giving it due consideration, mixing passing into the offense more often than ever. Green Bay, with Curly Lambeau in charge, had utilized the pass regularly for a decade. The Giants had turned the offense over first to Benny Friedman and then to Harry Newman. The Redskins had Baugh, and the Bears had Luckman.

Luckman was surrounded by exceptional players. Although Halas counted on him to lead, he was not the front man for an inexperienced crew that was also still learning on the job. Everywhere he looked he beheld a future Hall of Famer or a star on his side of the ball. "I was the luckiest guy who ever played football," Luckman said. "I came along at the right time, under a great coach with a great team. Our only thought was to win for each other, for the glory of the team."[1]

Many times, even in some crucial games, Coach George Halas preferred to play conservatively. Behind their stalwart line, the Bears could always be counted on to move the ball on the ground. When it came time for that key Green Bay playoff game, that is the approach Halas took. At times, despite his own previously professed support of the passing game, Halas seemed almost scared to let Luckman really cut loose. In that 33-14 trouncing of Green Bay, Luckman only threw nine times. The Bears scored 30 points by halftime and had the game salted away.

Luckman had moments early on in his career when he doubted himself, but he felt himself improving each season. Even as he got to pass a bit more in 1941, he recognized it was still the early stages for the T-formation and for quarterbacks being trusted to throw more and more. "The day for the pro passer was yet to come," Luckman said.[2]

He was right, but Luckman played a part in hastening that day's arrival. Although some believe the Bears may have been even better throughout 1941 than they were in smashing the Redskins, Luckman sometimes felt too much was expected of that year's club.

"We had made the T-formation appear almost simple, which was one of the illusions produced by success, as I see it now," he said. "Our chief trouble was the notion, at times, that we produced 100 percent perfect football. Of course, there never was such a critter. Whenever this attitude developed, we played a brazen, overconfident game, usually playing right into the hands of our opponents."[3]

Now that was an overstatement since the Bears hardly ever lost. Luckman always was a modest guy, however, so for the most part it was up to others to compliment him. What Luckman instinctively understood was a phrase that became part of NFL marketing in the future and is certainly accurate: "Any given Sunday." This phase suggests that no matter how good the best team is and how lousy the worst team is, no victory is guaranteed. That was how Luckman thought.

"All over the league they had the Bears tagged as a 'monopoly,'" Luckman said. "I guess they weren't far from wrong, but if you understand football teams, you know how greatly they despise a monopoly. It wasn't a safe calling-card by any means. They probably dished out twice as tough a brand of ball against the Bears as they did against each other. They switched and twisted defenses in trying to halt us."[4]

Any team the Bears played was lying in wait with a specially concocted plan and an extra layer of determination. Everyone had a very good player who took it personally when the Bears won. For the Redskins, that player was Baugh, in Luckman's mind. For the Packers, it was Don Hutson. Packers defensive lineman Buford "Baby" Ray seemed to take extraordinary pleasure in going after Luckman as well. "Ray once confessed that he never got a bigger thrill out of pro ball than in setting Mr. Luckman on the seat of his pants three times in one game," Luckman said.[5]

For all of the targeting of Luckman and the Bears that might have gone on during the 1941 season, except for that two-point loss to the Packers, they were above it all, the best team in the West, poised to capture another title. Their foe from the East was the New York Giants. New York went 8-3 that year under Coach Steve Owen.

The team that had showcased Friedman and Newman did not have a similarly qualified throwing specialist that year. Tuffy Leemans was the Giants' best all-around back, but he was not next in the line of prototypical new quarterbacks. He was more of a throwback to the pre–Friedman and Newman eras. That was the thing about the 1930s and 1940s. Quarterbacks with exceptionally honed throwing skills were not mass-produced from the colleges. They tended to come along singly, one by one in a given year, until much later.

Leemans stood 6-foot tall and weighed 195 pounds. He starred for George Washington University and twice made All-Star teams for the Giants before being enshrined in the Pro Football Hall of Fame. However, his skills were more old-school than Luckman's and Baugh's. That season, Leemans completed 31 out of 66 passes for 475 yards and four touchdowns. He also rushed for 332 yards, tops on the team.

The Giants came into the league later than the Bears and the Packers, but once they established themselves, they became one of the top teams, almost annually. New York won its first title in 1927 when the crown was based on regular-season play. They were runners-up to the Packers in 1929 and 1930. The Giants also lost to the Bears, 23-21, in 1933, in the first official NFL Championship Game.

Those same two teams were back for the league finale the next season, and on this occasion the Giants outsmarted the Bears. Playing on an icy field, the Giants switched to sneakers at halftime and ran away from Chicago for the 1934 title. New York lost the championship game to Detroit in 1935, beat Green Bay in 1938, and lost to Green Bay in 1939. So the Giants were always hovering near the end of the season, on the brink of claiming a title or at least battling the other division's best to capture one.

In 1941 the NFL Championship Game was scheduled for Wrigley Field on December 21. Just two weeks after Pearl Harbor was bombed by the Japanese, fans had pretty much lost interest in pro sports. Only 13,341 fans attended what turned into a rout. The Bears won easily, 37-9, though Tuffy gave them a tussle for a while.

The first points were put up by Bears kicker Bob Snyder on a first-quarter, 14-yard field goal. New York took the lead before the first fifteen minutes expired on a 31-yard pass from Leemans to George Franck. That gave New York a 6-3 lead after one quarter.

Chicago moved in front, 9-6, at the half after two more Snyder field goals at distances of 39 and 37 yards. New York kept battling and deadlocked the game at 9-9 on a 16-yard field goal in the third period. But that was the last time the Giants scored. The Bears' offense shook free and took over the game, with Luckman at the controls. Norm Standlee recorded two touchdowns on short runs of 2 and 7 yards. Both extra points were kicked, too.

In the fourth quarter the Bears expanded their lead. George McAfee scored on a 5-yard run, and Chicago capped the scoring when Ken Kavanaugh recovered a fumble and ran it back 42 yards for another touchdown.

Luckman did not show up on the score sheet at all, but he masterminded the game for the Bears. He was indeed a lucky man. He was also a much smarter player than he had been as a shaky rookie. He knew the ins and outs of the T-formation, which meant he knew which plays to call at which time—not necessarily just throwing passes, but picking spots for the runners.

"In all my years of football, I've never seen a player who worked as hard as Luckman," George Halas said. "When everyone else left the practice field, he stayed on. He practiced pivoting and ball handling by the hour. When he went to his room at night he stood before a mirror and practiced still more. He became a great player simply because he devoted about 400 percent more effort to it than most athletes are willing to do."[6]

Luckman developed a reputation for smarts in reading defenses, for calling plays, and for efficiency in making other teams pay when they committed a turnover or made a mistake. Snyder, the kicker, who was also a backup quarterback when Luckman starred, watched Luckman up close for several seasons and won two titles with him as a teammate.

"Sid can sit down and draw you every blocking assignment of the 10 other Bears on each of those plays," said Snyder, who later coached the Los Angeles Rams. "He knows exactly what every teammate is supposed to do, whether the assignment is against a five-, six-, or seven-man line. Any time you make a mistake against the Bears when Luckman is in there, it likely will cost you a touchdown."[7]

The Giants made more than their share of mistakes in the 1941 title game, and the Bears made sure they took advantage. When the final gun sounded, Luckman was a two-time champion.

Meanwhile, the other star quarterback who played in the eastern corridor, just a train ride away, was returning to form after his injury-plagued years. Sammy Baugh was rejuvenating the career that made him famous as a rookie four years earlier.

Baugh was still the marquee guy, the Texas drawler whom George Preston Marshall pictured as coming fresh off the range, wiping dust off his chaps, his rugged face creased by a lopsided grin.

That's how Hollywood pictured Baugh as well. He had the rugged visage and the lean build, and the moviemakers in California were in love with westerns as the new decade dawned. The Redskins were the losers against the Bears in 1940, but while Luckman began making investments in the business world that would eventually make him wealthy, Baugh was entertaining offers to make films.

Republic Pictures approached Baugh and offered him forty-five hundred dollars to film a twelve-part serial called *King of the Texas Rangers* in the off-season. Marshall pretty much said, "I told you so." He always saw Baugh as a leading man, and now someone else vindicated his judgment.

"He looked like the personification of every cowboy star who ever straddled a bronc," Marshall said, "only more so."[8] He did at that, even if Baugh was not an accomplished horseman as a young man, didn't rope cattle, and didn't fire six-shooters.

Baugh had never aspired to be an actor, and while he grudgingly thought it might be fun to spend part of the winter in California, he mostly signed on for the money.

When initially sounded out about appearing in the series of westerns, Baugh didn't even believe the offer was genuine. He thought he was being made the butt of a joke. That made more sense to him than being considered as an actor. His first answer was, "Hell, I'm a football player."[9]

For many decades, until after they unionized and pro football became a richer game, football players, like other professional athletes, almost had to work off-season jobs to support themselves and their families. For Baugh, this was the sweetest of part-time jobs, one at least worth a try. It beat construction work, or selling cars or insurance, it seemed.

Baugh reported for work and spent six weeks filming in Hollywood, but he was still a Texas boy and did not enjoy the experience of the work or the town. He didn't hang out with other celebrities, and he didn't see the attraction. When he left to report back to Sweetwater and Mona, he was glad to do it. Sometime later, Baugh also commented on the high prices of the Los Angeles area compared to what he knew of the small towns of Texas. He made the best comparison he knew how.

"It didn't make sense to be showboating all over Hollywood and spending a lot of money for a steak when I could take that money back to Texas and buy a whole cow," Baugh said.[10] Over time Baugh would do just that type of thing, getting his own ranch started and stocking it with cattle. He could eat filet mignon any time he wanted to have it.

Baugh came from a people who were stayers, the type of people who weathered the Depression and who saw people all over America being evicted. Baugh wanted his own land, his own place, and he wanted to develop it himself. He and his wife had earlier purchased a small spread with his Redskins money. Now with movie money, he bought seventy-five hundred acres, a place ten times bigger, and called his own operation the Double Mountain Ranch.

Not only was Baugh back in Texas after his Hollywood fling, he was home for good. If he could have built a stadium on the property and put a pro team in it, Baugh probably would never have strayed from his land except for NFL road trips.

CHAPTER 17 • 1942

Shortly after the National Football League's 1941 championship game, players across the league began swapping uniforms. They surrendered the outfits selected by their various teams for the uniforms of the US Army, Navy, or Marines.

The country was at war, and football players, like other professional athletes, were viewed as prime specimens of manhood. As the war unfolded in the South Pacific and in Europe, stretching from 1942 to 1945, more than sixteen million Americans would fight for their country against the clear and present danger of Adolf Hitler's Germany and the Nazi fanatics he nurtured and Japanese imperialism in Asia.

This was the costliest war in human history. Although it was not easy to pinpoint the number of deaths around the world, the total was estimated at sixty million people, civilian and military.

Football was clearly on the back burner for Americans. More was demanded on the home front from the citizen populace than in any other foreign war. Rationing of everything from gasoline to meat and sugar represented part of the sacrifices being made. For the first time on a broad scale, women took over the traditional roles of men in factories.

There was talk of suspending all sporting activities for the duration of the war. At the time, Major League Baseball was called the national pastime, and baseball commissioner Kenesaw Mountain Landis took the lead in inquiring of President Franklin D. Roosevelt whether it would be best for the nation if baseball ceased. Roosevelt replied with his so-called green-light letter. The statement concluded it was best for all if the country had some entertainment pursuits to follow. Baseball, he said, should play on, though no special courtesies would be extended to baseball players to avoid service.

The response to baseball was taken at face value by the leaders of other professional sports leagues. The NFL followed suit, teams holding together (though some barely), as did the then less significant National Hockey League, which had teams in only six cities, four in the United States. Professional basketball as we know it did not come into being until later in the 1940s.

From the immediate declaration of war until the end of hostilities in 1945, some 995 National Football League players wore the uniform of the United States in various branches of the service. Twenty-three players were killed in action during the war. Individuals overseas fought for their survival. So, in their own way, did teams in the NFL whose ranks were depleted and who filled rosters with 4F athletes, previously retired players, and the like.

George "Papa Bear" Halas was an ensign in the navy during World War I. He turned forty-seven on February 2, 1942, but used all of his political clout and influence with government individuals he knew to be activated again for World War II. Halas coached five of the Bears' games that season, and the rest of the campaign was administered by co-coaches Luke Johnsos and Hunk Anderson. Halas was given the rank of lieutenant commander and for twenty months was attached to Admiral Chester Nimitz and the Seventh Fleet.

Many of the star players from the Bears' 1940 and 1941 championship teams were also in different branches of the service. Not Sid Luckman at first, however. As teammates departed, Luckman stayed in the Bears' backfield during the 1942 season. He played in every game, completing 57 out of 105 pass attempts for 54.3 percent, 1,024 yards, and 10 touchdown passes.

That terrific Bears front line, which included Hall of Famers Bulldog Turner, Danny Fortmann, Joe Stydahar, and George Musso, kept the Bears tough. Plus several notable runners were still around, including Ray Nolting and Bill Osmanski. This was an extraordinary season for the Bears. Even with some players missing and the coach serving in the military across the sea, Chicago went 11-0 during the season.

The Bears romped through the West Division, and fans were even suggesting this version of the team might be better than the two recent championship clubs. Green Bay was the closest pursuer in the West with an 8-2-1 mark. In the East, the renewed Washington Redskins were back on top, capping their season with a 10-1 record. This pitted the Bears and the Redskins in a rematch of the 1940 massacre game.

The Sammy Baugh of 1942 was at the top of his game. He threw surprisingly often, 225 times. He completed 58.7 percent of his passes, best in the league, for 1,524 yards and 16 touchdowns. The Redskins and the Bears did not play during the regular season. Washington's only loss was to the New York Giants, 14-7.

So there they were again: Chicago and Washington were scheduled to meet for the NFL title on December 13, 1942, again at Griffith Stadium. Basically, with the memory of the 73-0 decision fresh in people's minds, this seemed like returning to the scene of the crime. Although Washington had been a first-class team, the unbeaten Bears were viewed as unstoppable. This was a team on a long run of success that had the mental advantage of having crushed the Redskins into the ground the last time the teams had met with so much at stake.

As player after player enlisted or was drafted, NFL team rosters were depleted. However, Washington was down only five regulars from the preceding season, and perhaps that familiarity, the collection of top players, and the comparative personnel losses of other teams contributed to that 10-1 mark. The key loss for Washington was end Wayne Millner, though Turk Edwards had retired and was acting as an assistant coach. Washington's motivation for vengeance was significant. The Bears had humiliated the team and many of these same players only two years earlier. The gaping wound had not healed.

In 1940, when Redskins owner George Preston Marshall insulted the Bears to sportswriters, his commentary appeared in newspapers and was used by George Halas to jump-start his guys. In 1942, Washington coach Ray Flaherty, who was in on the 73-0 beating, was as concise as possible in his pregame pep talk. Instead of speaking in heartfelt terms or yelling, he employed his own psychology. Flaherty wrote the numbers "73" and "0" on a blackboard and circled them. Enough said.

Attendance was listed at 36,006, very similar to the capacity crowd at Griffith Stadium in 1940. The temperature was a not-terribly-surprising fifteen degrees for mid-December, and the wind blew at twelve miles an hour. The overcast skies hinted at snow.

The Bears' Lee Artoe kicked off and Washington got the ball first-and-10 at its own 29-yard line. While it may seem like strange strategy in the modern era of pro football, the Redskins' Andy Farkas ran for 1 yard on first down, but then they punted on second down. It was a surprise quick kick by Baugh, who boomed a punt that rolled all the way to the Bears' 10-yard line. It seemed Flaherty was steeling himself for a defensive battle.

Chicago ran four plays and out, never obtaining a first down and stalling out at the 19. Washington took over at its own 31. Again, this time on third down, Baugh quick-kicked. Field position was a bit better for the Bears. They got the ball on their 40. The Bears' offense got moving somewhat. Nolting gained 18 yards on one run, and Luckman completed an 11-yard pass to Nolting on another play.

The Bears got as close as the Washington 37, and Artoe tried a field goal from the 45-yard line. It was no good, missing low. There was considerable back-and-forth in the opening period, but the score stayed 0-0. The quarter ended with Luckman, who did not have as strong a leg as Baugh, punting the ball to the Redskins' 38, where it was returned 5 yards.

That gave Washington possession on its own 43-yard line to start the second quarter. Back Ray Hare ran up the middle for 4 yards, and then followed one of the game's critical plays. Baugh faded back to pass and hit Dick Todd for an apparent 9-yard gain. But when Todd was hit, he fumbled. Most players believed the ball was already dead and there was no fumble.

Not Artoe. Artoe alertly picked up the ball and with a clear field ahead returned it for 52 yards and a touchdown. Although Artoe missed the extra point, presumably because he was still breathing hard, Chicago led 6-0. The turnover loomed as a potentially demoralizing play, bringing back bad memories from 1940 when the Bears kept stealing the ball from the Redskins on interceptions.

Washington did not panic or move away from its conservative strategy, though. On the next possession, situated at their 28-yard line, the Redskins again used Baugh to quick-kick. It was a punt extraordinaire. The ball did not stop rolling for 61 yards, or until it came to rest on the Bears' 11.

"That kick turned out to be a big play," Baugh said. "When I quick-kicked, I had the wind at my back, and that's why I did it. If the quarter had run out and we had to punt, we would have had to do it against the wind."[1]

Chicago started to move the ball, but any long drive was short-circuited when Wilbur Moore intercepted a Luckman pass intended for John Siegal. Washington took over in Bears territory at the 42-yard line. On third-and-7, Baugh heaved a pass to Moore at the goal line. He caught the ball and fell into the end zone for a touchdown. Bob Masterson kicked the extra point, and it was 7-6, Washington.

The score stayed that way into the half and right to the very end of the third period. Washington put together a solid drive, starting at the Chicago 43. This was not a Baugh throwing spectacle, but a ground drive that Baugh masterminded. The Redskin touchdown came on a 1-yard Andy Farkas plunge. The extra point was good, and Washington led, 14-6.

These were the mighty Bears, the Bears of 73-0 fame. Nobody thought this game was over, and everybody in the stadium felt certain the Bears were going to score again. They did not. The final score was 14-6, and the Redskins had their vindication. The numbers weren't as flashy, but the championship counted just as much as the 1940 one did for the Bears.

When the result was in the books, Baugh actually said he thought the 1940 losing Redskins had been better than the 1942 winning Redskins. "Our 1940 team was better," he said. "The best group of boys we ever had."[2]

After triumphing over the Bears, Baugh had two championships on his resume. He and Luckman were destined to fight things out often enough, but they became friendly rivals. It probably was the quarterback life they had in common.

"In all of our encounters," Luckman said, "Sam never has made a wild boast about the kind of game he was going to play, never said he would trounce the Bears, or make Luckman look sick, as a number of others have perpetually predicted. Sam doesn't like to look bad himself, and he knows that in football even the best passers have occasional sorry afternoons."[3]

Baugh preceded Luckman in the NFL by two years, but he also had a stronger pedigree as a passer coming out of Texas Christian than Luckman did coming out of Columbia. Baugh brought a reputation with him. Luckman had to create one. For pure talent, there was little doubt Baugh had more going for him. Even Luckman admitted that. But playing their roles for their respective top teams and going up against each other when it was winner-take-all for the title, they were more closely matched. The variables of weather, teammates, and defenses evened them out somewhat.

"After a long and hearty rivalry . . . I've learned to respect him as a sharp and able competitor," Luckman said of Baugh. "We may rub at one another, spreading a little malarkey on the side, but I do know this: When I reached Sam's level as a passer, it was the first major honor paid me in pro football. When Baugh and Luckman started to make twintypes on sports pages, I could finally tell myself that I had arrived as a football player."[4]

The 1942 game between the Bears and the Redskins still featured rosters with famous names. One by one, though, after that game, more and more figures on both teams disappeared into the Armed Services. Washington coach Ray Flaherty resigned from the team after the title game win and joined the navy.

Baugh's performance in the first championship win over the Bears was more impressive statistically than the second one, but he had grown as a quarterback from a rookie in need of experience into a savvy veteran who could turn games with less flashy numbers. After the battering he took in certain early seasons that left him limping, Baugh gained a broader appreciation for how blocking linemen could make his life easier.

As confident as Baugh was, he did occasionally come across as the aw-shucks brand of guy from Texas, wisely buttering up the players who helped make him look good. Once he said the best thing that a quarterback could have going for him was "a couple of nice, tall ends with good hands."[5]

Another time, after Turk Edwards succeeded Flaherty as coach, Baugh was in the boss's office with a young, untried large player. Edwards introduced the young man to Baugh, who quizzed him on what position he played while eyeing his jumbo-sized body.

"Gee, I dreamed of playing with the great Sammy Baugh," the young man said. "What position do you play?" Baugh inquired, discovering he was a tackle. "You knock hell out of some of those opposing linemen, and I'll dream of you," Baugh added.[6]

Baugh had long ago turned his back on baseball, and years had gone by since he said he didn't even know if he wanted to play football. Although his salary of about fifteen thousand dollars a year was minuscule compared to quarterbacks of the future, Baugh was a smart man with money, knew he could not equal his paydays elsewhere, and even began dropping hints that he actually liked to play football.

"When I find I'm taking too much punishment, I'll quit," he said. "But I'll throw as long as they let me and as long as I can."[7] Baugh came to realize that he had a golden arm and that there was gold in his arm.

In an era when football games were not televised constantly and sports news didn't run on a twenty-four-hour cycle on televisions and computers, many people didn't know that Baugh and Luckman had met for the first time in 1937 when Baugh dropped in on Columbia. Baugh had just starred in his rookie season, and Luckman was still a Lion seeking to improve his throwing. Luckman had the same inquisitive mind that he had possessed as a boy when he pumped Benny Friedman for information.

"It was natural for me to envy [Baugh] in those days," Luckman said. "He came to Columbia's campus on a visit one afternoon and a few of us tripped over a stack of helmets getting to him. We wanted to see how he worked his miracles. Baugh demonstrated various forms of passing. The way he held the ball stunned me. 'Mr. Baugh,' I exclaimed, 'you're throwing in the wrong style!' Then, as an afterthought, 'Or maybe it's me.'"[8]

Luckman was referring to the way Baugh held his thumb over the laces. Baugh accepted the comment with lighthearted amusement. He admitted coaches had tried to change his style, but he stuck with doing what he was most comfortable with and resisted their entreaties. Baugh told Luckman what he also wrote in advice to boys: As long as their style worked for them, do what felt best.

One of the funniest asides of that unheralded meeting between two future Hall of Fame quarterbacks who laid cornerstones in the foundation of the passing game was what Baugh told Luckman when the younger man asked about pro football life. Baugh told him not to do it. Going to the pros was a gamble, one where the odds were stacked against a player. It is intriguing to wonder if Baugh ever recalled that exchange when the two quarterbacks were battling for NFL supremacy.

CHAPTER 18 • Sammy and Sid in 1943

As World War II raged, spreading to islands in the South Pacific no one had ever heard of and to places in North Africa with unpronounceable names, people did not make the mistake of using the word "heroes" for football-player descriptions.

There were still sports stars, but they were secondary characters in the national mind. Depending on the city where they lived, and their reputation with the local newspapermen, a sports star was as likely to be questioned, if not criticized, for not being in the service as he was to be exalted for what he did on the field.

Still, President Franklin D. Roosevelt was right. The nation did need some entertainment, and everyone, from factory workers off shift to youngsters too young to serve, attended ball games.

Anyone in a sports uniform was subject to scrutiny, however. The prevailing thought—ahead of allegiance to a team—was to ask why an apparently healthy young man of supreme athletic skill was not at war while the questioner's own son was sent somewhere into the hinterlands.

Sid Luckman was 6 foot tall and weighed about 200 pounds. He had no existing major physical drawbacks. Sammy Baugh was 6-foot-2 and might have gained a few pounds up to 185. Outside of some football injuries suffered when larger men hit him in the backfield at full speed, he also was a healthy young man.

For some reason the United States never got around to drafting Luckman and he did not volunteer, sticking with the Chicago Bears throughout the 1942 and 1943 seasons. Immediately after the season ended, however,

Luckman volunteered for the Merchant Marine and went in as an ensign, although technically those who handle ships for that outfit are civilians.

Luckman was never stationed overseas. His full-time weekday job was with the Merchant Marine, but he had weekends off. That meant that in 1944 and 1945, as World War II continued, Luckman was free to play for the Bears. Home games did not present much of a problem, but for road games he sometimes flew to distant cities.

Baugh was in a different situation. He was married but also had two children for whom he was the sole support. In addition, as a cattleman his ranch provided beef for the Armed Services, so he was providing an essential civilian service. Baugh was not drafted and did not volunteer, but he did consult with his draft board in Texas to determine his role and to explore what he was able to do with his weekends. As long as he worked five days a week on the ranch, officials did not care if he played pro football on weekends for the Washington Redskins. So that's what Baugh did for the rest of the war.

"I love this place," Baugh said years later of his ranch. "Never wanted to be anywhere else. From the time I was a little kid in Bell County, I wanted a ranch of my own, and the best thing football did for me was to make that possible."[1]

One by one Bears' teammates of Luckman's and Redskins' teammates of Baugh's entered the Armed Forces. By 1943 the team rosters in no way resembled the squads' 1941 rosters. Even the coaches were gone, with George Halas of the Bears and Ray Flaherty of the Redskins both serving in the navy.

Halas returned stateside in 1943 for the NFL owners' meeting wearing a naval uniform, only to be admonished by George Preston Marshall, who ridiculed him for going off to fight at his age and showing up in uniform. Halas lunged across a table to take a swing at him.

Baugh never spoke much about being home on the ranch and the football field during the war, likely thinking he fulfilled his duty as the government saw fit by keeping that food coming for the army. Although Luckman's service did not begin until later, Baugh did not practice with the Redskins in 1943. Luckman did not practice with the Bears after 1943. For those coaching leaders who were strong believers in tough practices and hard drilling, Luckman and Baugh stood out as contradictory exemplars who, amusingly to some, played as well as ever without sharing practice fields with old teammates.

Despite the departure of proficient teammates, from a statistical standpoint Luckman and Baugh were better than ever in 1943. The caliber of players was down across the board, but while the quarterbacks lacked as many helpmates of a certain standard as they were used to, the men throwing the ball who were already better than anyone seemed to stand out even further.

In 1943, as his transportation complications mounted, Baugh missed one game and did not start a few others. Yet he led the National Football League by attempting 239 passes, completing 133, for a 55.6 percent rate—all of them league-leading figures. Baugh's other stats were top-notch, too, throwing 23 touchdown passes for 1,754 yards. If Baugh had been at full strength all season, his numbers might well have established new highs across the board.

Baugh also threw 19 interceptions. In the 2000s that would be a horrifying figure for a coach to contend with, but Baugh was under orders from his owner to throw and keep on throwing no matter what, and NFL rules tilted the playing field a little less in favor of quarterback success.

"There was no protection for the passer," Baugh said. "He could be hit until the whistle blew. A guy caught a pass across the field and the rushers put you on the ground. You could get hurt so damned easy with a rule like that. Back when I was playing, it was easier to intercept passes because the quarterback couldn't throw the ball away. We had to throw it down there and let them fight for the damn thing, more or less. We had to complete the pass to someone we thought would battle for it more than the other man."[2]

One player who emerged for Baugh as a go-to target was big end Joe Aguirre, a 6-foot-4, 225-pound graduate of St. Mary's. Aguirre was an eleventh-round draft pick from 1941 who made good. Among his 37 catches in 1943 were seven touchdown receptions. Aguirre caught 34 passes the next season as well. His career spanned the 1940s, with four seasons in Washington and four seasons playing for the Los Angeles Dons in the All-America Football Conference.

As a team, the Redskins in 1943 were not as good as some of their earlier squads, but their 6-3-1 record was good enough to win the East Division, although it took a playoff win over the New York Giants to advance to the title game. The Redskins slumped at the end of the season, losing their last three regular-season games, at least partially because Baugh was injured.

In the West, it was the Bears once again. Chicago finished 8-1-1, even with Halas working at another task thousands of miles away. He had left the team in capable hands with Luke Johnsos and Hunk Anderson coaching, and above all, Luckman at quarterback. In many respects, this was Luckman's finest season. He led the NFL in the categories Baugh did not, including two major ones: Luckman threw for 28 touchdowns, an unheard-of figure for the era, and 2,194 yards.

Baugh never topped that Luckman single-season touchdown record, though he did surpass the single-season yardage mark a couple of times. The first time Luckman's touchdown passing total was topped in the pros was in 1948, five years later, when Frankie Albert, a Stanford alum, threw 29 touchdowns for the San Francisco 49ers. However, at the time the 49ers were in the All-America Football Conference. It took until 1959 for Luckman's total to be surpassed in the NFL, when Johnny Unitas set the new record for the Baltimore Colts with 32 touchdown tosses.

With Flaherty resigning to join the navy, Dutch Bergman became the new Redskins coach in 1943, and they started well, winning their first four games. In that fourth game, on October 31, 1943, Washington met the Brooklyn Dodgers on the road. The game was played at Ebbets Field, and just 11,471 fans attended. The no-shows lost out. The Redskins won, 48-10, but the most notable aspect of the afternoon was Baugh throwing six touchdown passes.

That was a first and a new NFL record. Not so many years earlier, quarterbacks didn't complete six touchdown passes in a season. On that memorable day, Baugh threw for 376 yards in the game and he spread the touchdown wealth around, with Wilbur Moore as the biggest standout on the receiving end, pulling in seven catches for 213 yards.

The first touchdown throw of the day went for 44 yards to Joe Aguirre in the first quarter. Moore caught his first touchdown of the day on a 53-yarder in the second quarter, and Bob Seymour added a 23-yard touchdown grab before halftime. Aguirre opened things in the third period on a 10-yard toss, and Moore made his big play after that, collecting a 71-yard touchdown pass. The sixth touchdown throw went to back Andy Farkas on a 23-yard play.

Baugh, who was also a defensive back and the team's punter, was on the field for the Redskins for all sixty minutes that game.

As extraordinary as Baugh's performance seemed at the time, his record of six touchdown passes in a game lasted all of two weeks. On

November 14, 1943, Luckman threw seven touchdown passes in a game against the New York Giants.

Luckman was a native New Yorker, and on that day the city decided to honor him. It was Sid Luckman Day at the Polo Grounds when he showed up to play for the Bears. Gifts were presented to Luckman, including a one-thousand-dollar war bond. Fans in New York and Chicago contributed to that. No one could have predicted what occurred on the field that afternoon. Luckman erupted for the finest game of his career, leading the Bears to a 56-7 victory.

Unlike in the 73-0 triumph over the Washington Redskins a few years earlier, Luckman played a much larger statistical role for the Bears in this game. Chicago dominated the game, and Luckman was a huge part of the reason. His seven touchdown passes became a new NFL record. Although tied several times over the decades since, seven remains the mark for a single game. Luckman also threw for 453 yards, a statistical anomaly for the times. It was a spectacular and memorable day for Luckman.

The lead on the Associated Press game report read, "Sid Luckman put on the greatest air raid in National Football League history, Sunday." It added, "His seven scoring aerials for one game wiped out the old mark of six set up by Sammy Baugh of Washington only two weeks ago. . . . His 453-yard overhead advance smashed the existing previous high of 376, which Baugh also posted two weeks ago."[3]

Another game account read, "Sid Luckman, the kid who used to chuck a cheap football while dodging automobiles in the streets of Brooklyn, today pitched a pigskin as it was never pitched before."[4]

When the score reached 42-7 and Luckman had six touchdown passes in the bank, he was almost pulled from the lineup to slow down the slaughter. However, Bears teammates protested. They knew Baugh had the six-touchdown-pass record, and they wanted Luckman to get a shot at it. "Let Sid go for the record. This is his day," players on the sideline urged.[5]

Luckman did remain in the game and he did complete his seventh touchdown pass for the record. Luckman did it first, but as of the 2017 NFL season, seven others have accomplished the feat: Adrian Burk, Philadelphia Eagles, 1954; George Blanda, Houston Oilers, 1961; Y. A. Tittle, New York Giants, 1962; Joe Kapp, Minnesota Vikings, 1969; Peyton Manning, Denver Broncos, 2013; Nick Foles, Philadelphia Eagles, 2013; and Drew Brees, New Orleans Saints, in 2015.

Luckman compared his spectacular throwing day with hitting seven home runs in a Major League game. "Boy, I'll never forget it or lose the thrill of telling the story," Luckman said in picking this game and his effort as his greatest day in the sport for a book collection of such stars' experiences.[6]

It was certainly worth remembering, and more than seventy years later remains one of the greatest passing days by any quarterback in NFL history. "I just threw them and there was always a Bear around to catch the ball," is the way Luckman so casually dissected the passing game against the Giants. "They seemed to have glued fingers. There was no stopping the Bears. If the Bears were a perfect team against the Washington Redskins when we handed them that humiliating 73-0 defeat in 1940 they were close to perfect this afternoon."[7]

In the reduced NFL of wartime 1943, there were just eight teams playing with roster limits of twenty-eight men. The schedule was ten games long. A writer looking back at World War II and football history of that year made a telling observation about the league: "In 1943, you thought the greatest quarterback was either Sid Luckman of Chicago or Sammy Baugh of the Washington Redskins," an NFL game-day program noted. "There was no in-between, no alternative. And no matter who you chose you had the numbers to back you."[8]

As an aside, due to the manpower shortage during the war, the Bears doggedly pursued Bronko Nagurski to end his five-year retirement. Money talked, and Nagurski walked from Minnesota to Chicago. He was his usual old rugged self, at 235 pounds a massively strong performer as a tackler and a blocker. Nagurski was used more to guide the Bears' other runners than to run himself, and he didn't need a drill to make holes in the line.

"Anybody in the world could run behind him," Bears back Harry Clarke said. "All you have to do is step over the bodies."[9]

Clarke was right. The Bears did step over the heaps of bodies on the ground to run up a big score on the Redskins, familiar combatants in the title game. The December 26, 1943, contest was played at Wrigley Field in front of 34,320 people.

The game was scoreless after one period. The Redskins led in the second quarter after back Andy Farkas burst through the line for a 1-yard touchdown and Bob Masterson converted the extra-point kick. The Bears likely thought, *Enough of that.* The Bears did their growling thing and gained some benefits from their complaints.

Clarke scored on a 31-yard pass from Luckman, and Nagurski finished off another drive with a 3-yard run, culminating his comeback. That gave Chicago a 14-7 lead. Luckman did a lot more throwing in the second half, twice in the third quarter hitting Dante Magnani at distances of 36 and 66 yards. Baugh connected with Farkas on a 17-yard pass to end the period.

Luckman threw two more touchdown passes in the fourth quarter, one to Jim Benton for 26 yards. He also connected with Clarke for a 10-yard score. Washington kept plugging, and Baugh threw a 25-yard strike to Joe Aguirre. The final score was 41-21, Chicago. Luckman threw five touchdown passes in the game and gained 276 yards through the air.

Baugh missed parts of the game with injury. On one play, trying to tackle Luckman, Baugh hit his head and was knocked unconscious. Then he returned to the game. That was not surprising at all at the time, long before NFL concussion protocols would have sidelined him indefinitely. Luckman described the key play, saying he fielded a Baugh punt on the Bears' 20-yard line and was returning it when Baugh, in his defender role, streaked in for the hit.

"A clash of bodies was heard, as Sam and I collided solidly," Luckman said. "He lay there limp for a time and was carried from the field. With Washington's hopes weakened, its players took note of me and refused to call the play an accident. They were mighty angry."[10]

Later, when there was a time out, Baugh and Luckman were standing near one another. Baugh did not seem as agitated as his teammates. "I admired that hip or knee you handed out," Baugh told Luckman. "Guess I lost track of the fact you used to be a fair ball-carrier."[11]

The result gave the Bears and Luckman their third title in four years.

Luckman and Baugh always remained friendly despite the on-field rivalry producing hard-nosed play when the stakes were high for whoever won the game.

One time Baugh was making a public appearance in DC in the hours leading up to a game against the Bears at Griffith Stadium. He was signing autographs for kids, and the line was long. Baugh gave out the autographs and did not notice much about the line until, suddenly, there was Luckman handing him a football to be signed. Luckman told Baugh that he bet five dollars with George Wilson he could secure Baugh's name on the ball. Baugh signed to help Luckman win the bet and said, "Anything to help a friend fatten his bank account."[12]

CHAPTER 19 • Luckman's Steady Hand

The Chicago Bears, with Sid Luckman at the helm, won four National Football League titles in the 1940s—in 1940, 1941, 1943, and 1946. They also lost in the title game in 1942. That was the decade they became the Monsters of the Midway, and some believe if World War II had not interrupted the flow of the sport and many Bears players had not left the team to serve their country, then Chicago would have won more championships during the forties and would likely have been proclaimed the greatest dynasty in pro football history.

During that stretch, Luckman was the indispensable man. He was the one-and-only true leader. He and Sammy Baugh, on the other side of the country, were writing quarterbacking history. They shook up pro football and challenged the old precepts.

In 1944 Luckman missed games because of his involvement with the Merchant Marine, and his statistics declined accordingly. In 1945 and 1946 he again produced great seasons. Luckman threw for a league-leading 1,727 yards and 14 touchdowns in 1945, and in 1946 he tossed for a league-leading 1,826 yards and 17 touchdowns.

On December 15, 1946, at the Polo Grounds in front of 58,346 people, the Bears met the New York Giants in the Bears' fifth championship game of the decade. They won their fourth title that day, 24-14, after taking a lead in the first quarter and scoring a critical late touchdown in the fourth quarter when the Giants threatened.

Once again it was Luckman making the big play, but in an unexpected way. The score was 14-14 entering the fourth period. The Bears advanced to the New York 19-yard line. New York expected a run from someone coming out of the backfield or Luckman fading back to pass. Instead, Luckman shocked the stadium by keeping the ball, running a bootleg, and trotting into the end zone for the winning touchdown. Luckman did not run often, so this decision threw off everyone.

George Halas, who had returned to coaching in 1946, had called the play when the Bears were at the New York 34. It was named "Bingo-Keep-It." At first Luckman was skeptical of the call, but the Giants committed a 15-yard penalty, moving the ball to the 19. There was also a time out, and Halas talked directly to Luckman, telling him that's what he wanted to see.

The ball was hiked to Luckman. He faked a handoff to George McAfee, who ran left. While the defense concentrated on the back, Luckman strolled to the right with the ball. Only one defender had a shot at him, and Luckman faked him out. The Bears added a 26-yard field goal, and that provided the final score.

Luckman and the Bears had won their fourth title together, all since 1940. It would be the last one, although Luckman suited up through the 1950 season. He may have retired then because he was tired of getting his nose broken, which happened seven times in his playing days. In 1947 Luckman threw for a career-high 2,712 yards—and did not lead the league. Likewise, he threw 24 touchdown passes and did not lead the league. Baugh threw for 2,938 yards that season to top Luckman. Luckman's favorite receiver, Jim Keane, led the league in catches with 64.

The NFL was changing. More good quarterbacks were being manufactured by the colleges and more of them saw what Sammy Baugh and then Luckman could achieve in the pros. The genie was out of the bottle, which was a good thing for the forward pass.

Other fresh faces were imprinting their throwing game on the NFL. Paul Christman threw for 2,191 yards for the Chicago Cardinals in '47. Christman played college ball at Missouri. Although his career was not a long one, in 1947 he attempted 301 passes. Tommy Thompson came out of Tulsa and took over as quarterback for the Philadelphia Eagles. Although he never topped 2,000 yards in a season, Thompson threw 25 touchdown passes in 1948.

In 1948 the marvelous Charley Conerly, the University of Mississippi All-American, took over the controls for the New York Giants and threw for 2,175 yards. In the All-America Football Conference, which sprung up as a rival to the NFL, Otto Graham was the king of the position for the Cleveland Browns.

Although Luckman always admired Baugh and felt the Redskins quarterback was a better player than he was, Luckman said the outpouring of quarterbacks could not be solely laid at the Texan's feet. "No single passer, then, played the big role in getting this aerial wave started and forcing all professional clubs to hunt high and low for decent pitching arms," Luckman said. "But there it was."[1]

Luckman made the statement at the end of the 1940s, but from the vantage point of much later in the future, he was probably incorrect. Baugh, first, then Luckman, inspired those other teams. The college quarterbacks themselves likely saw what was going on at the next level, and they prepared for the pros based on what they viewed as possible. Luckman may have been too close to the changes.

"You might remember us as the same squirts who had been attracted to the aerial phase of the game when it had become so popular a decade before, when throughout the country hordes of youngsters had just naturally started to flip the ball about," Luckman said. "What had influenced us? Maybe the rash of newspaper stories describing what passers had accomplished with a twist of the wrist. Maybe the simple urge to cover distance without wasting time. Dropping into pro ball in a cluster, we found the welcome mat out."[2]

Before he retired from the Bears, Luckman had penned an instructional book for budding young quarterbacks. He was helping future generations along.

After World War II ended, hundreds of football players returned to the game. Some who served had been killed, and some had been wounded. Some had lost their skills. Some were ready for a career change. But many wished to resume right where they left off. There was competition for jobs with holdovers who had played during the war and helped their teams survive at the box office.

It was the beginning of a fresh wave of prosperity across the United States. Optimism dominated many industries. Risks were taken. A new professional basketball league, the forerunner of the NBA, was formed. And some people believed there was so much potential in pro football that they agreed to found a league to compete with the NFL.

Arch Ward, who was sports editor of the *Chicago Tribune* and possessed a creative mind and an entrepreneurial bent, was responsible for inventing the Major League Baseball All-Star Game in 1933. He was also the motivator behind the establishment of the new All-America Football Conference (AAFC). It opened for business in 1946 with eight teams.

Much like the future American Football League start-up in 1960, the American Basketball Association, and the World Hockey Association, all of which took on established pro leagues with high hopes, the AAFC approached players with checkbooks open. The plan was to siphon off top-name players to add star power and credibility to the new league.

One of the players who received an offer to play for one of the new teams was Luckman. He flirted with the league representatives but then signed a long-term contract with the Bears. Deep down Luckman knew he was never going to jump the Bears. He felt he owed his entire career to George Halas. In return, Halas, who was affiliated with the NFL for sixty-three years, looked upon Luckman as a son. In all of the time Halas ran the Bears, only a few other players became as close to him as Luckman did. No, Luckman was not going anywhere else to play football. When he retired Luckman had been NFL Player of the Year three times and an All-Pro seven times.

After 1948, Luckman's contributions on the field dropped significantly, and by 1950, his final season on the gridiron, he was mostly a bench player. He was only thirty-four, young in life. At first he rejoined the Bears as an assistant coach, though only as a part-timer who did not get paid. It was not surprising that he coached the quarterbacks. That made sense, because when Luckman was in his prime as a player Halas referred to him as "another coach on the field."[3]

Luckman didn't hang around the sidelines for long after retiring his cleats. But besides helping Halas on request, he often gave clinics at the urging of college coaches wanting to learn more about the T-formation. Luckman said that satisfied his desire to coach.

"The temptation to run a ball club can grow pretty strong," he said. "I've managed to resist it, despite some good offers, mainly because the playing bug never would quit biting me. I rightly considered it a privilege to travel and watch our system spread and take part in the missionary process."[4]

Luckman took much satisfaction out of watching the T-formation become the offense of choice and seeing how schools and pro teams executed it. The single-wing was extinct, and the T-formation became more popular yearly. "Just how far the system would go was anybody's guess," Luckman said. "By 1947, at least 90 percent of the colleges and almost every pro club had fallen in line, using a dozen variations of the T. It probably couldn't go much further than that."[5]

Luckman could, however. After he stopped playing and gave up coaching, Luckman devoted himself to his first interest, the business world. That worked out quite well for him. Despite not making nearly as much money as a pro football player as he would have early in a business career, Luckman became wealthy through company ownership. He ended up a millionaire through his involvement with Cellu-Craft, a food packaging company, and other firms. Luckman was a key investor in the famous Chicago restaurant Gibsons Steakhouse.

Even in retirement, Luckman was closely identified with the Bears. He never played or coached for another NFL team, and he was like a family member and a life long friend to Halas, who once called him his "second son."[6] Halas had one son by marriage.

There were rumors that Halas relied on Luckman for football advice relating to the acquisition and disposal of players, but anyone who said that probably did not know George Halas well. The Bears were his baby, and for better or worse he made the football decisions for the club. The first question of many Papa Bear watchers was, Did he listen to anybody?

"I have gone to him, maybe a thousand times from my playing days until now," Luckman said in 1982. "But I can truthfully say that he never has sought my advice on any big decision. Sid Luckman has no input in the operation of the Bears."[7]

One reason Luckman remained so popular in Chicago long after he stopped playing is because for decades—and even now—he is viewed as the best quarterback in franchise history.

Some sixty-five years after Luckman retired, he still was the most prolific touchdown passer in team history. The Bears have had some successful quarterbacks who had fine seasons. Billy Wade directed the Bears to the 1963 NFL title, their first since 1946 when Luckman held the job. Jim McMahon took the Bears to a Super Bowl title in 1986. Erik Kramer had some great stats. Jay Cutler had his moments. It took until the 2015 season for a Bears quarterback to match Luckman's career total of 137 touchdown passes in a Chicago uniform.

Still, when Bears fans think "quarterback," they think of Luckman first. It was surprising it turned out that way, because Halas, who had a great eye for talent, drafted some exceptional quarterbacks willing to follow

Luckman. Years-long lapses in judgments by Halas, (perhaps proof he did not heed anyone else), drove away or resulted in the trades of Johnny Lujack, Bobby Layne, and George Blanda, among others.

Admiration for Luckman in Chicago continued long after he swapped his number 42 jersey for a business suit. He was a big man in the Windy City for the rest of his life, although when he passed away at age eighty-one in 1998, he was in Aventura, Florida.

"Sid Luckman was one of the greatest quarterbacks of all time, an outstanding example to others, and a success in business," said Mike McCaskey, Halas's oldest grandchild, who took over as president of the team when Halas died in 1983.[8]

Periodically, when talking about his life story and how he reluctantly became a pro football player because of Halas's persuasive talents, Luckman could be quite amusing. Halas was never known as a big spender. When he convinced Luckman to try pro football with the Bears and hauled out the contract he brought to Luckman's New York apartment, Halas told him how rare it was for him to give a player more than five thousand dollars.

"When he gave me the contract, and I signed it," Luckman said, Halas added, "You and Jesus Christ are the only two that I would pay five thousand dollars." "Coach," Luckman said, "you put me in some pretty good company." There was irony in the comparison because Luckman was Jewish. "I had never been further west than Buffalo. I really thought that Chicago was where cowboys were still around."[9]

Stockyards, yes; cowboys, no, for Chicago.

Halas was in failing health for some time before he passed away in 1983. He put his affairs in order, the most important of which concerned the Bears. In 1982 Halas, who years before had had a falling-out with star tight end Mike Ditka, hired him to rebuild the Bears as coach. Halas did not live long enough to see Ditka lead his beloved team to a Super Bowl title, but he knew he had left the team in the right hands.

During the last year of his life, Halas also wrote a letter to Luckman. It showed a rare sentimental side in someone who had long ago been labeled a curmudgeon.

"My boy, my pride in you has no bounds," Halas wrote. "You were the consummate player. You added a luster to my life that will never tarnish."[10]

Despite guiding a passing book into print in 1948, Luckman knew that he did not own the perfect throwing form. He was often accused of coming up short on mechanics. While Luckman knew good mechanics and could coach them, that did not mean he could perform them. There is some irony that, in the book *Passing for Touchdowns*, Luckman concedes the status of best-ever to Sammy Baugh.

Luckman reflected on the evolution of the forward pass in the short period between Benny Friedman and Harry Newman with the Giants, and Baugh's debut:

> While Benny depended mostly on deep passes with his receivers running under the ball, Harry banked on a medium-distance pass with a lot of whip to it. Benny passed only a few times in a game and most of his heaves were somewhat on the long-odds variety. Strangely enough, following Newman's time there was a lapse of several years until passing really arrived. The man who was to take it over and develop it into the fine art it is today is the chap whom I consider the greatest passer I've ever seen. That would be Samuel Adrian Baugh—Slingin' Sam, of Texas Christian and the Washington Redskins.
>
> Why do I think Sam is the greatest of 'em all? First, he has a deadly arm. Second, he has a pair of exceptionally keen eyes. And third, his timing is perfect. I've always felt that Sammy's form when throwing out of a single-wingback formation was the nearest thing to passing perfection.[11]

In Chicago, Luckman was The Man. He had a pristine reputation as a quarterback and a gentleman and never did anything to tarnish it. He was a guy who almost skipped out on his true calling, threatening never to play a down of pro football. He was a New York guy, not a Chicago guy, but became one.

Late in life Sid Luckman reflected on the roads he took instead of the road not taken, and he concluded everything had worked out just fine.

"If I had to do it again, I would never change my life or lifestyle," Luckman said. "Throughout my life, having been in sports, I always try to be a role model to the young as well as to the old in our nation."[12]

Luckman even admitted in older age, long after he last threw a football with a purpose, that he still loved watching the game each season and still derived great pleasure from watching whatever the Chicago Bears did on the field. He was a Bear forever.

CHAPTER 20 • SLINGIN' IT TO THE END

Earl "Dutch" Clark once said of Sammy Baugh, "They don't come any greater than Sammy Baugh. He's the greatest passer I've ever seen."[1] Washington Redskins running back Cliff Battles said of teammate Baugh, "He's a wonder."[2] Green Bay Packer Lou Gordon said of Baugh, "Baugh is the greatest passer of them all."[3]

The most remarkable aspect of the compliments is that they all were recorded in 1937, Baugh's rookie year. That season concluded with him leading the Redskins over the Chicago Bears for the NFL title.

In 1970, seven years after the Pro Football Hall of Fame was created with Baugh a member of the inaugural class, the museum's director was Dick McCann. McCann had strong opinions about who was the greatest passer in NFL history:

> Pay no attention to anything else you hear. Slingin' Sammy Baugh was the best and will still be the best after the last pass has been thrown. Forget the passing. Sam Baugh was a football player, a whole football player and a full-time one. He left more than a page full of records for part-time specialists to peck at. He rewrote the whole book. He not only led the parade in passing year after year, but he was the game's greatest punter and he set records as a pass defender. Mr. Quarterback? Sammy Baugh was more than that. He was Mr. Football.[4]

In the years following the last showdown between the Redskins and Bears with Sid Luckman and Baugh as opposing quarterbacks, Baugh had some of his finest seasons. While it should be noted that in 1945 Baugh completed 70.3 percent of his passes, in those latter years he also threw more frequently. In 1947 he attempted 354 passes and completed 210 while gaining 2,938 yards and throwing for 25 touchdowns. All but the touchdown passes were league records that year.

Before one game that season, the Touchdown Club, an organization with a national membership, chose to honor Baugh. He was presented with the gift of a station wagon. Redskins coach Dutch Bergman took part in the ceremony, saying, "Today we are honoring a man who has made many a coach look awfully good."[5]

On the field that is, not with verbal flattery. Baugh never said ten words when five would suffice, and his acceptance speech was very brief, timed by one observer at thirty-three seconds.

"I can't tell you how much I appreciate this," Baugh said. "I want to thank all you people up in the stands who made this possible. And I want to thank all the fellows down on the field who made it possible. To you fans, and the Redskin players past and present, I am most grateful."[6]

The Redskins were on a losing streak, and they were taking the field against the Chicago Cardinals during that team's finest season, 1947, when it won an NFL crown. But that day Baugh completed 25 passes for 355 yards and six touchdowns.

The next season, 1948, Baugh attempted 315 passes and completed 185 for 2,599 yards. That included 22 touchdown passes.

Baugh led the NFL in punting five times, and his lifetime kicking average was 45.1 yards per boot. As a defensive back, Baugh intercepted 31 passes, including a league-leading 11 in 1943. Baugh played for the Redskins for his entire career. He remained active through the 1952 season, when he was thirty-eight years old.

For a time during his career, Baugh collaborated on a regular football feature for the *Washington Post*, with sports editor–columnist Shirley Povich doing some ghostwriting. "I am in the football business," Baugh said in one of those pieces, "throwing footballs, kicking them, and running with them, too, for the Washington Redskins of the National Football League. The club meets the payroll regularly, my teammates are real pals, the hours can't be beaten, and the whole business is a source of more fun than college football."[7]

Baugh compared his college playing days with his pro football days and said one big difference was that the Washington offensive line protected him from defenders better than he had ever been protected in his life. "Believe me, this was swell," Baugh said.[8]

Baugh was hired by George Preston Marshall, an owner who told him to keep on throwing the ball. Coach Ray Flaherty, the man in charge until World War II broke out, always built Baugh's confidence. He recognized what a weapon Baugh's arm was and wanted to use it to the utmost. Baugh threw low passes that traveled fast and had the sweetest of spirals.

"You just keep laying that ball in there, Sam, and if we don't catch it, it's our fault," Flaherty told his quarterback. "Keep 'em accurate and they'll be caught."[9]

Baugh threw for 187 touchdowns and 21,886 yards during his career. Those were fabulous totals for a man who came into the league in 1937, when passing was more an afterthought than an important aspect of the offense. But by the late 1940s Baugh was slowing down.

Marshall, who loved being right about both Baugh's potential and featuring the game's biggest star on his team, did recognize Baugh could not throw forever. He hoped to find an able successor through the draft.

Harry Gilmer was a star for Alabama and the Most Valuable Player in the 1946 Rose Bowl. He was Washington's first-round pick in 1948, but even Marshall was cautious about proclaiming him the next great quarterback. For a guy who liked star power and who had shown in the past that he often could not keep his mouth shut at critical times, Marshall's reticence was unusual. Marshall could have heaped so much praise on Gilmer that he might have weighted him down with concrete blocks worth of pressure, but he refrained.

"Of all the passers I've seen, this boy reminds me most of Sammy when I first saw him," Marshall said. He compared their sizes, weights, quickness, and throwing styles. "Yessir, this is the boy. But, mind you, he is no second Sammy Baugh. He's a first Harry Gilmer."[10]

That was accurate. At the time Gilmer looked pretty good, and Baugh thought so, too, informing his boss after some early workouts that Gilmer was the man to replace him. Gilmer had a good career—not a great one—and twice made the Pro Bowl. He remained with the Redskins from 1948 to 1954 when he was traded to the Detroit Lions, where he later coached.

Baugh remained the starter at first, partially because Gilmer got hurt in 1948. And the veteran stuck around to tutor Gilmer for a while as well. Anytime Baugh played healthy he was still good enough to leave an impression. That included delivering a message with his performance to New York Giant Charlie Conerly, then an up-and-coming star.

Supposedly, Baugh was approaching the end of the line in 1948, but he led the Redskins to a 41-10 romp over the Giants in Griffith Stadium. It so happened that the next day Conerly was appearing at a weekly football luncheon in New York at the famous Toots Shor's Restaurant. The schooling the Giants had taken from Baugh was still fresh in his mind.

"I learned more about forward passing in one day watching Sammy Baugh than I ever learned throughout my college days," Conerly said. "He's the greatest I ever saw."[11] The football world continued to agree on that topic more than a decade after Baugh made his debut in the NFL.

Sid Luckman, too, was always complimentary of Baugh. His Bears sometimes beat Baugh's Redskins, but the opposing quarterback always had tremendous respect for Baugh and what he was capable of doing behind center. Luckman understood that Baugh could just about single-handedly beat any team. "I like to just sit and watch Sammy," Luckman said. "Every time he throws, I learn something. Nobody is ever going to equal him. Not anybody."[12]

During the latter stages of Baugh's Redskins career, the team was not as good as it had been. Teammates came and went. Some retired because of age and others because of fading skills. Baugh persevered. While some of the old gang returned from World War II and suited up, not all of the players were as good as when they were younger. There was also the All-America Football Conference, where the team owners spent money to entice players to leave their old squads. Marshall was rich enough to keep his Redskins, but he did not have the willingness. Some important Redskin players jumped organizations.

In 1946 former star Turk Edwards was 'Skins' head coach, and the team finished 5-5-1. Washington was just 4-8 the next season. Things were a little bit better in 1948, when the Redskins finished 7-5. "If you play long enough," Baugh said, "you're going to play on a real good team, you're going to play on a mediocre team, and you're going to play on some bad teams."[13] That was the law of averages anyway, and Baugh saw that come true for him. Personnel losses meant the Redskins were not title contenders. Baugh held up his end and some other players were solid performers, but the team was not as good as it was in its heyday. Later in the 1940s, when Washington did not fare so well in the NFL standings and one of the team's flaws was its offensive line, Baugh was invited to speak to a meeting of FBI men. Baugh looked out at his listeners and quipped, "This is the most protection I've had all year."[14]

The more time that passed and the more new quarterbacks who came into the NFL, or even the AAFC, it was clear to old-time football fans that the forward pass was not only here to stay, but was on par with the running game for the teams that had the right guys at quarterback.

Baugh had presided over a revolution basically by being himself and doing what he did best. No more was the NFL dictated by a philosophy of three yards and a cloud of dust. Not that many coaches counted on the pass as their fundamental choice of offensive weapon. But neither could a coach any longer ignore passing's impact on the game. One thing Baugh could figure out rather easily was how much difference the T-formation made on his body. He had to block in the single-wing, and his body took a licking that would have shortened his career if he had to keep it up.

As football experts observed the changes, they came to the same conclusion. It was the talented Sammy Baugh who led them to think differently. Baugh knew what he could do, and his confidence was infectious. While the Texan's arm strength was prodigious, he also knew when to hold 'em and when to fold 'em. That's because he was also such an accomplished punter and the master of the quick kick.

That dual role made it easy for him to fool opposing defenses. Since it was Baugh who dropped back to kick and was going to receive the hike, he could easily pull off fakes and make first downs out of hopeless fourth downs. He began showing that skill as a rookie in 1937, making believers out of his teammates. The Redskins might appear to be pinned deep in their own territory, and out from the sidelines would strut Baugh to reassure them the circumstances weren't so bad after all. One instance that drew teammates' attention occurred when they were on their own 9-yard line, an obvious kicking situation. But Baugh's college coach Dutch Meyer did not call him the greatest gambler he ever knew without cause. "We're a-goin' into punt formation," Baugh told them, "but we're really goin' to pass."[15]

Who knows how they would have reacted to his harebrained idea the next time if this one didn't turn out successfully? But Baugh could back up his talk. He also thrived in the T-formation after the Redskins adopted the style of offense that only the Bears were using when Baugh broke into the league in 1937.

"Why, that's the easiest position in football, quarterback in the T-formation," Baugh said. "All you do is hand the ball off and pass. If they'd had the T when I started playing ball I could have lasted until I was 40 years old."[16] He practically did, anyway, staying in uniform until he was thirty-eight.

Football players played both ways back then, on offense and defense. The age of specialization lay in the future. It is impossible to determine how Baugh have would fit into the modern game without those defensive back and punting responsibilities. What would it have been like if Baugh came along later and all he had to do was lead an offense? He probably would have been bored from inactivity on the sideline.

As Baugh aged in the game, he did take note of the growing number of offensive geniuses who plotted to find the end zone. Whereas once it took X's and O's to diagram plans, practically the entire alphabet came into use to accurately describe the goings-on. "The algebra coach used to be the football coach," Baugh said. "Now the football coach is the algebra teacher."[17]

Baugh did take pride in his punting. He was far and away the finest punter of his era, and he held some kicking records for decades after his retirement. Baugh not only could kick for distance but he could punt for placement, which was often more important if it resulted in pinning the opposition inside its own 10-yard line. Field position could well turn a game compared to merely booming the ball into the end zone and seeing it come out and have it set down on the 20.

"Nobody really works at it the right way anymore," Baugh said in the 1970s. "We'd get out there in practice and work on it an hour at a time, standing on the 50 and putting the ball out in that coffin corner. I got pretty accurate. I think anyone can if he works at it. Trouble is, the pros don't work at it now. I see them stand back of that 50-yard line and punt the ball into the end zone. You would be surprised how often over a whole season it would have benefited that club to kick out around the 10 instead of trying to kick it dead somewhere between the 10 and the goal line. A punter thinks of that average."[18]

Nearing the end of his career, Baugh had some interesting contract negotiations with George Preston Marshall. When Baugh was a rookie and Marshall was desperate to have him join the Redskins, Marshall paid big money for the time. It wasn't until Baugh arrived in training camp that he realized he was getting much more money (eight thousand dollars) than accomplished veterans. That was one reason he steered clear of salary talk in the locker room.

Later, when Baugh no longer played defense full-time to save wear and tear, he agreed that he should be paid less than he had been paid in his prime. He left the figure up to Marshall, and Marshall did not cut his salary. "Money did not mean that much to me," Baugh said. "I had fun playing football."[19]

It was a little bit disingenuous to suggest money was not important to Baugh. He had wanted enough money to buy the ranch of his dreams, and he also gave money to Texas Christian as a thank-you for providing him with opportunity. But unlike some players who let ego get in the way of their game, Baugh was not bothered if he was not the highest-paid player on the Redskins. He said Marshall told him if he had to pay (or overpay) someone because of circumstances. Marshall did that as a courtesy, and he seemed nervous how Baugh would react. But Baugh did not turn around and demand more cash for himself when that happened.

Baugh set so many records—some punting and some on defense, as well as passing—that in retirement he could not remember all of them. In one game in 1948 Baugh completed 17 passes for 446 yards, setting the record at 18.58 yards per completion. He didn't recall that game at all.

He had a better memory of a 1943 game when he not only threw four passes for touchdowns, but intercepted four. Although that interception mark has been tied many times, more than seventy years after Baugh set it, the record still stood. Another time, in 1939, Baugh punted a record fourteen times in one game against the Philadelphia Eagles.

One of the best days of Baugh's life came in 1938 when the NFL changed the rule to prohibit the defense from hitting the quarterback after he threw the ball. Baugh had learned as a rookie that if he stood around admiring his throws, he risked injury. "You did that, you could get killed," Baugh said.[20]

There are now other rules in place that help protect the quarterback and ones that definitely aid in lowering the quarterback's interception percentage. "I played in the NFL sixteen years, and no coach ever told me to throw the ball away to avoid a sack," Baugh said. "You just couldn't do it. If you threw the ball out of bounds, or even halfway between two receivers, you got a flag for intentional grounding."[21]

One part of Baugh's career that defied something he said was about teams' ups and downs. Throughout his entire stay in the NFL, in his mind, the Bears never really regressed much.

"The Bears never really had a bad team in the sixteen years I played," Baugh said. "[George] Halas was a great coach and he had great players. Unlike other teams, when we played the Bears, they didn't assign anyone to block me at free safety. I didn't understand it." So he asked Bronko Nagurski what was up with that strategy, and the Bronk said, "Because Mr. Halas wants to use the extra blocker to get me through the line. Then I'm supposed to run over you."[22]

Nagurski was the toughest man for Baugh to tackle, a sentiment expressed by many others who likened the experience to going one-on-one with a train. "Hell, I used to get hurt more on defense than on offense," Baugh said.[23]

Baugh also said he probably should have retired earlier than 1952, but he stayed with the Redskins and was phased out at quarterback as he helped Harry Gilmer and then a young Eddie LeBaron learn the position. Many of the appearances were cameos at the end of the year, and when Baugh played in the last game of that season he knew it was over for him.

LeBaron came out of the College of the Pacific and he knew that spending time around Sammy Baugh could be beneficial to his career in the long run. LeBaron could have been rushed into the job, but it didn't perturb him at all to wait for Baugh to step aside. "The guy was in his sixteenth NFL season and he was amazing," LeBaron said. "He was the best thrower I ever saw. He was very fluid and he could throw overhand, sidearm, off-balance, and hit a guy on the run whenever he wanted to. It was incredible. Here was this guy winding down at the end of his career and he was phenomenal."[24]

The old man sure looked like he still had it in him to perform, but Baugh barely played in 1952 and knew he was headed back to Texas for good once the final whistle blew, not just for an off-season. "I played in the first three games of the season and made an appearance in the last game," Baugh said. "I went in for only a play or two. I knew it was to be the last game."[25]

When Baugh retired in December 1952, one thing was pointed out: he did so fourteen years after he was first inclined to get out. After his stellar rookie year Baugh told some listeners that he planned to compete in pro ball for only one more season. "One more year of gettin' banged around and then I'm gettin' out," he said.[26]

That thinking did not last, as Baugh hung around year after year. One Washington sportswriter gave Sammy Baugh, legend, a legendary sendoff, calling him "the Babe Ruth of pro football. The play-for-pay game will be missing not only its greatest box-office attraction and one of its greatest all-time stars, but also a guy possessed of a fine sense of humor."[27]

These days the NFL playbook is supposed to be as difficult to decipher as a NASA playbook. Quarterbacks are given IQ tests, and they are supposed to memorize a few hundred pages of maps, charts, X's, O's, numbers, and arrows and be able to summon them up in the huddle with about ten seconds to think it over.

In that farewell-to-playing-days story about Baugh, life in the Redskins' huddle was recounted, sounding much more like a playground game unfolding. "You ends go down about 20 yards and criss-cross," Baugh said. "You two halfbacks go down about 10 yards and buttonhook. That's it fellas, let's go." The fullback interrupted Baugh to ask what he should do, and Baugh replied, "Hell, I don't know, but just don't be in my way when I go back to pass."[28]

Nothing really bad ever happened to any of Baugh's teams when everyone else got out of the way to let him pass. The real secret of his success was the quick release of his passes, something scouts now routinely look for in young, untried quarterbacks. Also, well aware of how the defenses were trying to break his bones, Baugh mastered throwing on the run—not an advised approach to passing, but often a successfully improvised one.

Great athletes occasionally pass through a sport who seem as if they could play forever. The body gives out before the mind, usually, especially in football. Baugh maintained his football fitness physique long after he retired, and when football people saw him with the same lean frame as always, they would speculate on whether he could still play the hard game. It was just idle chatter, but sometimes Baugh played along. If he believed he could have kept playing pro football after 1952, he would have. But what he did think was that the game hadn't changed so much by the time he was fifty-five that he would be unable to bring the same strategy.

"If I went out to quarterback a team now," Baugh said in 1969, "I doubt that I'd do things much different than I did before. My theory, the way I was taught by Dutch Meyer at TCU, was you try to beat a defense. They're going to let you have a weak spot, so you find it and pick on it.

You keep going to a weakness until they adjust to cover it. Then they leave themselves open somewhere else and you go to that. That's where experience helps a quarterback. You've got to realize when they're stopping what you're doing and find out what else has opened up. You've got to beat defenses."[29]

Baugh did that very thing for a living, even as he was playing defense half the time. Then, in retirement, he played football in his head as a hobby, for anyone who asked. As great an all-around football player as Baugh was, the reason he is so revered, so well-remembered, is what he did with the ball in his hand.

When the Redskins' 1952 season concluded, Baugh did what so many cowboys did in the movies. He rode off into the sunset.

CHAPTER 21 • **OTTO GRAHAM AND FRIENDS**

The end of the era of the pioneer quarterback really came before Sammy Baugh and Sid Luckman even retired. They paved the way for the future, and by the mid-1940s, National Football League teams that read which way the wind was blowing were scouting to find someone who could carry them forward with the forward pass. It was no longer just Sammy and Sid: post–World War II it became Sammy and Sid and the new kids on the block. This new group of quarterbacks included Bob Waterfield, Norm Van Broklin, Y. A. Tittle, Bobby Layne, and the Cleveland Browns' legendary Otto Graham.

Bob Waterfield completed his eligibility at UCLA in 1944 and was a fifth-round pick of the Cleveland Rams (which would become the Los Angeles Rams, the St. Louis Rams, and then go back to Los Angeles). Although not a high draft choice, Waterfield started for Cleveland immediately and led the Rams to the NFL title in 1945, winning the Most Valuable Player award.

Waterfield threw two touchdown passes in the championship game as Cleveland topped the Washington Redskins, 15-14. The Rams believed in Waterfield and gave him a twenty-thousand-dollar-a-year contract, making him the highest paid player in the league.

Waterfield led the NFL in touchdown passes his first two seasons, though he never threw more than 17 in one year and retired as a relatively young man of thirty-two in 1952. Like Baugh, Waterfield was an accomplished punter, with a lifetime kicking average of 42.4 yards per boot. Despite the brevity of his career, Waterfield was elected to the Pro Football Hall of Fame in 1965.

A little bit younger was the quarterback who overlapped with and then succeeded Waterfield for the Rams: Norm Van Brocklin, a rookie out of Oregon in 1949. Van Brocklin led the NFL once each time in completions, attempts, completion percentage, and yards. He also led the Philadelphia Eagles to the championship in 1960, his last season.

Van Brocklin, who was just thirty-four when he retired, was also a proficient punter with a career 42.9-yard average. He threw 24 touchdown passes in his final season and threw 173 in all before turning to coaching. Van Brocklin, who was selected for nine NFL All-Star teams, also had one of the greatest single-game passing days in league history. On September 28, 1951, with the Rams facing the New York Yanks, Van Brocklin threw for a record 554 yards in a game. Some sixty-six years later, Van Brocklin, who in 1961 became the expansion Minnesota Vikings' first head coach, still owns that record.

Yelberton Abraham (Y. A.) Tittle was drafted by the Baltimore Colts in 1948 after a college career at Louisiana State. Those were the original Colts of All-America Football Conference fame, but that team folded and Tittle became a star for the San Francisco 49ers in the 1950s and then the New York Giants in the early 1960s. Although he never won a championship, Tittle was a dominant figure in the game well into his thirties.

He tied Luckman's record of throwing seven touchdown passes in one game and in 1962 threw 33 touchdown passes. A year later he broke that record by throwing 36. Tittle was elected to the Hall of Fame in 1971.

In 1948, when it became apparent that Luckman was nearing the end of his career, George Halas was searching for a replacement. He thought he had his man when he obtained Bobby Layne out of Texas. Layne had been drafted by the Pittsburgh Steelers, but he didn't want to play for them. Halas traded for Layne, then made him a third-string quarterback, which did not sit well with Layne. Layne tried to cut his own deal with the Green Bay Packers, but Halas exiled him to the lowly New York Bulldogs of the All-America Football Conference.

This was one time when Halas outsmarted himself. By Halas's standards—and most of conservative America's standards—Layne was a wild man. He liked to drink and carouse and keep crazy hours. But on the field he could be a marvel. Halas did not believe Layne had it in him to be a winner, but the coach was wrong.

In 1950 Layne surfaced with the Detroit Lions instead and led the Lions to championships in 1952 and 1953 before eventually starring for the Pittsburgh Steelers. Detroit coach Buddy Parker knew what Layne could do. Layne was a riverboat gambler, a daring player who often skirted disaster on the field but regularly pulled off the improbable. Layne threw as many as 26 touchdown passes in a season and for as many as 2,500 yards. He was a six-time Pro Bowl player, elected to the Hall of Fame in 1967.

Halas's rejection of Layne sent the Bears into a tailspin that lasted years as Halas made misjudgment after misjudgment about the quality of the quarterbacks he had on his roster. They kept turning up with other teams and becoming all-stars.

Not Otto Graham, however. Halas never had a shot at him. Graham was born in Waukegan, Illinois, about fifty miles north of Chicago. He enrolled at Northwestern University, made an instant impact in 1941, and then split his time between the Wildcats and the US Navy Air Corps for the duration of World War II.

When he left Northwestern, Graham was the Big Ten's all-time leading passer. But in 1945, when approached about turning pro, Graham was tied up with his naval obligation. Paul Brown, the innovative coach who led Ohio State against Graham's Northwestern teams, was a founder and coach of the Cleveland Browns of the new All-America Football Conference.

Brown agreed to pay Graham some living expenses until the war was over and he could officially sign with the Browns. There was a brief in-between period when Graham played guard for the Rochester Royals in the new National Basketball League. Rochester won the championship, and the NBL soon merged with the National Basketball Association. Graham was discharged from his military service in 1946 and moved right on to the Browns' training camp.

It was the 6-foot-1, 200-pound Graham who, in terms of being a winner, was next in line. However, his choice of signing with the Browns in the fledgling AAFC kept him out of the limelight at first. Nobody knew whether the competing AAFC would make it or not. All Graham did was play, and all the Browns did was win.

Graham was already twenty-five years old as a rookie, and he played for one decade, all with the Browns. The Browns put up with comments that they were not good enough to play in the NFL and were in a minor league. But when the AAFC folded, the Browns were just as good in the established league as they had been in the new one. Graham led Cleveland to seven championships in ten years, four in the AAFC and three in the NFL.

"In sheer passing ability Otto may have been second to Baugh," wrote one author. "In cold brilliance he may have been second to Luckman. In the qualities of character and leadership, he was second to no one."[1] It was no myth that Graham was a hard-core competitor. It was no sportswriter's idle comment that winning is what fueled him. "I hate it when my wife beats me at croquet," Graham said.[2]

Truly, all great quarterbacks have the risk gene in their makeup. In one AAFC game against the Buffalo Bills of that pre–American Football League team of the same name, the Browns had the ball at their own 1-yard line. Everyone in the building thought the Browns would have to run their way out of poor field position—except for Graham, of course. Those in the huddle were even skeptical when Graham said, "I think we'll try a little screen pass. Look, there's nothing to worry about. I'm not going to let them trap me. If I see I'm getting rushed, I'll throw the ball in the stands. All they can do is penalize me half the distance to the goal line, and the ball is on the 1-foot line now."[3]

Notice should be taken of Graham's statement. Such strategy was not something Baugh considered because the rule against intentional grounding was in effect. After the snap, the Bills rushed Graham like a herd of enraged buffalo. But Graham anticipated that, and he flipped the ball to Mac Speedie on the goal line. Speedie lived up to his name and raced the entire length of the field, officially a 99-yard touchdown.

Waterfield did okay during his second season with the Rams as well. He was a natural as the face of the franchise. He grew up in Southern California, played college ball in Southern California, and was good looking enough to be wooed by Hollywood filmmakers for part-time jobs. Waterfield threw 17 touchdown passes in 1947. In 1948 Waterfield rallied the Rams back from a 28-0 deficit with four touchdown throws. The quarterback, who married actress Jane Russell, began sharing his on-field job with Van Brocklin in 1949, not a comfortable arrangement for either man. The Rams reached the NFL title game in 1949, 1950, and 1951, losing the first two, but winning the third time.

"There's no thrill in football like popping the ball to a receiver who has a step on his man in the open," Waterfield said.[4]

Although his career was not a very long one, Waterfield got off to that fast start as a rookie. The results left people gushing as he led the Cleveland version of the Rams to their only crown before moving West. "Bob Waterfield is the greatest T-formation quarterback in the world," said Rams coach Adam Walsh.[5] Sammy Baugh and Sid Luckman had apparently slipped Walsh's mind in the euphoria of the moment.

Among the receivers Waterfield and Van Brocklin had were stars Elroy "Crazy Legs" Hirsch and Tom Fears, guys who knew how to get open downfield and who could hold onto the ball. These were the early stages of opening up the passing game even more, not just completing the short ones beyond the line of scrimmage or hitting the running back coming out of the backfield.

Van Brocklin was lucky he came along when he did because he was no runner. He was neither fast nor impressive looking when he had to tuck the ball under his arm and take off. Before the phrase was coined, although not before the first time two quarterbacks on one team dueled for the first-string job, Van Brocklin and Waterfield were part of the first true genuine NFL quarterback controversy. Fans took sides.

It would still be some time in the future before interceptions would be viewed as deadly as hand grenades, but throwing accuracy was becoming more prized. "In this league the difference between a touchdown and an interception is whether the ball comes down over the receiver's right shoulder or left shoulder," Van Brocklin said.[6]

Van Brocklin was often viewed as crotchety when he was a coach with the Vikings and Atlanta Falcons, but even as a player he could alienate opponents with insults. Once he got into a back-and-forth with younger defensive tackle Floyd Peters, then of the Browns. Peters said to Van Brocklin, "You're an old man, and you're all through in this league." Van Brocklin retaliated as quickly as if he was firing a line drive pass over the middle. "You're a rookie and you're punchy already," Van Brocklin said in 1959.[7]

Bobby Layne was a leader on the field. Men followed him. After hours he took absolutely no care of his body, which is one reason he died at age fifty-nine. As an individual, Layne seemed more likely to be hanging out with Johnny Blood and the other old-timers of the game, but his reckless desire for striking fast and effectively was more of a new-age thing. Like Baugh, he spoke with a Texas drawl, but his feelings translated this way: "I don't like to lose ball games," Layne said. "I don't like to lose ball games. Dammit, I don't like to lose ball games."[8]

Layne was known for his acts of generosity to those in need, to those in need of a party, and to teammates. He never hid his partying ways. Once when he was with the Lions he was arrested for drunk driving. He requested a trial by jury, hired a sharp defense attorney, and in the most memorable line of the trial—after which he was acquitted—Layne said, "I'm not drunk, I'm from Texas," as a way of explaining the slur in his words.[9]

They say that after that verdict, many bars around Detroit posted signs reading, "I'm not drunk, I'm from Texas."

Tittle at first made it big with San Francisco, the franchise that introduced the shotgun formation. The quarterback did not put his hands on the center's butt but stood about 5 yards back and accepted a short, line-drive toss for the hike. The shotgun was popular for a little while some sixty years ago and in more recent years has made a resurgence, mostly used by teams on passing downs. It was intended to provide the quarterback with another second or two to survey the defense when it was third-and-long for a first down.

Tittle was drafted by the Detroit Lions but signed with Baltimore in the AAFC. When that league folded, the NFL held a dispersal draft, which is what sent him to San Francisco to play for a decade. With a young John Brodie in the fold, the 49ers began to phase out Tittle in 1960.

Although Brodie became a fine player, Tittle's reputation was greatly enhanced by his shift to New York. He had his greatest passing seasons there and led the Giants to three NFL title games, although they could not win a championship.

In 1962 Tittle threw 33 touchdown passes and for 3,224 yards. Tittle was even better in 1963, throwing 36 touchdown passes for 3,145 yards and a completion percentage of 60.2, which led the league. Tittle said he was a better quarterback with New York, even at ages thirty-six and thirty-seven, than he had been in San Francisco because of Coach Allie Sherman and the serious way the Giants approached studying for games.

"Nothing is overlooked," Tittle said. "Nothing is left undone. We might get beat, but when we do it is because the other club has beaten us physically, and not because we went into the ball game unprepared. He [Sherman] is a perfectionist when it comes to details."[10]

Tittle's Giants lost twice to the Green Bay Packers and in 1963 to the Chicago Bears. That was the most frustrating defeat of his life. The final score was 14-10, and Tittle injured a knee in the first half. Rather than leave the game for treatment he kept on playing. "I kept trying, but I was not maneuverable," Tittle said. "I could not get back away from the center. I like to fly back there, plant myself, find my receiver, and get rid of the damned ball. I was still putting the ball in the air when the game ended. But it was no use. I felt as low as at any time in my career."[11]

There was no fourth try. In 1964 everything came unglued for the Giants. The team fell apart, and Tittle, who had long been prematurely bald, finally looked his age. When the year ended, he retired.

During seventeen seasons, including time spent in the All-America Football Conference, Tittle threw for 248 touchdowns and 33,070 yards. Whereas not so many years earlier any quarterback throwing for 2,000 or more yards in a season was an anomaly, Tittle topped that milestone nine times, twice clearing 3,000 yards. In the last years of his career Tittle benefited from having a coach who believed in him more than the coach he had during the early stages of his career. The results were fantastic, passing totals he had never before approached. An opportunity to play for a supportive coach and in a system designed to take advantage of their skills often can be the backdrop for quarterbacks' success.

As a Cleveland Brown in the AAFC and the NFL, Otto Graham's record was 114-20-4, including playoffs. Graham never played for any pro team other than the Browns, nor any other head coach besides Paul Brown. As a rookie, Graham learned that if the Browns were trailing at the half, the coach did not berate players so much as introduce adjustments to facilitate a comeback. "Paul Brown didn't waste time with pep talks at halftime," Graham said. "He utilized the time to teach, not preach."[12]

Brown was regarded as one of football's great innovators, a brilliant coach, and a winning one. One thing his quarterbacks, from Graham on, resented was not being allowed to call their own game signals. Brown insisted on calling the plays. He employed a messenger system with one guard running in from the sideline each play with his instructions.

"Paul Brown sent in the plays with alternating guards from day one," Graham said, "only the frequency changed. It was the only aspect of his philosophy on which we disagreed. I thought the quarterback, caught up in the flow of the game, had a better feel for another team's weaknesses and should call the plays. I made no bones about my feelings, but they never came between Paul and me. It was his team and his decision, and so long as we won, how could I argue?"[13]

Paul Brown did it his way, and the Browns were remarkably successful doing it his way. He needed the right guy at quarterback, someone who would not resist his calls any more than Graham's light protests.

Graham said his favorite sport was actually basketball, but he was better at football. He did injure a knee in high school and had an operation, which slowed him down briefly. However, he won eight letters at Northwestern in football, basketball, and baseball. In Cleveland, Graham was not known as a hard thrower so much as an accurate one. He was blessed with fine receivers like Mac Speedie; Dante Lavelli, whom he affectionately called "Spumoni"; and Dub Jones.

Jones, who made two all-star teams, caught 43 passes from Graham in 1952. Speedie, a three-time All-Pro, had seasons of 67, 62, 58, and 62 catches for 349 receptions in his career, a very high total for his time. In 1947, the season he caught that 99-yarder from Graham, he gained 1,146 yards on catches. Lavelli, another three-time All-Pro, was elected to the Pro Football Hall of Fame. He caught 386 balls, averaging 16.8 yards per catch.

Graham suffered another knee injury before the 1948 AAFC championship game. Brown told him, "Don't even bother to dress for the game."[14] Graham had his knee taped up, tested its firmness, and demanded to start. On the Browns' first offensive play he tossed a touchdown to Lavelli.

When Graham signed for the 1954 season he said it was going to be his last. The Browns emphatically ended the two-year run of the Lions, 56-10, in the championship game. Graham intended to carry through on his intentions although he was naturally asked why then. "You've got to quit sometime," Graham said. "And it's good to quit when you're on top."[15]

When the Browns gathered for training camp in 1955, Graham was sitting at home. Exhibitions don't mean much of anything in terms of a team winning or losing, but when the Browns lost all but one preseason game, Paul Brown realized he did not have a Graham replacement in hand. He telephoned Graham with a request. "Come back, Otto! We need you," Brown said.[16] They did, and he did. The Browns finished 9-2-1 and won one more championship, besting the Los Angeles Rams.

Only fans with long memories or students of history recall the AAFC and that the Browns were part of it. That was the first chapter of the Browns' existence. Next they joined the NFL in 1950 when the AAFC folded. Later, the Browns that everyone knew moved to Baltimore and became the Ravens. Ultimately, the NFL granted the Browns an expansion team of the same nickname in 1999. Fans were furious at the initial departure, joyous at the return of pro football, but frustrated pretty much ever since because of the failures of the Browns in their second coming.

After moving from the AAFC to the NFL, the Browns were dismissed as a fluky team that feasted on weaker opposition in the start-up league. No one believed the Otto Graham–led team would be much of a factor in the NFL. Those experts underestimated the Browns' talent level; they sent seven players to the Pro Bowl right away. Cleveland went 10-2 and shockingly won the championship.

Graham remembered well the insults that greeted the Browns as that season began. Their old league was called the "All-Amateur Conference" and the "Red Ink" league.[17] Commissioner Bert Bell said he thought the Browns would be fortunate to win three games, which annoyed the team. They were incredibly hungry to prove themselves when the season began, and they were scheduled to go up against the defending champion Philadelphia Eagles. As predicted, the game was a rout. As was not predicted, it was Cleveland doing the routing, 35-10.

"We would have played that game for a milkshake," Graham said, adding that Paul Brown posted on a bulletin board every negative story about his team that he found in newspapers. "It was painless, almost child's play," Graham said of the Browns' first touchdown on a 59-yard pass.[18]

When it was over, the losers were stunned. It shook the foundations of the NFL the way the New York Jets did a little more than a decade later in their upset of the Baltimore Colts in the Super Bowl. "Jeez, they've got a lot of guns," said Eagles coach Earle "Greasy" Neale, "a lot of guns."[19]

That was the first NFL title. The last Graham NFL title occurred when he was summoned from retirement by Brown. The New York Giants were the main practitioners and creators of the umbrella defense. The umbrella defense sprang from the imagination of Giants coach Steve Owen, who designed a 6-1-4 defense. It called for six down linemen putting pressure on the quarterback and four men back while just one defender roamed the middle. Up until then the standard NFL defense called for a five-man front. Graham and the Browns picked that formation apart.

The umbrella defense was successful in some instances but it was soon superseded. During an era when assistant coaches were luxuries, Owen counted on his star defensive back Tom Landry to teach a new 4-3 defense. Those three men in the middle had flexibility to either halt the run or cover the pass.

Landry, who later became the Hall of Fame leader of the Dallas Cowboys, graduated to full-time assistant coach with New York before taking over the 1960 Cowboys as their first head coach.

Paul Brown, being Paul Brown, countered the umbrella with the invention of the two-minute offense. The hurry-up scheme worked so well for Cleveland that the Browns could work around the umbrella, and the Browns even wondered if they should play that style all game long. "Paul, the great innovator, had devised the now-commonplace two-minute drill for those occasions to keep defenses on their heels and allow our offense to eat up huge chunks of yardage in a hurry," Graham said.[20]

The Rams, the 1955 title game opponent, had used the umbrella, but it did them no good in this season finale versus Cleveland. Graham and Dub Jones met with Paul Brown and suggested the Browns go the whole game with the two-minute offense. "It always goes well when we do use it," Graham said. "Why keep it just for emergencies? Why not play the whole ball game that way? If we have something that good, why hold back on it?"[21]

They convinced Brown it was a smart idea, and the Browns tore apart the Rams using the forerunner of the hurry-up offense. Cleveland won, 38-14, in front of more than eighty-seven thousand fans at the Los Angeles Coliseum. It was known that this was Graham's last game, and Rams fans gave him a standing ovation.

"When I got to the sidelines, I simply said, 'Thank you, Paul, but no more promises,'" Graham told Brown. "He smiled, patted me on the shoulder, and said, 'Thank you, Otto.'"[22]

Paul Brown meant that, too. Sometime later when he was asked about quarterback contributions and skills, Brown said this to a sportswriter: "The test of a quarterback is where his team finishes in the league standings. Every year Graham quarterbacked Cleveland they finished No. 1. He was the best of them all."[23]

CHAPTER 22 • JOHNNY U.

Johnny Unitas's NFL quarterback beginnings almost sound like a fictional story.

A college player at Louisville, Unitas was born in Pittsburgh in 1933 and, after finishing his college career, felt sure he was good enough to help his hometown Steelers. The Steelers made what could be described as a courtesy draft pick when they chose Unitas in the ninth round in 1955.

At that time, as Otto Graham was playing out his last season with the Cleveland Browns, no one in America would have predicted Unitas would be the heir apparent, the successor as the National Football League's next great quarterback.

Unitas reported to the Steelers training camp believing he could make the team. He barely got a look-see before he was cut. In what was perhaps the biggest personnel goof in NFL history, Coach Walt Kiesling never gave Unitas a chance and ushered him out the door. Unitas was not happy to go either. He felt shabbily treated.

"Just before the season was to start, Kiesling called me in and said he was sorry, but he couldn't use four quarterbacks," Unitas said. "I told him, 'I don't mind if you gave me the opportunity to play and I screwed up. But you never gave me the opportunity.' He told me he would try to put me on the reserve list for $100 a week, but I never heard from him again."[1]

Nobody around the NFL called Unitas on the phone to invite him to another team's camp. Discouraged, Unitas signed on for the chance to play semipro football as he worked in construction in Pittsburgh to support his family. He needed that labor work because lining up for the Bloomfield

Rams was definitely not paying the bills. Unitas, making six dollars per game, was mostly playing football for fun, but also with hope in his heart that he would be discovered, as unlikely as that was.

Lightning struck when Unitas was asked to join Bloomfield lineman teammate Jim Deglau in trying out in the Baltimore Colts' training camp before the 1956 season. The duo did not even have gas money to make the short trip and had to borrow it. But whereas the Steelers ignored Unitas and ranked him fourth out of four quarterbacks in their camp the year before, the Colts were smarter and gave him a chance to play.

There had been some talk that Paul Brown and his Cleveland Browns were interested in Unitas. Brown was the kind of man who could spot talent where others couldn't, and he was quarterback-shopping in the post–Otto Graham era. But Unitas made the cut with the Colts, first as a backup to George Shaw. Shaw was an All-American quarterback out of the University of Oregon who won the starting role in 1955. He played fairly well, completing 50.2 percent of his passes at a time when making good on half your throws was a barometer of success, for 1,586 yards and 10 touchdowns.

Shaw was only twenty-three in 1956, the same age as Unitas, and Coach Weeb Ewbank must have been confident that he had found the quarterback who could lead his rebuilding team all the way to a championship. Unitas was raw and untried, but eager and smart. As the second-stringer he did not figure to see much action, and in the Colts' first few games he appeared only briefly.

However, in a development that closely mirrored the fate of a 1920s New York Yankees first baseman named Wally Pipp, Unitas got a break. Pipp was the regular in 1925 when he came to the ball park one day and told his manager he had a headache and could not play. A young player named Lou Gehrig was inserted into the lineup and that was it. Pipp was outclassed and outshone by probably the greatest first baseman of all time. Gehrig, as it turned out, never needed a rest. Once installed at first, Gehrig stayed for 2,130 straight games, a record that stood for fifty-six years.

What happened to Pipp is pretty much what happened to Shaw. Shaw played in five games for the 1956 Colts and was completing 60 percent of his passes when he broke his leg. Unitas became the emergency replacement. Unitas's start, against Chicago, was a messy one. He threw an interception on his first pass that was returned for a touchdown. He also screwed up a handoff for a fumble on the next play, and the ball was recovered by the defense. The Bears demolished the Colts that day, 58-27.

Knowing he had not shown well and feeling his status was shaky, Unitas was down in the locker room afterward. He was surprised and encouraged, however, when owner Carroll Rosenbloom stopped by to give him a pep talk. It was one complimentary visit that stuck with Unitas over the years.

Unitas was lucky he still had a job after that harsh of a start. But he settled down, performed well, and completed 55.6 percent of his passes that season for 1,498 yards and nine touchdowns. At the time the completion percentage was the best-ever mark for a rookie. The next season, 1957, Unitas won the starting job and relegated a healthy Shaw to the backup spot.

Once Unitas found his rhythm, it was all over for Shaw or any other Colt quarterback contender for years. That season Unitas completed 172 passes in 301 attempts, more often than any other quarterback passed that year. He completed 57.1 percent of his tosses for 2,550 yards and 24 touchdowns.

Unitas was also in the right place at the right time for the Colts. Ewbank had been hired to build a championship team from scratch, and by that year he had most of the building blocks in place. Ewbank believed in a balanced offense; he had the tools for a good running game with Lenny Moore and Alan Ameche, a good passing game with Unitas, and good receivers in Raymond Berry, Jimmy Orr, and Jim Mutscheller. Unitas was the trump card, wily enough to call a pass when it could be a big gainer, and savvy enough to rely on the run when circumstances demanded it. In a sense, Unitas was his own system, seizing upon circumstances to drive the team.

The 1957 campaign was a turnaround year for the Colts. They finished 7-5 and believed they were on the cusp of something significant. Baltimore was loaded with talent just coming into its own. Ameche, Berry, Gino Marchetti, Gene "Big Daddy" Lipscomb, Art Donovan, Moore, and Jim Parker were just some of the big names on the squad.

In 1958 the Colts were just two games better in the standings, going 9-3, but that was enough. They captured the Western Division and advanced to the NFL Championship Game against the New York Giants for a contest that became known as "the greatest game ever played."

That title game introduced the concept of sudden-death overtime to the nation. It drew a tremendous television audience and was so exciting that it became known as the most important game in NFL history. The Colts won 23-17 in overtime, and Unitas was cool and collected under pressure, so much so that his national profile and reputation were enhanced fiftyfold.

Unitas missed a few games because of injury that season, but still threw for 2,007 yards and 19 touchdowns against just seven interceptions. Those who played against Unitas regularly understood he was a special talent. He stood 6-foot-1 and weighed 195 pounds, but Unitas did not look chiseled. He had a hunched-over manner that also detracted from first impressions. But he was brilliantly accurate with a football in his hands, with the guts of a gunfighter and the personality to lead and rally a team.

While every smart quarterback throws to whoever is open, the best quarterbacks frequently have what is described as a favorite receiver, the end who gets open most often, the player with the best hands, the best moves, the go-to guy who is trusted more than anyone else because he has been there, done that.

For Unitas and the Colts, that player was end Raymond Berry. Berry was not even a star in college at Southern Methodist University. He was such a long shot to make it in the pros that the Colts picked him in the twentieth round of the league draft. But through hard work, repetition, good hands, and an ability to read defenses, Berry made himself into a Hall of Famer. When Berry retired in 1967, he had 631 catches on his resume, then the NFL record.

The Giants were favored in the 1958 championship, and for much of the game it appeared they would win. When the Colts rallied to send the game into overtime, Unitas-to-Berry changed the game's complexion. Baltimore trailed, 17-14, with time running out in the fourth quarter. But Unitas guided the Colts downfield, mostly on medium-range passes to Berry. "It certainly was the best game Unitas and I had together," Berry said.[2]

Steve Myhra kicked the tying field goal to send the game into overtime. The sudden-death rule was new and had never been used. At the end of regulation, many of the players thought the game was over and that the teams would be co-champions. Officials had to explain to the teams that the first team to score was the winner. Baltimore got the ball, and once again Unitas, the field general, masterminded a long drive that pierced the Giants' vaunted defense and set the Colts up with a try for the win on the New York 1-yard line. Although Ewbank had not wanted Unitas throwing, the quarterback took what defenders gave him on the previous play, hitting Mutscheller for 6 yards.

At the 1, when Unitas accepted the snap, he turned and handed the ball to Ameche, the fullback. Expecting turbulence ahead, he ducked his shoulder and plowed toward the goal line. However, the Colt line opened such a large hole that Unitas could have driven an Edsel through. Ameche scored easily, and the Colts were champs—famous champs at that. In an instant Unitas went from being just another NFL quarterback to a star in demand by sportswriters and even Ed Sullivan, whose Sunday night show was the most popular variety TV event of the time.

"They couldn't have stopped us if we needed 10 yards," Unitas said.[3] Although Unitas was awarded a Corvette as the game's Most Valuable Player he turned down Ed Sullivan because it would have meant not being able to travel back to Baltimore with his teammates.

Members of the national press corps learned, upon meeting Unitas for the first time in the game's aftermath, that he was a very self-assured, confident young man, as quarterbacks tended to be. Someone raised the question of the element of risk in Unitas throwing to Mutscheller, but Unitas made it sound as if the call was a no-brainer.

"It wasn't a gamble," he said. "They didn't see what I saw. When you know what you're doing, you're not intercepted. The Giants were jammed up at the line and not expecting a pass. It was no sweat. They were playing one on one, looking for a run. All I had to do was flip it up there for Jim and let him catch it. I don't expect a pass like that to fail, and it didn't. No matter how good a defense is, you can always find a weakness somewhere."[4] So there.

Unitas was the man of the hour. In two years he had gone from semipro to the best of the pros. He was the toast of Baltimore and suddenly the most famous player in the nation. No one knew exactly what the Pittsburgh Steelers were thinking when they watched Unitas lead the Colts to victory, although by 1958 they were coached by Buddy Parker, not Walt Kieseling. It was too late for Parker to claim Unitas, but he did go out and trade for Bobby Layne.

The Giants were a star-studded team with numerous Hall of Famers in the lineup, no one more prominent on a terrific defense than linebacker Sam Huff. "The man was a genius," Huff said of Unitas. "I never saw a quarterback that good on those two drives."[5]

Unitas was just getting established, but from that championship demonstration on, he was a hero in Baltimore. Baltimore was a blue-collar town, and Unitas was a blue-collar guy. Sure, appearing on Ed Sullivan might have been okay, but only if he had nothing better to do than to hang with his guys.

During seventeen seasons in Baltimore and one rather strained one with the San Diego Chargers, Unitas recorded an extraordinary career. He had two nicknames—the simple "Johnny U." and the more laudatory "The Golden Arm." He wore a flattop haircut and black high-top shoes with white laces. In neither case were those indications of high fashion. Johnny U. was just Johnny U. He didn't care much for celebrity frills, although he was in fact a celebrity, one of the faces of the NFL.

Unitas led the league in completions three times, yards passing four times, and touchdown passes four times. His 32 touchdown passes in 1959 set a league record. He passed for 40,239 yards in his career. He also threw 290 touchdown passes. Unitas's longest-lasting record was an intriguing one. He completed at least one touchdown pass in forty-seven straight games between 1956 and 1960. That record stood for fifty-two years, until it was broken by the New Orleans Saints' Drew Brees in 2012.

Of Lithuanian descent, Unitas was a true American success story of overcoming odds. He was elected to the Hall of Fame in 1979. Unitas, whose number 19 jersey was retired by the franchise, was in loud sympathy with Baltimore fans when owner Robert Irsay uprooted the franchise and moved the team to Indianapolis in 1984. Unitas never had anything else to do with the team after that. He remained a Baltimore guy.

A ten-time Pro Bowl player, Unitas seemed more modest than most football stars. When he retired after eighteen years and innumerable accomplishments, he said he preferred to do so without fanfare. "I came into the league without any fuss," Unitas said. "I'd just as soon leave it that way. There's no difference I can see in retiring from pro football or quitting a job at the Pennsy Railroad. I did something I wanted to do and went as far as I could go."[6]

Given that he weighed 145 pounds in high school, that he played at Louisville before Louisville played major college ball, and that he was cut by Pittsburgh, Unitas took things pretty far. He was determined and capable, and all he asked for was a chance. Weeb Ewbank gave it to him, as did the fate of Shaw's broken leg. "The most important thing of all about Unitas," Ewbank said, "is that he had a real hunger. This was a kid that wanted success and didn't have it so long, he wasn't about to waste it when it came."[7]

Today Unitas can be seen as a bridge figure in the passing game, from the days of Sammy Baugh, Sid Luckman, Arnie Herber, Cecil Isbell, and Otto Graham into the 1970s, when passing became so important. The pass's more frequent use in the offense then led to the out-of-control 1990s and 2000s, when the air game for some teams would almost eclipse the running game completely.

Later in life, Sid Luckman, who had always insisted that Baugh was the best thrower ever, changed his tune and anointed Unitas the next greatest of them all. Luckman said the Unitas he watched was the best quarterback of all time.

"Better than me," Luckman said. "Better than Sammy Baugh. Better than anyone."[8]

Unitas put up better numbers than Baugh and Luckman. He put up better numbers than any old-timers. But others came along, and, as the NFL schedule expanded from twelve games per season in Unitas's prime to fourteen and then to sixteen, passers threw more than ever. Unitas's best statistical seasons went by the wayside, receding from impressive and untouchable to run-of-the-mill. It was merely representative of the change in the sport, not a true reflection of the greatness of the individual. Everybody outthrows Baugh's and Luckman's numbers these days as well: one reason is just that every team throws more than teams used to throw.

The author of a Unitas biography summed up the impact the player made on football during his early years when the game was changing, when TV was just starting to boost its popularity, and when he led his Colts to that stunning overtime win over the Giants. "He carried professional football on his sloping shoulders to the pinnacle of sports in America almost overnight during his first five years with the Baltimore Colts," the author wrote. "It took skill and courage, and Unitas used both to become the greatest quarterback who ever played the game."[9]

Johnny Unitas was not one to go around bragging that he was the best, but deep inside, knowing how the flame burned, how proud and confident he was, surely he believed it.

CHAPTER 23 • Joe Namath and the AFL

Until the T-formation swept the National Football League, the quarterback was not even the glamour player in the lineup. Once the quarterback became the focal point of the offense, the stature of the man with the powerful arm would grow in prominence.

Sammy Baugh helped make the quarterback a star. Sid Luckman did, too. More college players graduated to the NFL and became standouts. But until Joe Namath joined the New York Jets and earned the nickname "Broadway Joe," the quarterback was still a bit more like the other guys than not. Certainly, Johnny Unitas always viewed himself as more teammate than individual icon.

Namath introduced the era of the quarterback as celebrity, an athlete transcending his sport altogether, a hipster in tune with the times and habits of society at large. Namath stood out not only because he was a talented football leader but also because he enjoyed standing out.

Joe Willie Namath wore white football shoes. That alone should have told people he was a different type of cat. He grew his hair long, more in line with hippie style than the flat-top military style favored by many older players, Unitas included, if not Unitas especially. His name appeared in the gossip columns of New York tabloids, not that he minded. Namath realized he played football in the media capital of the universe, and he didn't mind cooperating with the media.

Namath was portrayed as the most eligible bachelor around, and in the

1960s, the decade of free love, he seemed to be a willing participant in that loosening of social mores. It was a big deal when Namath in 1965 signed a New York Jets contract for four hundred thousand dollars, making him the highest-paid football player, which helped make him not only the face of the franchise but the face of the upstart American Football League.

As far back as the 1920s, the National Football League had been challenged by a competing league. The NFL wasn't even yet on sound footing when the first American Football League was formed. That was a by-product of Red Grange teaming up with promoter C. C. Pyle on his grand tour of America.

After Grange participated in that swing around the hinterlands with the Chicago Bears, owner George Halas wanted to sign him for good. But Pyle thought Grange was worth more money than Halas was offering, which wasn't particularly surprising, since Halas wasn't typically generous to the stars he already had under contract.

So the original AFL was created as a showcase for Grange. The organization played out one season in 1926 with nine teams. Grange competed for a team known as the New York Yankees, a club that hoped the popularity of the baseball team would rub off. It did not.

Periodically, optimists with deep pockets (though rarely deep enough) pulled together a coordinated act to thrust a new league in the NFL's face. Typically, owners of these teams were rich enough to be members of the NFL's exclusive club but were spurned because the league was not interested in expansion at the time.

The All-America Football Conference was a genuine challenger when it began play in 1946. The idea for the establishment of the league came from Arch Ward, the sports editor of the *Chicago Tribune*, who also drove the creation of baseball's All-Star Game and the annual college-pro football charity game. Ward's record was pretty good.

Initially, NFL leaders did not take the AAFC seriously. NFL commissioner Elmer Layden, a member of the Notre Dame "four horsemen" backfield in the 1920s, scorned the other league when he learned of Ward's plan in 1944. Layden advised the AAFC to "first get a ball, then make a schedule, and then play a game."[1]

He was not alone. George Preston Marshall, who always had to say something loudly, and frequently offensively, had the same kind of harsh thoughts. "I did not realize there was another league, although I did receive some literature telling about a WPA [Works Progress Administration] project," Marshall said with sarcasm.[2] He just figured the NFL would run the other guys out of business in short order. Later, Marshall said, "The worst team in our league could beat the best team in theirs."[3] That must have made him the most surprised guy around when the Browns would whip the league's best come 1950.

The AAFC ceased to exist as an entity in 1949. However, that league spawned the Cleveland Browns with famed quarterback Otto Graham. Other teams were good enough and played in solid enough markets to be absorbed by the NFL.

The second American Football League began play in 1960. There were eight teams, and most of them had serious money men as backers, businessmen of note who wanted in to the NFL, especially oil man Lamar Hunt. These owners were not happy to be rebuffed and were not patient enough to wait for potential expansion teams to be awarded. Hunt was the biggest mover and shaker. The NFL actually told him it had no place for him.

"The idea just hit me while I was flying home from my last attempt to buy the Cardinals," Hunt said. "I knew that other cities were interested in getting pro football teams and I decided the answer had to be a new league."[4]

So the new league began—with the Boston Patriots, Buffalo Bills, Dallas Texans, Denver Broncos, Houston Oilers, Los Angeles Chargers, New York Titans, and Oakland Raiders. Fifty-seven years later all of those teams are still around: Boston became New England, the Titans became the Jets, the Oilers moved to Tennessee, and the Chargers moved to San Diego (but ultimately moved back to Los Angeles).

Only eleven years had elapsed since the demise of the AAFC. Some NFL old-timers like George Halas, who had lived through that uncomfortable period of competition, were wary of these newcomers. The AFL had a few things in its favor compared to previous leagues that had taken a shot at the NFL. While this did not apply to all owners, most of them were rich enough to sustain financial losses for a while. The league was formed right after the Baltimore Colts–New York Giants sudden-death 1958 championship game that demonstrated a large public appetite for televised professional football. The AFL was kept afloat by its own TV contract. Also, the AFL seemed determine to play a more exciting brand of football.

To a large extent, especially with the flagship Green Bay Packers at the time, the NFL was still ground-bound. AFL teams took to the air, no team with more enthusiasm than the Chargers under Sid Gillman. Gillman believed in throwing deep and deeper, and some called him "The Father of the Passing Game." Al Davis, the Hall of Fame Raiders leader, hung that nickname on him as a compliment. Perhaps the nickname should be amended to apply it to only the modern era of passing, given the decades of throwing history featuring Benny Friedman, Sammy Baugh, Sid Luckman, and the others.

Gillman was born in Minnesota in 1911. He had an extensive coaching background in college, then was head coach of the Rams in the 1950s and the boss of the Chargers from 1960 to 1971.

"Sid Gillman is still the father of the modern-day passing game at all levels of football: the National Football League, collegiate football, high school football, and even down to Pop Warner," said Ron Jaworski, a quarterback who played for Gillman for three seasons but was also an esteemed analyst for ESPN. "The concepts that he developed are still being used at every level of football."[5]

Jack Kemp was the first notable quarterback for the Chargers under Gillman. He was followed by John Hadl. The 1963 Chargers blasted the Patriots in the AFL title game, 51-10. Veteran Tobin Rote was the backup that year. Of course, Hadl had Lance Alworth to throw to, perhaps the finest receiver during the AFL heyday. Alworth was built to go long. Gillman wanted his throwers to find him, and they did.

"We had the master of offense, what I think was the early West Coast offense," Alworth said, "that Sid Gillman designed and put into play." Alworth had high praise for Hadl. "It really helps the receiver knowing that the quarterback knows exactly what's going to happen and when it's going to happen and he can adjust if necessary and still get the ball to you."[6]

Alworth also had a theory about receivers. He believed pass catchers were born, not made. He apparently did not know Raymond Berry, but that's what Alworth felt. "If a man can catch the ball, he can catch it, and that's all there is to it," he said. "Coaching may make him a little better, but not much. It's born to a person. It's innate."[7]

The Chargers were not the only AFL team that could throw and wanted to make a splash that way. George Blanda, one of the most remarkable players in pro football history, surfaced as quarterback of the Houston

Oilers in 1960 after Halas ill-advisedly treated him poorly and failed to recognize his skills. Blanda ended up playing pro ball between 1949 and 1975, not retiring until he was forty-eight years old. He scored more than 2,000 points, mostly as a kicker; forty-two years after his eventual retirement, Blanda still ranked seventh on the NFL's all-time points list. In 1961 Blanda threw for a record 36 touchdowns (before Y. A. Tittle did so in 1963) and gained 3,330 yards passing.

Blanda kept playing long after what was the accepted norm. As he aged he enhanced his reputation as one of the most successful clutch players in NFL history. When Blanda died, his *New York Times* obituary quoted the *Sporting News* on his legend. "He never got older. He just got better. He was the epitome of the grizzled veteran, the symbol of everlasting youth."[8]

During Blanda's big 1961 season, receiver Charlie Hennigan caught 82 of Blanda's passes for an impressive 1,746 yards, or a 21.3-yard-per-catch average. In 1964 Hennigan caught 101 passes. That was even outdoing Don Hutson.

Meanwhile, Lionel Taylor, wearing the fashion-objectionable striped socks of the Denver Broncos, caught 92 passes in 1960 and 100 in 1961, and for six years in a row caught no fewer than 76 passes in a season. Frank Tripucka, a Notre Dame grad who had been playing professional football since 1949, was the man at the front end of those throws. He topped 3,000 yards in the AFL's first year. He heaved 24 touchdown passes but also an unfathomable 34 interceptions, not as much of a concern back then.

Gillman, as he had for years, led the way with setting a passing tone for the AFL, but the entire atmosphere was different. To the new guys, the NFL was old, established, and stodgy. The minds calling the plays in the AFL might have been more agile or felt less restricted. Bombs away! Go for it! Those were themes of the new league.

All of this led up to Namath parachuting into the upstart AFL. Namath was born in 1943 in Beaver Falls, Pennsylvania. Western Pennsylvania has been called the cradle of quarterbacks because the coal country produced so many of them. Among those spawned in that region were passers such as Dan Marino, Joe Montana, Unitas, many other non–Hall of Fame pros, as well as Namath.

Namath went to college at the University of Alabama and played for legendary coach Paul "Bear" Bryant. The Crimson Tide won a national championship in 1964, Namath's senior year. Even before he graduated, however, Namath had right knee problems. Later, during his pro career, Namath would be almost as famous for his weak knees as for his strong arm.

The Jets took Namath with their first-round pick, which happened to be the overall number-one pick of the AFL. The Jets had been the woebegone Titans during the early years of the league and under different ownership. The new owner was Sonny Werblin, who also spent time as chairman of Madison Square Garden, but more prominently was a figure in the entertainment world spotting and managing talented performers.

By offering Namath $427,000 coming out of college, Werblin was pretty much doing what he always had done, albeit in the sports world. The interesting thing about Namath's negotiations with the Jets was that he did not begin his professional life thinking he would collect anywhere near that much money. When Namath's college eligibility was up, the Jets made him their top pick in the draft. But the St. Louis Cardinals of the NFL also drafted him. Before Namath spoke to any representative from any team, he consulted with Bear Bryant and an attorney. They quizzed him about how much money he was going to ask for. He said $100,000, but Bryant told him to aim higher and ask for $200,000.

The Cardinals got to Namath first, and he asked their guys for $200,000 and a new car. They seemed taken aback at first, but then agreed if he signed right away. Namath demurred, saying he hadn't talked to the Jets yet. Namath promptly reported on the talks to Bryant, who said, "They went for it, huh? Well, you got something pretty good going. You've got to talk to the Jets now."[9]

That seemed like a good idea, and that's what Namath did. When he and Werblin began talking business, the owner offered $300,000. Namath was shocked. He said the money was getting so big he was overwhelmed, but he still told Werblin he couldn't take any step without first discussing it with his lawyer. Negotiations continued, but now Namath's attorney, Mike Bite, was heavily involved. Bite got the Jets and the Cardinals to keep bidding. Bite's comment to Namath was, "Just like blowing in a balloon. You got to go as far as you can without breaking it."[10]

The final deal called for $427,000 over three years, although it was most commonly reported as $400,000. Werblin encouraged use of the catchy phrase, "The $400,000 Quarterback." A Lincoln Continental was part of the action, and the contract included a no-trade clause and a no-cut clause.

The big-money, high-profile signing was a statement by the American Football League that it was in the game to stay and that it could afford to pay top dollar for new talent. The contract made history at the time, but the impact of Namath choosing the AFL over the NFL was more significant over the long run. It helped further establish the league as the rumblings of a potential merger began.

As a player, Namath was a five-time Pro Bowl selection. It probably would have been more, but as often as not Namath had to hobble along in the pocket, mobility ruined by perpetual knee woes. When he was sound, though, he was very, very good. In 1967, when Namath completed a league-leading 258 passes while throwing nearly 500 of them and completing 26 for touchdowns, he became the first quarterback in history to pass for more than 4,000 yards in one season. He hit 4,007 that year.

It did not hurt that one of Namath's targets was Hall of Famer Don Maynard, who scored 88 touchdowns in his career, was the first receiver to surpass 10,000 yards, and retired with 633 receptions. "I don't look at it like I'm the greatest receiver," Maynard said, although he definitely was high on the list. "After you play a while, anybody can break certain records. Longevity is the key. The record I'm proudest of is being the first guy to get 10,000 yards in receptions. Others may do it, but I'm the first, and only one guy can be the first."[11]

His dashing good looks, his derring-do on the field, his big contract, and the publicity received for squiring around babes, Namath's biggest claim to fame—and once again, the immeasurable value it brought to the AFL—was what he did before and during Super Bowl III.

The game was played on January 12, 1969, at the Orange Bowl in Miami. The Jets were the AFL champs, matched up against the Baltimore Colts, a team regarded as one of the greatest on the NFL side. The Colts were an 18-point favorite, but Namath shrugged at the odds and created a sensation in the days before the game by not only predicting New York would win, but guaranteeing it.

By then a merger of the two leagues was set to go into effect in 1970, ending a decade's worth of strife and skyrocketing salaries. As a preliminary step, the champions of each of the leagues had been playing for a larger title for two years at that point. Both times, the Vince Lombardi–led Green Bay Packers, with Bart Starr at quarterback, dominated the opponent from the AFL. In Super Bowl I (although it hadn't acquired a Roman numeral yet), the Packers clobbered the Kansas City Chiefs, 35-10. In Super Bowl II, the Packers handled the Oakland Raiders, 33-14.

Many football fans believed that the Jets–Colts result would be similar, with the old-line team finishing way ahead. Many of those same fans were not relishing the merger because they thought the AFL was inferior and that the newer league's teams would water down the quality of play.

Namath was 50 percent surer of victory than confidence would allow. He was positively chortling that his Jets could control the Colts and beat them. Of all Namath's accomplishments, the manner in which he spoke up for his team and then led it on the field was both his most famous and finest hour.

For starters, only a day after the Jets defeated the Raiders for the AFL crown and the right to advance to Miami, a friend of his told him the point spread at that moment was 18. "Hell, that's crazy," Namath said. "We should only be favored by 9 or 10."[12] Namath said he was kidding about that, but he never thought the Colts should have been made big favorites. "I couldn't believe anyone would be dumb enough to give us 17 points," he said.[13]

Once the Jets knew who their opponent would be, they did what teams do now as well: they studied film. Namath liked what he saw of the Colts' defense. He picked up some tendencies, and while Baltimore had a reputation as a first-rate blitzing team, Namath saw those defenders being successful because of a lack of adjustments by other NFL teams. "I just prayed that the Colts would blitz us," Namath said. "If they did, I figured they were dead. Our backs are just the best there are at picking up the blitz."[14] He cited Matt Snell's, Bill Mathis's, and Emerson Boozer's talent for doing so.

Namath—who, as always, needed knee treatment in Florida leading up to the Super Bowl—was invited to a luncheon to accept an award at the Miami Touchdown Club and speak. There he uttered one of the most famous comments in football history: "We're going to win Sunday. I'll guarantee you."[15]

Namath's remarks created a bit of a frenzy. Up until then, just about nobody in sports history ran around predicting triumphs, except for heavyweight fighter Muhammad Ali, who was often criticized for doing so. Namath did not shy away from his beliefs that had been formed by film study. "I was just telling those people the truth," Namath said.[16]

Not many other football people outside the Jets' locker room believed that Namath knew what he was talking about. But he did. He was a big talker, but he backed it up. By the end of the first quarter, people were pondering what Namath had said. The score was 0-0, which in itself was a surprise. The Jets' defense had blocked the Colts at every turn.

At 9:03 of the second period the Jets went ahead, 7-0, on a 4-yard run by Snell and a Jim Turner extra point. That was the halftime score, and the buzz was strong as people wondered what was wrong with the Colts. It was as if the Jets led 30-0.

New York added six more points in the third quarter as Turner hit field goals of 32 and 30 yards. Still, the Colts could not get on the scoreboard, and the Jets led 13-0 after three periods. Again in the fourth, Turner booted a field goal, this one traveling 9 yards. With barely more than three minutes left in the game, the Colts finally scored. Jerry Hill broke into the end zone on a 1-yard run, Lou Michaels kicked the extra point, and that was it. The Jets won, 16-7.

It was an efficient performance for New York. The Jets notched more first downs than the Colts. The Jets outgained Baltimore through the air, with Namath completing 17 of 28 passes (Babe Parilli was 0 for 1) and Baltimore's Earl Morrall and Johnny Unitas going a combined 17 for 41. Snell rushed for 121 yards. George Sauer caught eight passes, but Maynard did not catch any. He was playing with an injured knee and spent the game as a decoy.

The Colts intended to make Namath eat his words. They failed, and Namath grinned ear to ear. "The only thing that really upset me all day was that, after the game was over and we'd won, 16-7, we didn't have any champagne in our locker room," Namath said.[17]

The reason? AFL higher-ups didn't want the players to be shown drinking on television. Namath said he got his celebratory drinks in later—Johnnie Walker Red.

Namath was already widely known, but his guarantee and victory increased his Q rating, public visibility, and popularity probably tenfold. Now everybody across the land knew Broadway Joe.

CHAPTER 24 • COACH BAUGH

When Sammy Baugh was playing for the Washington Redskins between 1937 and 1952, as soon as each season ended, he promptly fled Washington for Texas. Hollywood notwithstanding, Baugh rarely left his ranch.

Baugh loved having his own property, his own ranch, and he had no wanderlust beyond Texas's borders. He figured out a way to stay in football and close by when he accepted an assistant coaching job at Hardin-Simmons University. The school is located in Abilene, Texas, in Baugh's part of the state.

That job lasted a few seasons, and five years after he left pro football, Baugh received an intriguing offer to become the head coach at Hardin-Simmons. Appropriately enough, the school nickname is the Cowboys, and by then it could be said that rancher Baugh really was a cowboy.

Baugh's old friend and neighbor Bulldog Turner played his college ball at Hardin-Simmons and gained his first fame competing for the school. Turner is a member of the university's Hall of Fame.

Baugh became head coach for the 1955 season and led the purple and gold to a 5-5 record. The Cowboys never showed much improvement during Baugh's five seasons in charge. During the next four years Hardin-Simmons went 4-6, 5-5, 6-5, and 3-7. Mixed in was a Sun Bowl invitation in 1958, but that was a loss. While Hardin-Simmons was a Baptist school of about fifteen hundred students, the school scheduled over its head because it had a big name in Baugh at the helm.

After the losing year in 1959, Baugh was finished with the Hardin-Simmons Cowboys. However, another opportunity beckoned. In 1960 the American Football League began play, and Baugh was hired by the New York Titans and owner Harry Wismer. The team finished 7-7, in second place in the AFL East.

Wismer had been a star high school athlete in Michigan, played college football at both Florida and Michigan State, had a solid broadcasting career, and had been a part owner of the Washington Redskins and Detroit Lions. He was the majority owner of the Titans as the AFL prepared to launch, and he also was behind the plan for the new league to share broadcast revenue equally. Without that proviso, the AFL might not have survived the decade until the full NFL merger.

In December 1959, soon after the conclusion of Baugh's final season at Hardin-Simmons, Wismer offered Baugh the job as head coach of the Titans. Wismer had been searching for a big name he wished to exploit in the New York media market and had nearly hired others before his roulette wheel stopped on Baugh.

When Wismer summoned the sportswriters and broadcasters on December 18, it was with a teaser: "One of the biggest names in the history of football will be announced as the head coach of the New York Titans."[1] Baugh was his man, and it was no surprise that when he thought of offense as a head man, he thought of passing first and running second. The Titans averaged 27.3 points per game, the highest-scoring outfit in the league. However, the Titans also gave up 28.5 points per game, the league's worst defensive mark.

Fittingly, Baugh did have a quarterback who could throw in Al Dorow. Dorow completed 201 passes for 2,748 yards and 26 touchdowns. Dorow was thirty-one years old at the time with a sound background. He played college ball at Michigan State and had been in the pros since 1954, playing for the Redskins (he missed Baugh by a couple of years), the Philadelphia Eagles, and the British Columbia Lions of the Canadian Football League.

Baugh was a players' coach in that he was no gruff hardliner. He did not blame the Titans for their mistakes. He looked upon them as adults trying to do a job and taking responsibility for their actions. He was not a screamer on the sidelines. "I never liked to chew on anybody if they made a mistake," Baugh said. "I've made too damn many myself. I was taught at TCU to never chew one of your players out if he misses a ball, misses a block, misses a tackle. As long as he's doing the best he can do, that's all you can ask. That's how I feel about it today."[2]

By most football coaching standards, where the head coach wanted to show everyone who's boss, Baugh's approach made him a laissez-faire guy. Being an all-time great also put Baugh into the category of an all-star who may have expected too much automatic reaction from his players to situations. He was not a teacher.

Tackle Buddy Cockrell compared Baugh the coach to such other successful pro coaches as Paul Brown and Weeb Ewbank. "Sam knew more football than all of them," Cockrell said. "His problem was that he knew football so well, knew what every defensive man's reaction should be on every play, that he had a problem getting it across to players. He assumed everyone knew what he did."[3]

When Baugh's early players, and other early AFL players, spoke about him, they complimented his knowledge of offensive play. You didn't hear many raving about his defensive savvy, but no one was surprised that the Titans led the league in points scored. "Sammy could draw better plays in the dirt than most coaches could draw on the board," said star linebacker Larry Grantham.[4]

Quarterback Cotton Davidson never played for Baugh in New York, but he was the starter for the Dallas Texans in 1960 and had a long pro career. He admired Baugh's sharpness from afar. "Offensively, I don't know too many people who had a better mind than he did," Davidson said.[5]

There was no doubt Dorow had material to work with when he faded back. Don Maynard, the Hall of Fame receiver just coming into his own, caught 72 passes for 1,265 yards in 1960, and young Art Powell caught 69 passes for 1,167 yards. Having two guys on the same team accumulate so many yards through the air was virtually unheard of at that time.

The Titans played their home games at the old Polo Grounds, which only a few years earlier had been abandoned by the New York Giants baseball team when it moved to San Francisco. The Titans had their moments, starting 3-1. They hit a rough patch in mid-season, dropping four straight games. But they entered the final regular-season game at 7-6 with a chance for a winning record before losing to the Los Angeles Chargers, 50-43, on the road.

That 0-4 stretch irritated Baugh. For once, out of character, he really gave it to the players about how lousy they were playing. Linebacker

Roger Ellis maintained a vivid memory of that harangue. "He spent an hour and basically went around the room and chewed our ass," Ellis said. "He told the prima donnas who they were in front of everyone. He ripped every one of the 35 guys."[6]

Dorow had been around some and seen a lot. He was pleased to be the starter and happy to be a quarterback for the great Sammy Baugh, especially since Baugh let him call his own plays. It would have been difficult to see Baugh sending in signals from the sidelines. He would have resented it as a player, and given his personality he was no martinet control freak. In Dorow, Baugh had a man he could trust and who appreciated being given the responsibility. "That's why I play," Dorow said. "There is much more satisfaction to me in making a good call on third-down, 2-to-go situation and fooling some linebacker than throwing a 60-yard touchdown pass. This is a brain game."[7]

Just as the Titans had in 1960, they finished 7-7 in 1961. They were 7-5 with two games to go and lost both. Dorow was again the quarterback, and while he played most all downs, his efficiency declined a bit. He completed just 45 percent of his passes, as compared to 50 percent the year before, for 2,651 yards and 19 touchdowns. He also threw 30 interceptions. Powell caught 71 passes, but his yardage total dipped to 881, and Maynard caught just 43 passes. The Titans needed a break and couldn't buy one.

Two years into league play, the AFL was still at war with the NFL, with one area of contention being the player draft. The Titans made some good choices in 1961, but they lost out on some fine players who decided on the NFL. Those included second-round pick Herb Adderley, who starred at defensive back for the Green Bay Packers; third-round pick Tom Matte, who became an indispensable player for the Baltimore Colts; and fourth-round pick Bill Brown, who emerged as an excellent fullback for the Minnesota Vikings.

Receiver Bernie Casey, the ninth-round choice, went for the San Francisco 49ers. Tenth-round pick Joe Scibelli spent fifteen seasons playing offensive line for the Los Angeles Rams. Defensive back Irv Cross, the fifteenth pick, chose the Philadelphia Eagles. And seventeenth-round pick, offensive lineman Mike Pyle, hooked up with the Chicago Bears. With the twenty-eighth-round pick, the Titans selected Fred Cox out of the University of Pittsburgh, who went on to score 1,365 points as a kicker for the Vikings. Also, New York's number-one draft pick was Tom Brown, the winner of the Outland Trophy as the best lineman in the country, of the University of Minnesota. Brown did not even play in the NFL but spent his entire pro career in the 1960s with the British Columbia Lions and was inducted into the Canadian Football Hall of Fame.

That was one draft! What a team the Titans would have had with the influx of all of those players at once. But none of those guys helped out Baugh.

Harry Wismer was not an easy man to get along with when he believed his team should be playing better ball and moving up in the standings. He and Baugh saw their relationship become testy. Wismer wanted Baugh gone after the second 7-7 season, but he had a problem. He had signed Baugh to a three-year contract and didn't want to pay him to go away. What he really wanted was for Baugh to resign so that Wismer wouldn't have to fulfill the third season in the deal. At stake was twenty thousand dollars.

Baugh was honest to a fault, which meant he wasn't as discreet as he should have been when sportswriters asked questions. If he felt Wismer was hindering progress, he said so. That steamed Wismer.

"He tells me he's unhappy about some of the things I've been doing," Wismer said. "Well, if anybody is unhappy with his job, there's a simple way of taking care of that—quit. I'm paying him $20,000 to be disloyal. That's a fine situation, isn't it?"[8]

During the period when Wismer and Baugh were slinging barbs, Wismer came up with an idea for how Baugh could earn his salary with the Titans. Wismer had already decided to make Bulldog Turner, of all people, his next coach, but Wismer suggested Baugh stick around the staff as assistant backfield coach. Not surprisingly, the thought did not resonate with Baugh. "I'd rather be a ticket taker," Baugh said.[9]

More oddly, although Turner did know it when he accepted twenty thousand dollars to become head coach for the 1962 season, Baugh was still on the payroll. Turner and Baugh went way back, and Turner felt the awkwardness of the situation as talk turned to Baugh sticking around as a consultant. "I have the highest respect for Baugh and will welcome any help he can give me," Turner said. "We will go over our player personnel as soon as possible and start making plans for 1962. I don't know how he feels about it, though."[10]

The sniping between Wismer and Baugh continued. Wismer told sportswriters that Turner had been his first choice for a coach back in

1960 and Baugh had been only his fourth choice. Baugh fired back. “Wismer makes a big fuss over name players,” Baugh said. “He puts out publicity about the big money he’s going to pay them. And while we’re fooling around with the big names, the NFL is picking off the top players which we had a chance of signing.”[11] Perhaps he was thinking of that draft when so many good players were on the Titans draft list but ended up signing elsewhere.

At last, in July 1962 Baugh and Wismer brokered a peace treaty. They met the press as friends. Wismer agreed to pay Baugh twenty thousand dollars for the third season of his contract. Baugh was going to be an adviser and a kicking coach.

“I think the world of Sammy, so this is the way to do it,” Wismer said. “We’re both good friends. He’ll be paid in full for the remaining year of his contract.” Baugh responded, “I think the world of Harry. I’ll take it. Harry gave me my chance to coach in pro football. The Titans are going to have a heck of a ball club this season.”[12]

Baugh did not rule out seeking another pro coaching job, but he and Wismer said they agreed he would be paid for this year no matter what happened. “I may even make him a director of the club,” Wismer said. “If he gets a job, God bless him. In fact, I’ll do anything I can to help him land one.”[13] The lovey-dovey scene was almost as bizarre as the insults that had flung back and forth in the months preceding it.

If Baugh knew anything about kicking, it was punting, but that was not a role that would engage much of his time and he knew it. “I will be mighty happy teaching boys how to kick for $20,000 a year,” he said.[14]

The kickers did not make much of a difference for Turner during the 1962 season. New York finished 5-9.

Baugh got his money, but the Titans were a failing business. Their attendance was low from the beginning and never got better. The Titans drew just ten thousand fans to their first real game. Only twice during the 1960 season did New York, a franchise the other NFL owners hoped would be a flagship operation, draw more than twenty thousand fans to a game. Wismer was looking for investors and couldn’t find any.

By the 1963 season Turner was gone, replaced by Weeb Ewbank, the championship coach from Baltimore. The Titans name was gone, changed to the Jets. And Wismer was gone. A five-man business group bought the club for $1 million with Sonny Werblin as the lead owner.

Baugh's connection with the New York AFL team was severed, but he left a mark on those he coached as a fair man worthy of admiration. "Sammy is one of the nicest gentlemen I have ever met in my life," said Thurlow Cooper, an end out of the University of Maine. "That's why he didn't last. He was just too nice a guy to be a pro coach."[15]

Backup quarterback Dick Jamieson expressed fondness for Baugh. "Most of us loved the guy," he said. "He held the team together in spite of a lot of tough things that happened to us."[16]

Not everybody loved Wismer, including Baugh, who later clarified his feelings about the owner. His comments did not match what was said in the press conference announcing he was getting his third year of pay, despite being put out to pasture with his cows.

"Harry was one of those guys who seemed to go out of his way to be his own worst enemy," Baugh said. "He was always coming into the dressing room trying to give us a pep talk that nobody ever listened to. It was embarrassing just to be around him, and before long a lot of people started hating him."[17]

It should also be said that Baugh was a mismatch for New York. He didn't spend any time in the city when he wasn't actually coaching, and he alienated Wismer by refusing to make public appearances to sell the team to prospective fans.

Baugh spent one season as an assistant coach at Oklahoma State in 1962 and one year at Tulsa in 1963. That year the Pro Football Hall of Fame opened in Canton, Ohio, and Baugh was chosen as a member of the first class. Baugh did not really even want to leave Texas for that induction ceremony. But Baugh went to Canton. In his induction speech he spent much of his time praising the owners who stuck with pro football when it was on shaky financial footing as pioneers who deserved credit more than players like him.

Even in 1963, football experts recognized the special role Baugh played in the evolution of the forward pass. When the Hall of Fame produced its first profile of him, part of the content read that he was a "premier passer. Obviously, such a change emphasizing the pass could not be brought about by one individual. But Baugh was the catalyst that changed the game. No one had seen a passer who could throw with such accuracy."[18]

A year later Baugh was back at the helm of a pro football team: the Houston Oilers. He might have coached the Oilers forever if he hadn't had to travel to away games outside the state. Houston finished 4-10. That season provided a one-year pairing of Baugh and George Blanda, two Hall of Fame quarterbacks working together.

It was a time of change in pro ball, with the AFL forcing the NFL to spend more money and the AFL playing a more wide-open style with more passing. Blanda's career dated to the 1940s, before Baugh retired, and when he was with the Bears as backup quarterback, he recalled playing some time on defense, as well as kicking. In this 1960s' era of increasing specialization, Blanda said teams needed to have three quarterbacks on the roster in case of injuries.

In 1964, his lone AFL year with Baugh, Blanda attempted 505 passes and completed 262 of them, both statistics career highs. He also threw for 3,287 yards and 19 touchdowns—at age thirty-seven.

In 1966, when even Baugh probably thought he would never coach in the NFL again, he joined the Detroit Lions as an assistant coach for his old Redskins teammate and quarterback successor Harry Gilmer. Baugh's deal called for six months of work.

After that fling, Baugh returned to his beloved ranch, not anxious to ever again step foot outside of Texas. He rarely did again.

CHAPTER 25 • Brett Favre and the New World

The numbers at the position of quarterback recorded by Brett Favre—and others—in the decades after Sammy Baugh retired would have astounded him. They are mind-boggling. It would have taken Baugh thirty years to match them. Each year, it seemed, as the 1960s matured into the 1970s, 1980s, 1990s, and then into the twenty-first century, quarterbacks became more and more important and their arms more and more treasured.

They were all men with golden arms, capable of throwing passes 70 yards in the air, of threading the needle to receivers in double coverage, of throwing 30, 40, or more touchdown passes every season.

Baugh played when the forward pass was evolving, but it became part of a full-fledged revolution. There was no longer any such thing as passing too much during a game. Seasons of more than 100 catches for wide receivers, and even running backs, became commonplace. Quarterbacks began using the pass the way older offenses used to employ the run. Instead of three yards and a cloud of dust being run three downs in a row, quarterbacks threw 5-yard passes to inch their way down the field on drives. Instead of softening up defenses with fullbacks pounding up the middle, the fullback was almost eliminated from the offense, turned into just another blocker. The old T-formation notion of three running backs lined up behind the quarterback crossing that T vanished.

Receivers flooded downfield zones, and innovations such as the West

Coast offense, which called for those shorter touch passes to advance the ball more than the long bombs, came into vogue. Taking the thoughts of Sid Gillman a bit further, another Chargers coach, Don Coryell, loosed the original West Coast offense. His throw, throw, and throw game plans became known as "Air Coryell."

Relying on the arm of Dan Fouts, the Chargers led the NFL in passing for six seasons in a row between 1978 and 1983 and, after a year off, once again in 1985. The Chargers passed so successfully that Fouts and receivers Kellen Winslow and Charlie Joiner would end up in the Pro Football Hall of Fame. Coryell actually introduced this daring offense with the St. Louis Cardinals first in the mid-1970s and then brought it with him to San Diego. Gillman introduced the notion that the offense should really spread out the defense and make opposing defenses cover the entire field. Coryell built upon that theory. One of Coryell's innovations was putting his receivers in motion so that defenders at the line of scrimmage could not hit them to slow down their patterns.

Coryell also used his tight end, mostly Winslow, in much the same manner as his wide receivers. Starting in the 1960s with Mike Ditka of the Chicago Bears, the tight end was often kept busier catching the ball than he had ever been. Coryell expanded on that as well. Less a blocker and more of a player relied on for good hands, the tight end's job grew in the West Coast offense. Coaches who had the personnel to send multiple receivers downfield became Coryell disciples.

Bill Walsh, the Hall of Fame coach for the Cincinnati Bengals and most prominently with the San Francisco 49ers, actually was developing his West Coast offense as an assistant coach with Cincinnati while Coryell was still coaching in college. When Walsh took over the 49ers in 1979, Coryell was already throwing like a madman. It took a couple of years for Walsh to implement the offense with the 49ers as the club matured into Super Bowl champions.

The full-fledged embracing of this offense as run by Coryell and Walsh transformed football. As others sought to emulate their success, more quarterbacks were given the freedom to throw and more receivers were needed to run the routes. By 2010 or so, the running game was clearly eclipsed as the most important offensive facet of the game. Modern players were the most prolific receivers on NFL all-time leader charts, from most catches, to most yards gained, to most touchdown passes caught.

When Raymond Berry retired as a player in 1967, he held the record for most catches with 631. As of the 2016 season he ranked fifty-seventh on the list. The top thirteen men had caught at least 1,000 balls. Only two players in the top thirty retired before the year 2000: Art Monk and Steve Largent. As proof of how far ahead of his time he was, Don Hutson still ranked eleventh on the career touchdown receiving list, and he had been retired for more than seventy years. Only one player in the top ten—Largent, in ninth—retired before 2000. Basically, it was a new world out there for passers and pass catchers. Much of that can be attributed to the popularity of the West Coast offense, which put such a high premium on accurate throwers given a wide variety of possibilities as receivers.

More all-star-caliber quarterbacks than ever before were coming out of college, many of them so good they started their first season in the pros. The onetime concept that a quarterback had to serve a three-year apprenticeship evaporated. If a rookie was given the starting job and played like a rookie, everyone from the coaching staff to the media to the ticket-buying public wanted to know what was wrong. Careers were written off in a single season. Other careers were made in sixteen games.

There was no longer patience, nor any time, to wait for a quarterback to grow into the job. He was either ready-made or a benchwarmer. As rookies tend to be erratic, the same guy might be a star one week and then play a has-been type of game the next. It was no longer good enough for a quarterback to complete just 50 percent of his attempts; 60 percent was borderline acceptable. Throwing an interception was a mortal sin. Throwing two in one game practically got you benched and maybe forgotten.

Brett Favre was born in Gulfport, Mississippi, in 1969. He spent one season on the bench for the Atlanta Falcons after being drafted out of Southern Mississippi: in 1992 he became the starter for the Green Bay Packers. Favre completed 64.1 percent of his passes for 3,227 yards and 18 touchdowns as an inexperienced player. He got better from there, becoming a legend in northern Wisconsin.

Certain stories written about Sammy Baugh referred to him as a gunslinger because he was from Texas and because he threw on the run. Favre really was a gunslinger. He threw early and often, near and far, stationary and on the run. He took gambles and turned the risks into valuable payoffs.

Favre was a Mississippi country boy. He loved to hunt, hang out with friends and have a few beers, and was a friendly, fun-loving guy. He also had a gun for an arm, as anyone knew who saw him play football. Favre's vital stats were listed as 6-foot-2 and 225 pounds. He was not known as a fast runner, but he could complete long-range passes that other quarterbacks wouldn't even try.

The young player did have some hiccups in his early years, sometimes making his audience impatient because he threw too many interceptions, which had become almost a zero-tolerance error. But the Packers had committed to Favre when they acquired him, and Coach Mike Holmgren bolstered Favre's confidence whenever he was mentally down. "I had to tell him straight out that he was the guy," Holmgren said. "I didn't want him to worry about looking over his shoulder. I let him know that he and I were joined at the hip. I more or less said, 'Brett, if you go in the dumper, I'm going with you.'"[1]

That circumstance did not arise. Instead, Favre and Holmgren won a Super Bowl together.

Before that, there were some doubts about how well Favre could adjust to the pros from Southern Miss. He was selected for the East-West All-Star Game, and future Green Bay general manager Ron Wolf was more impressed with how Favre handled himself than with his statistics. He felt Favre possessed the intangibles of a winner.

"All I could think of is that about once a generation a quarterback comes along who has this particular quality," Wolf said, "and that's the ability to make it seem as if the whole field is tilting one way whenever he's out there."[2]

Ironically, Wolf was scouting for the New York Jets, his employer of the moment, and the Jets did not have a number-one draft pick. After Wolf became the Packers' general manager, he remembered Favre from those days and pulled the trigger on the trade with Atlanta.

"He had so many things you're looking for at the quarterback position," Wolf said. "He seemed to be a natural leader, a win-at-all-costs player. He had great skill and ability. It was just a matter of harnessing that talent. I thought he would be an outstanding player."[3]

That was one time a personnel executive got it right—actually, two times with one guy. Wolf saw the potential when he was with one team, and he found a way to obtain the player with a second team.

Favre–Green Bay was an interesting match of young player and building club. Holmgren even said he knew the Packers had to take chances and thought the best way to win was to obtain a big-time quarterback, and if it had to be a young, developing quarterback, that was okay, too.

If Baugh was a great offensive mind whose teammates thought he could get by drawing up plays in the dirt, Favre was the same type. He didn't bother to improvise in the dirt, but he had instincts and vision in his head. Holmgren wanted Favre to stick to the play plan. Favre didn't mind if a play fell apart and he had to try something else.

"Here's Mike from San Francisco and I'm from the Bayou," Favre said. "He's cultured and I'm country. He went to USC and I went to USM. He probably eats calamari and I eat crawfish. So coming from a background like that you know he thinks he's smarter than I am. He's a pretty sharp guy, but with me he's chasing a pretty fast rabbit and I'll always be just a little ahead."[4]

Favre played in the NFL from 1991 through 2010, most of that time with the Packers, in addition to that sit-on-the-bench year with the Falcons. He also spent one season with the New York Jets and two seasons with the Minnesota Vikings at the end of his career.

After twenty seasons in the pros, Favre retired with 508 touchdown passes, then a record. Nine times he threw for at least 30 touchdowns in a season, including 2009 when he was age forty. Favre also retired with a record 71,838 yards passing. He had six seasons of throwing for at least 4,000 yards, including a 1995 best of 4,413. Favre attempted 10,169 passes, including 613 in 2006. (In Baugh's sixteen seasons he attempted 2,995 passes.) Favre retired with the glitziest of records, but he came along during a golden era for quarterbacks.

During the bridge years, the football world was introduced to the creative Fran Tarkenton. He was built like the earlier guys, 6-foot tall and weighing 190 pounds. Tarkenton was known for his scrambling ability, his talent at eluding the rush and keeping plays alive. He played eighteen years, most of them with the Vikings, but in two stints wrapped around a five-year stay with the New York Giants.

In five of Tarkenton's last six seasons, he completed more than 60 percent of his passes, better than in any other single year of his career. He retired with 342 touchdown passes and 47,003 yards. Unusual as an athlete going out at the top of his game, Tarkenton led the NFL in pass attempts, with 345 completions and 3,468 yards during his last season. Tarkenton was also good for 300 yards or so rushing each year, although the plays seemed to unfold accidentally.

"I scramble because I'm good at it," Tarkenton said, "because I can twist and dodge those big pass rushers better than most guys and we get a lot of touchdowns that way. A quarterback has to maintain his cool while a 300-pound pass rusher is firing at him like a Sindwinder missile, and at the last second, before his feet get knocked out from under him, he has to stick that ball right on some receiver's left ear."[5]

The man who had held many of the passing records before Favre was Dan Marino. An All-American at the University of Pittsburgh, Marino was a local guy. He was drafted by the Miami Dolphins and moved into the lineup right away in 1983. A nine-time Pro Bowl selection, all with the Dolphins, Marino played with that one team his entire career, ending in 1999.

Marino threw for 61,361 yards and 420 touchdowns. In 1984, Marino's second season, he had a mind-boggling campaign, throwing for 5,084 yards and 48 touchdowns, both records at the time. He was just one season removed from being the nervous twenty-two-year-old rookie when he broke into the lineup. Marino was very edgy when he knew he was going to start against the Buffalo Bills.

"To be honest, I was a little nervous," he said. "I stood on the sidelines. I remember a veteran, a veteran safety coming up to me, Lyle Blackwood. He came up to me with a serious look and he shook my hand and said, 'Dan, good luck today. And I don't want you to feel any pressure, but remember this one thing: If you play bad, we'll lose.' Now that's pressure on a rookie."[6] And that's exactly what the pressure is like on a young quarterback, if not all of them, these days.

John Elway came out of Stanford and also broke in with the Denver Broncos in 1983, the same year as Marino. He played through the 1998 season and was also a nine-time Pro Bowl selection. He played at 6-foot-3 and 215 pounds—just like Marino, the prototype of the modern quarterback, bigger and stronger than the Baughs and Luckmans of the past.

Elway threw 300 touchdown passes over his career and gained 51,475 yards through the air. He led Denver to five Super Bowls and won two rings by capturing the title in his last two tries late in his career. He was elected to the Pro Football Hall of Fame and become executive vice president of football operations and general manager for the Broncos. "I think probably the thing I am most proud of is that I was able to hang in there long enough to win a couple of Super Bowls," Elway said.[7]

It seemed that just about every team found a quarterback good enough to be a Hall of Famer. Terry Bradshaw led the Pittsburgh Steelers to four Super Bowl crowns. Jim Kelly led the Buffalo Bills to four Super Bowls. Troy Aikman led the Dallas Cowboys to three Super Bowl titles. In addition to his passing wizardry, Steve Young, a seven-time Pro Bowl choice, was one of the greatest rushing quarterbacks of all time.

Young also somehow pushed Joe Montana out of San Francisco. Most view Montana as one the best quarterbacks ever. He led the 49ers to four Super Bowl crowns while being selected to eight Pro Bowls. Montana was a western Pennsylvania guy, Joe Namath territory, and starred at Notre Dame. He was listed on rosters at 6-foot-2 and 205 pounds. Montana was not known for his cannon of an arm, but his precision, his coolness in making comebacks, and making his team a winner.

Another Hall of Famer, Montana threw for 273 touchdown passes and 40,551 yards. He led the league in completion percentage five times, including in 1989 when his percentage was 70.2 percent. Montana's main target was Jerry Rice, the NFL's greatest receiver. Rice was a thirteen-time Pro Bowl invitee who scored 208 touchdowns, caught 1,549 passes, and gained 22,895 yards on receptions. In 1995 alone, Rice totaled 1,848 receiving yards. He and Montana—and then he and Young—made for deadly combinations.

It took only until Montana's second year for him to lead the NFL in pass completion percentage. Then he did it again the next year. In that way he was an immediate hit. But he was not a bombs-away guy. He was a more careful passer at first, and his work did not excite everyone immediately. "It took quite a while for Joe to get the kind of respect he deserved," said Ken MacAfee, a 49er teammate, "and I think it was something he used as a motivational tool."[8] Many great athletes, most notably basketball star Michael Jordan, were known for motivating themselves by interpreting a minor comment or even some accidental slight and using that as fuel.

Montana's other great partner in his success was San Francisco coach Bill Walsh, a creative-thinking, offensive-minded coach. Walsh's West Coast offense played upon Montana's strength of hitting the open man short to move the chains instead of counting so much on the running game.

Montana and Walsh were key figures in the 49ers' first Super Bowl victory in 1981. San Francisco topped the Cincinnati Bengals, 26-21. Montana was the game MVP after throwing one touchdown pass and scoring another touchdown on a run. After the game, Walsh said of Montana, "He's one of the coolest competitors of all time and he has just started. He will be the great quarterback of the future."[9]

Walsh was right. Montana was just starting. Soon he was admired for his accuracy, his proper touch on his throws, his ability to read defenses and change plays at the line of scrimmage, and his ability to play even better when the stakes were high and the pressure was most intense. When a team is trailing but still thinks it is in the game, or when a clutch play is imperative, that is when the best quarterbacks shine and when their teammates expect them to make magic. Johnny Unitas's Colts had that faith in him. Elway's Broncos always believed he would manufacture a last-minute drive. Montana had the same kind of command in the huddle, and his teammates always figured that if something could be done to save the day, Joe would do it. "Joe was just a natural leader," 49ers fullback Johnny Davis said. "He had a presence. You could feel it."[10]

As the years passed and Montana's achievements mounted, his stature increased. Not nearly as flamboyant as some of the NFL's top stars, and not nearly as talkative as Favre, Montana played the game with dignity and accumulated respect. The longer he played, the better the 49ers did, and the more successful he was in running up big numbers, Montana became a sort of icon within the sport without retiring. Of course, although it was an aside, Montana had a great name for a quarterback, too. If the name did not belong to a rodeo cowboy, then it was a darned fine thing that the possessor of the name was a hotshot quarterback. One thing Montana did not fit was the image of a cocky ringleader. Sometimes he was self-effacing to the extreme, almost too much so.

"I'm just an ordinary Joe," Montana said once. "I can't even throw that hard. I'm just fortunate to be in a great system surrounded by some great players. I just hope I'm worthy of this game."[11] If someone else had said that about Montana, he would have taken it as an insult and used it to light a fire the next time he played that talker's team. But Montana wouldn't lighten up much. He definitely was no ordinary Joe on the football field.

Montana was extraordinary, not ordinary, during the 1984 season. The 49ers won their third Super Bowl and finished 18-1. Montana had his usual stellar passing season, completing 64.6 percent of his passes for 3,630 yards and 28 touchdowns.

San Francisco met the Miami Dolphins in the Super Bowl. The game was billed as Marino versus Montana. Montana threw for 331 yards and three touchdowns and won the MVP award. Marino actually earned more of the pregame attention because that was his crazy-good season with 48 touchdowns and 5,000-plus yards. Miami came into the game at 16-2.

When the game was over and the 49ers were gazing victoriously at a 38-16 final score, Montana spoke up. "All week, all we heard was, 'Miami, Miami, Miami,'" Montana said. "What about us? That motivated the entire offense. It wasn't so much me against Dan. Our whole offense was overlooked the last two weeks."[12]

Montana's tenure in San Francisco ended strangely. Injuries played a role, as did the hovering presence of a younger Steve Young, aching to start and needing to start after waiting around as a backup. Montana exited to the Kansas City Chiefs for the last chapter of his career. He went out on top as a player, though not as a champion again, with an excellent performance for a thirty-eight-year-old quarterback. He completed over 60 percent of his passes that year for 3,283 yards.

In 2000 Montana was elected to the Hall of Fame. He was a young man by general standards and said he felt too young for the final step of his football career. Then he reanalyzed his opinion. "I had a very difficult time of it at the beginning," Montana said in his induction speech. "I don't think I was looking at it in the proper perspective. I felt like, well, I'm only forty-four years old. I feel like I'm being in my grave, in my coffin alive and they're throwing dirt on me. And I can feel it and I'm trying to get out. This is not an ending point. This is a beginning point. This is the beginning of the rest of my life with a new team. Take a look at these guys [other Hall of Famers]. What a team it is."[13]

CHAPTER 26 • Manning and Brady

If Sammy Baugh and Sid Luckman were the standout quarterbacks of their era, Peyton Manning and Tom Brady became the standard-bearers of the 2000s. They became legends in their own time, players who would each receive mention as possibly the greatest quarterback of all time.

In 2016 Manning, after playing a fourth season with the Denver Broncos following a long career with the Indianapolis Colts, retired just shy of age forty. He had surpassed some of Brett Favre's career records and went out as a Super Bowl champion. Much of his final season was interrupted by injuries, but Manning was in the lineup for the title game.

Brady is still a fixture with the New England Patriots, the leader of a club that has won five Super Bowls with his signal-calling. He is viewed as one of the sport's ultimate winners.

Brady's first season was 2000. He was only a sixth-round draft pick out of the University of Michigan, proving that not even the most astute scouts around the league know what they are doing all of the time. Brady began his Patriots career behind Drew Bledsoe, also an all-star. Brady was thrust into a starting position when Bledsoe was injured, and Brady never would relinquish the starting job. As of the end of the 2017 season Brady has been selected for thirteen Pro Bowls.

Peyton Manning, son of former New Orleans Saints quarterback Archie Manning and older brother of New York Giants quarterback Eli Manning, was an instant starter and star when he came out of the University of

Tennessee in 1998. Manning retired after the 2015 season as a fourteen-time Pro Bowl selection.

They were not lonely at the top either. On any given Sunday, players like Green Bay's Aaron Rodgers, successor to Brett Favre; the Pittsburgh Steelers' Ben Roethlisberger; and especially the Saints' Drew Brees might have a better day than anyone else. During the 2015 season, Brees had one game where he threw for 505 yards and seven touchdowns, tying Luckman's long-standing single-game touchdown pass record in a 52-49 victory over the Giants.

As of the end of the 2017 season, Brees had thrown for 70,445 yards and 488 touchdowns. Brees has already passed Brady in yards, and he is tied with him in touchdown tosses.

"One of the craziest games I've ever been a part of," is what Brees said of his seven-touchdown performance.[1] One reason it was so crazy was that Eli Manning threw six touchdown passes and for 350 yards and lost—on a 50-yard field goal. It should be remembered that Peyton Manning is one of the other partners in the seven-touchdown record.

Brady stands 6-foot-4 and weighs 225 pounds. He is an unflappable guy on the field, one of those cool leaders with the deep-seated belief that if he throws the ball in the air it should be caught. As he has improved, Brady has proven likely to go through an entire NFL sixteen-game regular season with a single-digit total of interceptions, even when attempting more than 600 passes.

Playing for an acknowledged whiz of a coach in Bill Belichick, as partners Belichick and Brady have in some ways made the Patriots a role-model franchise, even during the salary-cap era when players are often rented for a year and hardly ever stay with one team for an entire career.

Yet Brady has had to play musical receivers, with guys catching more than 100 balls from him in a year and then leaving the team for elsewhere, either by their choice or Belichick's. The Patriots just plug in fresh faces. Brady is so talented that as long as he is matched up with receivers that have half-decent hands, he can make them look good. And if he is teamed up with a genuine star receiver, look out.

Except for going 1-for-3 for his entire season output as a rookie in 2000 when he entered just one game, Brady has never had a season where he completed less than 60 percent of his passes. He is rapidly climbing the touchdown pass ladder and with 456 in his career and is tied with Brees.

Although Brees still likely has a few years to go, he has just one Super Bowl championship on his resume, fewer than either Brady or Manning.

In 2007 Brady had one of the greatest years ever for a professional quarterback. He threw for 50 touchdown passes, breaking Dan Marino's record of 48, and 4,806 yards. He completed 68.9 percent of his passes. As of the 2017 season, Brady had two regular-season MVP awards and four Super Bowl MVP awards among his accomplishments.

By early 2017, Brady had led the Patriots to seven Super Bowl appearances, and they had won five of them. Seventeen years into his career, Brady was accumulating the kinds of statistics that steadily moved him ahead of previous stars. Like Manning had and Brees was doing, Brady kept climbing the all-time lists. Brady has thrown for as many as 5,235 yards and three times has completed more than 400 passes in a season.

Once a decade of head-to-head play was in the books, and with the Patriots and Colts regularly fighting it out to be top dog in the American Football Conference, analysts and fans began raising the matter of who was better, Brady or Manning. Brady had more big wins. Manning had more overwhelming statistics and was on his way to the finest body of work in NFL history.

"I fear Tom Brady more than anybody," former New York Giant defender Michael Strahan said. "Tom Brady, there is just something about Tom, not taking anything away from Peyton Manning at all. I don't want to face him either. But there's just something about Tom. Maybe because we've seen him do it time and time again."[2]

Several years ago, when a magazine interviewer asked Brady why he was not the face of the NFL, he explained it by saying that football wasn't like pro basketball. He wasn't even on the field half the game because he didn't play defense (Sammy Baugh and Sid Luckman did!). "There's one guy whose game I love," Brady said.[3] He was talking about Peyton Manning.

One thing Brady became years into his career, besides reclusive, was a fanatic about exercise and nutrition. By taking care of his body to the utmost he hoped to play into his forties. He was forty years old for the 2017 season, and there certainly was no drop-off in performance. Brady, like so many other athletes, wanted to prove that age was more a state of mind than a foregone conclusion of a deteriorating body. "That's where they get, 'No quarterback can play past 38 or 37,'" Brady said, dismissing the conventional wisdom as age bias.[4]

Peyton Manning was trying to make the same kind of statement with his performance as Brady. In 2013, at age thirty-seven, during his second season as quarterback of the Denver Broncos after his Indianapolis Colts booted him out the door and questions arose about Manning's ability to keep playing because of a neck injury, he recorded the finest season of his career.

Manning put up insane statistics. He completed 450 passes (for the second time in his career), for 5,477 yards and a record 55 touchdown passes, breaking Brady's old mark of 50.

By 2015, some critics were saying that Manning was washed up and should retire. His interceptions exceeded his touchdown passes through the first half of the year. That was very unlike Peyton. Yet it was impossible to determine if nagging injuries were ruining him or not.

What had been consistent about Peyton since his rookie year of 1998 was his brilliant field generalship, fantastic accuracy, and performance under pressure, often bringing his team back from deficits. The Colts with Manning won the Super Bowl over the Chicago Bears in 2007.

"We've won as a team," Manning said. "Everybody did their part. There was no panic. We really won this championship as a team."[5]

Growing up in the house of Archie Manning, pro quarterback, Peyton never really dreamed of becoming anything else in life but a quarterback. No fireman or police officer for Peyton. By the time he was three, he was emulating his father throwing the ball.

Manning was renowned for his work ethic, his willingness to invest time watching film and studying the playbook. He looked for every edge and poured his heart into preparation. His motto was to do whatever it took to be the best and to make sure his team was well-positioned to win a game. This all went to his ambitious side. Peyton wanted to start and start right away. He wanted to determine outcomes.

The Mannings grew up in New Orleans because that's where their dad had made his career. And they did grow up, both Peyton and Eli. Peyton is 6-foot-5 and 230 pounds. He would tower over many of the top quarterbacks of the past. Manning exhibited a rifle arm, but what he really had was a keen eye for developing action. He was the king of audibles, changing the offense's play at the line of scrimmage.

Manning studied so long and hard that just about each time he stepped behind center, he was able to recognize opposing formats and tendencies and adapt. Over the years, Manning developed a soft public image, as a nice guy with a big heart who signed autographs for kids and gave millions of dollars to charitable projects. He has even acted as a comedian in commercials and as host of *Saturday Night Live*, demonstrating to the world that he has a sense of humor.

Manning never had a sense of humor about game preparation. He parked the jokes and delved into material the way a computer programmer might. Data in, results out. Manning was good enough as a freshman at Tennessee to chase off others who never thought they could really compete with him for the quarterback job. They transferred to other schools. Todd Helton, who became a standout Major League Baseball player, read the handwriting on the wall with Peyton's arrival and wisely cast his lot with the Volunteers' baseball team and ultimately the Colorado Rockies.

The Indianapolis Colts could have botched it. They had the number-one draft pick, but they weren't wedded to Manning. Many football people felt Ryan Leaf was a better pro prospect. The Colts avoided the big mistake by choosing Manning. Leaf, from Washington State, was drafted by the San Diego Chargers. He got into embarrassing trouble, didn't perform on the field, and even after his short NFL career got into more legal entanglements.

It only took about ten minutes of his rookie year for Manning to prove he was a better player than Leaf. He spent the next two decades reminding people who had even tried to equate the two players just how foolish their thinking went.

In a famously reported exchange, when Manning met with Colts owner Robert Irsay and the boss still seemed to hesitate who to select with his number-one pick, Manning turned to him and said, "You know, Mr. Irsay, I'll win for you."[6] It was a simple enough statement, but the Colts hadn't done much winning for a while. Losing big was the reason they were even in the Peyton Manning sweepstakes. Something about the way Manning said it, with sincerity and commitment, helped sway Irsay into believing Manning was the right man for the job.

Manning did not win the Heisman Trophy as a senior in college, but he did win the Sullivan Award as the best amateur athlete in the country.

The honor was special for him, given its long history. "It's really very humbling when a person is selected to receive an award for something he loves to do," Manning said. "It's even more rewarding for me to receive the Sullivan Award today because its voters traditionally look beyond statistics and highlights. Instead they look at the person and what he or she represents."[7]

It didn't take very long at all for Manning as a rookie to impress NFL critics. After watching him play just a few games, sportswriters were telling readers how he was one of the all-time great passers. That was early in Manning's third season, and he thought his rooters gushed too much when they said he was great. He might have been right about that glib commentary then, but after a number of years running the show with the Colts, Manning would have been able to use the word "great" with impunity. Manning certainly grew into the role.

He spent enormous amounts of time studying film—his thirst for knowledge was legendary—both at Tennessee and with the Colts, gaining the nickname "Caveman." It was applied because he spent so much time sitting in the dark watching game films, trying to pick up every edge he could. That also gave Manning a nerdlike image for a while. It wasn't just the film preparation either. At times he sounded like a goal-oriented college student. "An athlete has to have goals—for a day, for a lifetime—and I like to put mine in writing so that afterward I can check the design against the finished product," he said.[8]

Manning was viewed as straitlaced, but he began doing TV commercials where the lighthearted side of his personality shone through. When he hosted *Saturday Night Live* in 2007, it was also clear he was a big star who could make fun of himself. Some of his skits were hilarious. That night changed his image forever. He would appear on the show again in 2008 and 2015.

When Manning split with the Indianapolis Colts, he faced an uncertain future. He assured people he would be healthy, and he was proven right. But the Colts did not want to lock into an expensive deal with him to keep him around. There were some questions about his neck, but by 2015 he had been with the Denver Broncos for four seasons. For the first three years Manning continued to rack up the yardage and the touchdown passes, and he led Denver to a Super Bowl, even though the Broncos lost to the Seattle Seahawks.

In 2015 Manning endured some of the most difficult stretches of his career. There were plenty of flashes of brilliance on the order of what he had shown for seventeen years. Yet although the Broncos kept winning, Manning was throwing an unusually large number of interceptions and a surprisingly low number of touchdown passes. The overall performance did raise the question of whether Manning was in his final season.

The common belief was that for sure, if Denver won it all, he would retire. Whether this was a false alarm and Manning would catch fire during the second half of the season, or play out the string with nagging little injuries and at somewhat less than full power, it almost did not matter in the long-run analysis of his career.

He was going to go out with the most wins by a quarterback, the most yards thrown, and the most touchdown passes thrown, as well as being the sport's only five-time Most Valuable Player. Manning set his records, notably his single-season mark of 55 touchdown passes, after he underwent four surgeries on his neck, had numbness in his hand, and had aged beyond the point where most quarterbacks fade out.

Manning was nearing the end of a stupendous career. Whether he was reluctant or not, he did retire after a second Super Bowl championship. There is no question that he will forever be in the mix for the title of greatest quarterback of all time, no matter who else comes along.

CHAPTER 27 • Home on the Range

After Sammy Baugh completed his assignment as an assistant coach with the Detroit Lions in the mid-1960s, he returned to his ranch in Rotan, Texas, just as he always did during the off-seasons when no football was being played. Over the decades, Baugh told everyone how he felt about Texas and his home range. He didn't want to leave it if he didn't have to be anywhere else. More and more over the years, he found fewer reasons to do so.

Baugh also decided he didn't much like flying, so he gave that up almost entirely. The invitations came to make appearances, but Baugh rarely ventured outside of Texas. As he aged and his children grew up, it took more than a tow truck to haul him off the ranch. It was his favorite place in the world, his own special place, and Baugh didn't see much else out there in the wide world that interested him.

Baugh did not crave bright lights. Celebrity status did not define or woo him. He knew what he had done, and he didn't much brag about being a great quarterback or a pioneer thrower. But he wasn't beyond reminiscing, especially if a sportswriter made the trek to his West Texas ranch for a visit. He would entertain with tales of his Redskins days, also telling stories about riding horses and how he did actually eventually become a cowboy, though many years after George Preston Marshall talked him into dressing like one.

Baugh's body rhythm was well-suited to the farmer-rancher lifestyle. He rose at 4:30 a.m., possibly beating any rooster in the neighborhood to early crowing. He dressed in jeans and a cowboy hat and boots and saddled his horse. Over the years Baugh kept expanding his ranch and built it up to thirty-five thousand acres. There was always plenty of room to ride.

As far as his wife, Edmonia, was concerned, the ranch was the best place to be as well. She was no big-city gal, and she got used to the lifestyle in a small town where most of the company on a daily basis was the cattle. Baugh did not grow up in the saddle, but he adapted. Later, after he was done with football, Baugh became a decent roper and competed in rodeos. Marshall's throwaway comment about Baugh being the Texas state roping champ was premature by decades.

The sportswriters who visited Rotan ate up the color that they translated to their home audiences in NFL cities a thousand or more miles away. It was a pretty neat moment for one of them when Baugh extended his arm and hand in the air as all those who live off the bounty of rainfall do to test any waters falling from the sky, even if it was only a few drops trickling down.

"We sure could use a lot of rain," Baugh said once. "Been pretty droughty down this way and there just isn't enough grass on the range for the cattle to keep going."[1] Baugh half-sounded like Walter Brennan playing a role on the big screen as he assessed his Herefords.

That rain comment was actually made during one of the earliest of all visits by a writer to Rotan. Baugh was still dabbling in coaching. At least he kept a close watch on pro football and the quarterbacks who started out before he retired or soon after. He had kind words for Otto Graham, Bobby Layne, and Norm Van Brocklin. Baugh may have been far removed from the pro football scene—more and more so in the ensuing years—but he did keep up with developments.

The Washington newspapers, the *Post* and the *Star*, and the big Texas papers were the most avid suitors for a moment of Mr. Baugh's time. Baugh never was forgotten in Washington, nor should he have been, and every once in a while whoever was running the sports department of a local paper sent a man with a compass and a map to West Texas to cajole Baugh into talkative nostalgia.

The Double Mountain Ranch was close by the mountain of the same name and the Brazos River. Rotan's population was about twenty-four hundred in the 1970s. You can bet that a stranger showing up in town was noticed. Probably most of the residents figured out quickly that any newcomer had to be looking for Sammy for a chat about the good old days or the current NFL days.

Baugh didn't drink or smoke, although in his younger days he was sometimes caught on camera with a cigar in his mouth. He did cuss, though, always did. In rereading old Baugh quotes, one must wonder if they were uttered in that form or had been edited for public consumption, given that four-letter words were common in his vocabulary.

Baugh wasn't one to pretend that all of the players from his era were better than all of the younger players. He also didn't believe football was as exciting during his career as it became when he was a senior citizen. He appreciated the faster players, the more aggressive offensive style, and even players being specialists instead of being impressed into handling three jobs per game—as he did as quarterback, defensive back, and punter. "Football is a great game today," Baugh said in the 1970s.[2]

After the loud and vituperative back-and-forth newspaper war with Harry Wismer that ended with a truce and the announced commitment for Baugh to be paid the final year on his New York salary, many years later Sammy said he never did get paid all he was owed. "I was goldanged mad at the time," Baugh said. "But later I felt sorry for Harry. He lost a lot of money in that team. He began to drink and you couldn't talk to him and make sense unless you caught him in the morning."[3]

As Baugh aged, he not only put away any footballs lying around, but he retired his rope and took up golf. It was a way to kill time and yet still was a sport. He needed to fill his days after his wife died in 1990. He hung on in the cattle business, switching to the Beefmaster brand, even when he wasn't up to riding anymore. Before that he did break an arm once when a bull ran into him.

One thing those visitors always wanted to talk about was the 73-0 game. The Chicago Bears' unbelievable triumph had grown in stature and was entrenched in NFL lore. The score was never going to change. Baugh reprised his comment that if the Redskins had scored the first touchdown, the final score would have been 73-7.

However, nearly sixty years after the game was played, one of those writers caught Baugh thinking differently about the 1940 game. Baugh was eighty-five years old when he gave an interview to the Associated Press during which, for the first time, he said he wondered if the game was on the up-and-up. Baugh said he suspected that teammates angry with Marshall stopped trying. Baugh said he had no proof of his allegations that the Redskins threw the game but thought that players may not have given their all in retaliation for Marshall's inflammatory remarks about the Bears.

"He put things in the paper running the Bears down," Baugh said of Marshall in 1999. "You don't want to help the other team. You shouldn't say things like that. It made us so mad. They decided not to play."[4]

At the time, having lost by 73 unanswered points, Marshall made a similar comment that was chalked up to sour grapes. That insult was coming out of the mouth of an owner who had made so many ill-advised statements in recent weeks that it didn't have a long shelf life. Baugh did not speak up for six decades before giving interviews to a Texas TV station and the wire service. "I never said anything," Baugh said. "I never had anything to go on except for the way the team played. I just said I had doubts about how the game was played."[5]

Most of the players who participated in the game had died by the time Baugh talked about a sort of fix being in. He seemed not to truly be aware of what a sensation his words would cause. One still-living teammate was lineman Clyde Shugart, who expressed disbelief about what Baugh said. "Was he drunk when he said that?" Shugart asked.[6]

Since Baugh was not a drinker, it didn't seem likely. "They turned on Mr. Marshall," Baugh said of the Redskins. "They had been running him down for a year. I swear I think they wanted to hurt Mr. Marshall more than anything. I never talked to the league because I didn't have any proof and I still don't. It doesn't keep me from thinking, though."[7]

There was an outcry that Baugh should have stayed quiet without proof and a belief in some quarters he was imagining the whole thing. Baugh otherwise never created controversy with his football talk from down on the ranch.

Before Baugh's moratorium on visits to Washington took full effect, he occasionally appeared in DC for events. There was one account of Baugh visiting a Redskins practice when Bill McPeak was coaching in the early 1960s. McPeak invited Baugh onto the field to talk to that generation of Redskins. Another time Baugh attended the National Press Club banquet, and his assigned seat was next to Joe DiMaggio, a baseball legend.

The story goes that DiMaggio, apparently unaware that Baugh had played the sport, picked up a baseball sitting on the table and said, "Sammy, I'll bet you wouldn't know what to do with this ball." Baugh could have mentioned his minor-league baseball experience, but instead joked around. He said, "Just pump a little air into it and I'll show you."[8]

When the Pro Football Hall of Fame opened in Canton, Ohio, in 1963, Baugh was still in the coaching ranks. They threw a big shindig to honor the first class. That group consisted of seventeen men, many of them legends like Baugh. Marshall went in with Baugh. So did Bears founder and owner George Halas, Red Grange, Bronko Nagurski, Jim Thorpe, Ernie Nevers, and Don Hutson.

In late June 1997, Hutson, the great Green Bay Packers receiver, died, and as a courtesy the Hall of Fame telephoned Baugh at his ranch. What he was told, much to his surprise, was that he was the last surviving member of the charter class. At the time Baugh was eighty-four.

"I was shocked," Baugh said. "I knew a lot of the others had died, but I sure didn't know I was the last. You know, it feels kind of strange. Well, in this case, last is a hell of a lot better than first."[9]

Late in life Baugh was more reluctant than ever to leave Rotan and the ranch, even when an organization like the Redskins was honoring him for his deeds on the gridiron. "I appreciate everything people want me to do," Baugh said. "But I just don't want to leave home any more than I have to. And I don't have to."[10]

Baugh lived long enough to see the sports collectible world explode. He turned down invitations to card shows and for public appearances. What Baugh did do, periodically, was sign autographs for people who mailed him memorabilia. He saved up a bunch and then did them all at once, always signing "Sam," not the longer version of his first name. "People have always wanted me to sign 'Slingin' Sammy Baugh,'" he said. "But I can sign 'Sam Baugh' twice as fast. And I try to sign everything. It just may take a while."[11]

As an illustration of how the demand for star players' autographs had changed, indeed providing a fairly good living for many players who did not earn big salaries during their playing days, Baugh said he was once offered twenty thousand dollars to sign autographs for two hours in Dallas and Fort Worth. He turned down the opportunity. "I wouldn't trust any sumbitch that claimed he was going to pay me that much money to sign my name," Baugh said.[12]

Well into old age, Baugh watched football. He frequently praised the modern-day player for his skill. He believed Joe Namath besting the Baltimore Colts was one of the best-executed, most masterful performances by a quarterback of all time. When Namath was still young, Baugh predicted he could become the best of all time, even better than Sammy Baugh, as long as his knees stayed healthy, which did not occur.

Baugh was eighty years old in 1994 when he made himself available for some pictures throwing a football. He tossed a few and admitted he hadn't thrown a ball since 1966. "I gotta admit," Baugh said, "that felt pretty goddamned good. If I threw a few times a week my ol' arm might feel all right."[13]

Baugh said he promised himself that when he could stay on the ranch, he would stay on the ranch. But once in a great, great while, he could be enticed off the land. He was honored when chosen for the NFL's seventy-fifth-anniversary team, which brought an avalanche of attention. He did not duck that attention, and year after year he would talk football with anyone willing to find the way to Rotan.

Many said Baugh was a recluse, but that's not how he saw it. "Hell, anybody who wants to find me knows I'm right here," he said of being on the ranch. "I don't like a city and I don't like a town. I spent half my life away from home playing football and I said when I was finished I would never leave here."[14]

One of the attractions of the ranch, besides peace and quiet, and all of the cattle, was looking up at Double Mountain. Baugh was comforted by the sight of it. When he was middle-aged and ranching and went for long horseback rides, he said he rode up the mountain once a week.

"I fell in love with that damn mountain," he said. "I just like to see it."[15]

It was one of the great loves of his life, along with Edmonia, his wife of fifty-two years, playing football, and being a ranch owner. Baugh died on December 17, 2008, at the age of ninety-four. Sammy Baugh, the man who might be the greatest legend in National Football League history for lifting the passing game out of the dark ages, kept gazing at that damn mountain as long as he could.

NOTES

Introduction

1. Booton Herndon, *Football's Greatest Quarterbacks* (New York: Bartholomew House, 1961), 91.

Chapter 1

1. Vahe Gregorian, "SLU Was the Pioneer, Sept. 5, 1906," *St. Louis Post-Dispatch*, September 4, 2006.
2. David Nelson, *The Anatomy of a Game: Football, the Rules, and the Men Who Made the Game* (Newark: University of Delaware Press, 1994), 128–29.
3. Gregorian, "SLU Was the Pioneer."
4. Eddie Cochems (with editor Walter Camp), *How to Play Football*, Spalding Football Guide (New York: American Sports Publishing Co., 1907), 51.
5. Eddie Cochems, "Football Like an Airship Would Open Up the Game," *Washington Post*, December 5, 1909.
6. Brian Kunderman, "Football's Forward Pass Turns 100 Years Old," St. Louis University Public Relations Office, September 4, 2006.
7. Kevin McGuire, "Bradbury Robinson, Father of the Forward Pass," www.no2minutewarning.com, March 7, 2013.
8. Ibid.

Chapter 2

1. Brian Kunderman, "Football's Forward Pass Turns 100 Years Old," St. Louis University Public Relations Office, September 4, 2006.
2. Ibid.
3. "Greatest Coaching Decisions," ESPN.com, December 23, 1999.

4. Frank P. Maggio, *Notre Dame and the Game That Changed Football* (New York: Carroll & Graf, 2007), 84.
5. Harry Cross, "Inventing the Forward Pass," *New York Times*, November 1, 1913.
6. Ibid.
7. Maggio, *Notre Dame*, 90.
8. Ibid., 100.
9. Ibid., 111.
10. Ibid., 117–18.
11. Ibid,. 192–93.

Chapter 3

1. Joe Holley, *Slingin' Sam* (Austin: University of Texas Press, 2012), 14.
2. Mike Cochran and John Lumpkin, *West Texas: A Portrait of Its People and Their Raw and Wondrous Land* (Lubbock: Texas Tech University Press, 1999), xi.
3. Ibid., 92.
4. Holley, *Slingin' Sam*, 20.
5. Michael Barr, *Remembering Bulldog Turner* (Lubbock: Texas Tech University Press, 2013), 13.
6. Ibid.
7. Ibid., 33.
8. Ibid., 35.

Chapter 4

1. Murray Greenberg, *Passing Game: Benny Friedman and the Transformation of Football* (Philadelphia: Public Affairs Books, 2008), 30.
2. Ibid., 60.
3. Ibid., 61.
4. Ibid., 74.
5. James Tuite, "Benny Friedman, Star Passer at Michigan and with Pros," *New York Times*, November 24, 1982.
6. Greenberg, *Passing Game*, 151.
7. Tuite, "Benny Friedman."
8. Eric Kennedy, "Benny Friedman: The QB Who May Have Saved the New York Giants," www.bigblueinteractive.com, February 13, 2008.
9. George Halas, "Halas Calls Friedman Pioneer Passer—Rest Came by Design," *Chicago Daily News*, February 4, 1967.
10. Barry Gotteher, *The Giants of New York: The History of Professional Football's Most Fabulous Dynasty* (New York: G. P. Putnam's, 1963), 65.

Chapter 5

1. Richard P. McCann, *The Life Story of Sammy Baugh* (St. Louis: C. C. Spink & Son, 1949), 7.
2. Ibid., 8.
3. Whit Canning, *Sam Baugh: The Best There Ever Was* (Indianapolis: Masters Press, 1997), 24.
4. Ibid.
5. Ibid.
6. Ibid.
7. Mark Rea, *The Diehard Fan's Guide to Buckeye Football* (Washington, DC: Regnery Publishing, 2009), 56.
8. Canning, *Sam Baugh*, 29.
9. Joe Holley, *Slingin' Sam* (Austin: University of Texas Press, 2012),.52.
10. Ibid., 55.
11. Ibid., 57.
12. Canning, *Sam Baugh*, 47.

Chapter 6

1. Jim Dent, *Monster of the Midway* (New York: Thomas Dunne Books, 2003), 105.
2. Ibid., 108.
3. Ibid.
4. Cecil Dodge, "Sports Shots," *Lowell* (MA) *Sun*, January 9, 1935.

Chapter 7

1. David Zimmerman, *Curly Lambeau: The Man behind the Mystique* (Hales Corners, WI: Eagle Books, 2013), 29.
2. Ibid., 57.
3. Pro Football Hall of Fame, www.profootballhof.com/hof/member.
4. Zimmerman, *Curly Lambeau*, 88.
5. Ibid., 89.
6. Green Bay Packers, www.packers.com.
7. Zimmerman, *Curly Lambeau*, 89.
8. Martin Hendricks, "Herber Earns a Place in Packers Folklore," *Milwaukee Journal-Sentinel*, June 7, 2007.
9. Cleon Walfoort, "Packers of The Past: Herber Couldn't Thread Needle with Ball, but—," *Milwaukee Journal*, September 1, 2012.

Chapter 8

1. Steve Gelman, *Pro Football Heroes* (New York: Scholastic Book Services, 1968), 57.

2. David Zimmerman, *Curly Lambeau: The Man behind the Mystique* (Hales Corners, WI: Eagle Books, 2013), 111.
3. Zimmerman, *Curly Lambeau*, 113.
4. Gelman, *Pro Football Heroes*, 51.
5. Ibid.
6. Ibid., 54.
7. Zimmerman, *Curly Lambeau*, 125–26.
8. George Sullivan, *Pro Football Greats: Pass to Win* (Champaign, IL: Garrard Publishing, 1968), 84.

Chapter 9

1. David Zimmerman, *Curly Lambeau: The Man behind the Mystique* (Hales Corners, WI: Eagle Books, 2013), 132–33.
2. Ibid., 133.
3. Ibid.
4. George Sullivan, *Pro Football Greats: Pass to Win* (Champaign, IL: Garrard Publishing, 1968), 77.
5. Ibid., 88.
6. Ibid.
7. Ibid., 90.
8. Murray Goodman and Leonard Lewin, *My Greatest Day in Football* (New York: A. S. Barnes and Company, 1948), 124.
9. Ibid., 125.
10. Ibid.
11. Ibid., 126.
12. Peter Jackel, "Hutson's Greatness Apparent on, off Field, Say Friends, Teammates," *Racine* (WI) *Journal Times*, July 6, 1997.
13. Ibid.
14. Goodman and Lewin, *My Greatest Day in Football*, 114.
15. Ibid., 115.
16. Ibid., 116.

Chapter 10

1. Richard P. McCann, *The Life Story of Sammy Baugh* (St. Louis: C.C. Spink & Son, St. Louis, 1949), 27.
2. Ibid.
3. Ibid., 28.
4. Joe Holley, *Slingin' Sam* (Austin: University of Texas Press, 2012), 98.
5. Ibid.
6. Ibid., 99.

7. Ibid., 104–5.
8. Ibid., 107.

Chapter 11

1. Jack Doyle, "Slingin' Sammy, 1930s–1950s," pophistorydig.com, December 21, 2008.
2. Ibid.
3. Ibid.
4. Joe Holley, *Slingin' Sam* (Austin: University of Texas Press, 2012), 111.
5. Slingin' Sam Baugh, "A Football Hero's Own Story: Second in a Series," North American Newspaper Alliance, October 18, 1937.
6. Slingin' Sam Baugh, "A Football Hero's Own Story: Third in a Series," North American Newspaper Alliance, October 19, 1937.
7. Ibid.
8. Ibid.
9. Ibid.
10. Ibid.
11. Ibid.
12. Slingin' Sam Baugh, "A Football Hero's Own Story: Fourth in a Series," North American Newspaper Alliance, October 20, 1937.
13. Ibid.

Chapter 12

1. Ted Brock, "Air Show on a Frozen Midway," National Football League game program, November 6, 1977.
2. Ibid.
3. Jim Dent, *Monster of the Midway* (New York: Thomas Dunne Books, 2003), 212.
4. Ibid., 187.
5. Ibid., 210.
6. Ibid., 210–11.
7. "Sammy Baugh Idol of Fans; Team Mobbed," Associated Press, December 12, 1937.
8. Bernie Harter, "Another Angle," *Washington Herald*, December 12, 1937.
9. Brock, "Air Show."
10. Shirley Povich, "This Morning, Slingin' Sammy Baugh, a Real Hero," *Washington Post*, December 12, 1937.
11. Joe Holley, *Slingin' Sam* (Austin: University of Texas Press, 2012), 135.
12. Ibid.

Chapter 13

1. Jim Kluttz, "How Baugh Got $25,000 from the Redskins—For Three Years," *Washington Post*, June 24, 1994.
2. Ibid.
3. Ibid.
4. Wilfrid Smith, "Bears Find Out Why They Call Baugh the Best," *Chicago Tribune*, December 13, 1937.
5. Ibid.
6. Ibid.
7. Joe Holley, *Slingin' Sam* (Austin: University of Texas Press, 2012), 143.
8. Ibid., 145.
9. Murray Goodman and Leonard Lewin, *My Greatest Day in Football* (New York: A. S. Barnes and Company, 1948), 20.
10. Ibid.
11. Ibid., 20 and 22.
12. Ibid., 22.
13. Ibid.
14. Ibid., 22–23.
15. Ibid., 23.
16. David Elfin, "Redskins Recover 1937 Glory," *Washington Times*, March 2, 1996.
17. Richard P. McCann, *The Life Story of Sammy Baugh* (St. Louis: C.C. Spink & Son, 1949), 29.
18. Holley, *Slingin' Sam*, 154.

Chapter 14

1. Bill Jauss and Ed Stone, "Bears' Luckman Dies," *Chicago Tribune*, July 6, 1998.
2. Sid Luckman, *Passing for Touchdowns* (Chicago: Ziff Publishing, 1948), 8.
3. Ibid.
4. Ibid., 8–9.
5. Ibid., 9.
6. Ibid.
7. Sid Luckman, *Luckman at Quarterback: Football as a Sport and a Career* (Chicago: Ziff Publishing, 1949), 1.
8. Ibid., 1–2.
9. Ibid., 2.
10. Ibid., 16.
11. "Yesterday's Heroes: Clyde 'Bulldog' Turner," National Football League game program, December 28, 1980.
12. Jauss and Stone, "Bears' Luckman Dies."

13. Ibid.
14. Luckman, *Luckman at Quarterback*, 32.
15. Ibid., 56.

Chapter 15

1. Michael Barr, *Remembering Bulldog Turner: Unsung Monster of the Midway* (Lubbock: Texas Tech University Press, 2013), 101.
2. Ibid., 101–2.
3. Ibid., 102.
4. "Pro Football's Most Famous Game—Or Was It Infamous?" *The Fifth Down* newsletter, Pro Football Hall of Fame, citing Dwight Chapin of the *Los Angeles Times*, 1975.
5. Ibid.
6. Bill Jauss, "'40 Title Rout of Redskins Defined Age of Luckman," *Chicago Tribune*, July 6, 1998.
7. Morris Siegel, "Luckman Recalls 73-0 Holocaust," *Washington Star*, August 17, 1963.
8. Ibid.
9. Robert Cannon, "Sid Luckman and the Destruction of Washington," *Sports Collectors Digest*, March 10, 1995.
10. "Sid Luckman Recalls Historic NFL Rout," United Press International, December 7, 1980.
11. Joe Holley, *Slingin' Sam* (Austin: University of Texas Press, 2012), 170.
12. Ibid., 171.
13. Ibid.

Chapter 16

1. "Sid Luckman Hall of Fame Biography," Pro Football Hall of Fame, www.profootballhof.com, permanent section.
2. Sid Luckman, *Luckman at Quarterback: Football as a Sport and a Career* (Chicago: Ziff Publishing, 1949), 105.
3. Ibid.
4. Ibid., 106.
5. Ibid., 107.
6. Tommy Devine, "Brain of the Bears," *Sportfolio*, September 1947.
7. Ibid.
8. Joe Holley, *Slingin' Sam* (Austin: University of Texas Press, 2012), 173.
9. Ibid., 173.
10. Ibid., 174.

Chapter 17

1. Joe Holley, *Slingin' Sam* (Austin: University of Texas Press, 2012), 198.
2. "Pro Football's Most Famous Game—Or Was It Infamous?" *The Fifth Down* newsletter, Pro Football Hall of Fame, citing Dwight Chapin of the *Los Angeles Times*, 1975.
3. Sid Luckman, *Luckman at Quarterback: Football as a Sport and a Career* (Chicago: Ziff Publishing, 1949), 130.
4. Ibid., 128.
5. Bob Addie, "What Makes Sammy Baugh?" *Sportfolio*, December 1947.
6. Ibid.
7. Luckman, *Luckman at Quarterback*, 129.
8. Ibid.

Chapter 18

1. Jerry Coffey, "At 77, Sammy Baugh Remembers His Passing Fancy," *Fort Worth Star-Telegram*, October 6, 1991.
2. Jonathan Moore, "Slingin' Sammy," Associated Press, September 2, 1994.
3. "Luckman Pitches 7 Touchdowns," Associated Press, November 14, 1943.
4. "Bears Win, 56-7; Luckman Sets Pass Record," Chicago Tribune Wire Services, November 15, 1943.
5. Booton Herndon, *Football's Greatest Quarterbacks* (New York: Bartholomew House, 1961), 39.
6. Murray Goodman and Leonard Lewin, *My Greatest Day in Football* (New York: A. S. Barnes and Company, 1948), 140.
7. Ibid., 140, 142.
8. John Wiebusch, "There Was War on the Homefront, Too, in 1943," *NFL Gameday Magazine*, November 3, 1986.
9. Ibid.
10. Sid Luckman, *Luckman at Quarterback: Football as a Sport and a Career* (Chicago: Ziff Publishing, 1949), 131.
11. Ibid.
12. Ibid., 132.

Chapter 19

1. Sid Luckman, *Luckman at Quarterback: Football as a Sport and a Career* (Chicago: Ziff Publishing, 1949), 135.
2. Ibid., 135–36.
3. William N. Wallace, "Sid Luckman, Star for the Bears, Dies at 81," *New York Times*, July 6, 1998.
4. Luckman, *Luckman at Quarterback*, 184–85.

5. Ibid., 186.
6. Bill Jauss and Ed Stone, "Bears' Luckman Dies," *Chicago Tribune*, July 6, 1998.
7. Ibid.
8. Bess Winakor, "More Than 40 Years after His Brilliant Football Career Ended, Sid Luckman Is Still a Legend around Chicago," *Chicago Tribune*, July 11, 1995.
9. Ibid.
10. Ibid.
11. Sid Luckman, *Passing for Touchdowns* (Chicago: Ziff Publishing, 1948), 26–27.
12. Winakor, "More Than 40 Years."

Chapter 20

1. "Baugh Greatest of All—It's Unanimous," United Press International, December 1937.
2. Ibid.
3. Ibid.
4. Jim Garner, "Slingin' Sammy—Mr. Quarterback," *Texas Christian University Game Program*, 1970.
5. Richard P. McCann, *The Life Story of Sammy Baugh* (St. Louis: C.C. Spink & Son, 1949), 65.
6. Ibid., 67.
7. Sammy Baugh and Shirley Povich, "Dealing 'Em off the Arm," *Washington Post*, (date missing) 1937, in Pro Football Hall of Fame Library Archives.
8. Ibid.
9. Ibid.
10. McCann, *Life Story of Sammy Baugh*, 67.
11. Ibid., 71.
12. Steve Gelman, *Pro Football Heroes* (New York: Scholastic Book Services, 1968), 77.
13. Joe Holley, *Slingin' Sam* (Austin: University of Texas Press, 2012), 222.
14. "Sammy Baugh: Greatest of Passers Changed the Game," *Washington Star*, November 22, 1966.
15. Ibid.
16. Ibid.
17. Ibid.
18. Sam Blair, "Kick It Again, Sam," *Dallas Morning News*, April 29, 1974.
19. Charles Richards, "Slingin' Sammy: Baugh's Marks Came under Tougher Conditions," Associated Press (date missing), in Pro Football Hall of Fame Research Library.

20. Ibid.
21. John McClain, "The Last Gunslinger," *Houston Chronicle*, July 26, 1998.
22. Ibid.
23. Bud Buczkowske, "Slingin' Sammy," *Benecia* (CA) *Herald*, August 6, 1991.
24. Holley, *Slingin' Sam*, 244.
25. Morris Siegel, "Slingin' Sam Quits—14 Years after He Planned 'Retiring,'" *All Sports News*, December 17, 1952.
26. Ibid.
27. Ibid.
28. Sam Blair, "First of the Great Passers," *Quarterback Magazine*, 1969.
29. Ibid.

Chapter 21

1. Booton Herndon, *Football's Greatest Quarterbacks* (New York: Bartholomew House, 1961), 44.
2. Ibid., 45.
3. Ibid., 54.
4. "Bob Waterfield Biography," Pro Football Hall of Fame, www.profootballhof.com.
5. Rob Fernas, "Complete Package," *Los Angeles Times*, December 25, 1999.
6. Herndon, *Football's Greatest Quarterbacks*, 135.
7. Ibid., 136.
8. Ibid., 73.
9. Ibid., 78.
10. Y. A. Tittle and Don Smith, *I Pass!* (New York: Franklin Watts, 1964), 243.
11. Ibid., 258.
12. Duey Graham, *OttoMatic: Otto Graham* (Wayne, MI: Immortal Investments Publishing, 2004), 75.
13. Ibid., 77.
14. George Sullivan, *Pro Football Greats: Pass to Win* (Champaign, IL: Garrard Publishing, 1968), 57.
15. Ibid., 64.
16. Ibid.
17. Graham, *OttoMatic*, 109.
18. Ibid., 112.
19. Ibid.
20. Ibid., 140.
21. Herndon, *Football's Greatest Quarterbacks*, 63.
22. Graham, *OttoMatic*, 140.
23. Sullivan, *Pro Football Greats*, 67.

Chapter 22

1. Lou Sahadi, *Johnny Unitas: America's Quarterback* (Chicago: Triumph Books, 2004), 45.
2. Ibid., 20.
3. Ibid., 23.
4. Ibid.
5. Ibid., 25.
6. "Johnny Unitas Biography," Pro Football Hall of Fame, www.profootballhof.com.
7. Bob Carter, "Unitas Surprised Them All," ESPN.com (n.d.).
8. Ibid.
9. Sahadi, *Johnny Unitas*, 219.

Chapter 23

1. David Boss, Jim Campbell, Seymour Siwoff, Rick Smith, and Bennett Wiebusch, *The NFL's Official Encyclopedic History of Professional Football* (New York: Macmillan, 1977), 245–51.
2. Michael McCambridge, *America's Game: The Epic Story of How Pro Football Captured a Nation* (New York: Random House, 2004), 13.
3. Ibid.,.64.
4. Joe Horrigan and John Thorn, *The Pro Football Hall of Fame 50th Anniversary Book: Where Greatness Lives* (New York: Grand Central Publishing, 2012), 129.
5. "Sid Gillman, Airing It Out," ESPN.com, June 10, 2013.
6. Horrigan and Thorn, *Pro Football Hall of Fame 50th Anniversary Book*, 26.
7. Ibid., 127.
8. Frank Litsky and Bruce Weber, "George Blanda, Hall of Fame Football Player, Dies at 83," New York Times, September 27, 2010.
9. Joe Willie Namath and Dick Schaap, I Can't Wait until Tomorrow . . . 'Cause I Get Better Looking Every Day (New York: Random House, 1969), 205.
10. Ibid., 206.
11. Horrigan and Thorn, *Pro Football Hall of Fame 50th Anniversary Book*, 128.
12. Namath and Schaap, *I Can't Wait until Tomorrow*, 49.
13. Ibid.
14. Ibid., 55.
15. Ibid., 58.
16. Ibid., 59.
17. *New York Daily News*, "Superduper!" January 13, 1969

Chapter 24

1. William J. Ryczek, *Crash of the Titans: The Early Years of the New York Jets and the AFL* (Jefferson, NC: McFarland and Company, 2009), 37.

2. Ibid., 41.
3. Ibid.
4. Ibid.
5. Ibid.
6. Ibid., 42.
7. Ibid., 198.
8. Ibid., 199.
9. Michael Barr, *Remembering Bulldog Turner, Unsung Monster of the Midway* (Lubbock: Texas Tech University Press, 2013), 160.
10. Ibid.
11. Howard M. Tuckner, "Titans to Pay Off Baugh in Full; Owner, Ex-Coach Part Friends," *New York Times*, July 18, 1962.
12. Ibid.
13. Ibid.
14. Ryczek, *Crash of the Titans*, 43.
15. Ibid., 42.
16. Joe Holley, *Slingin' Sam* (Austin: University of Texas Press, 2012), 262–63.
17. Ibid., 270.
18. Pro Football Hall of Fame profile, Sammy Baugh, 1963 (upon induction).

Chapter 25

1. Steve Cameron, *Brett Favre: Huck Finn Grows Up* (Indianapolis: Masters Press, 1997), 126.
2. Ibid., 131.
3. Ibid.
4. Ibid., 153.
5. Joe Horrigan and John Thorn, *The Pro Football Hall of Fame 50th Anniversary Book: Where Greatness Lives* (New York: Grand Central Publishing, 2012), 130.
6. Ibid., 230.
7. Ibid., 221.
8. Keith Dunnavant, *Montana: The Biography of Football's Joe Cool* (New York: Thomas Dunne Books, 2015), 105.
9. Ibid., 132.
10. Ibid., 146.
11. Ibid., 175.
12. Ibid., 179.
13. "Montana Has His Day at Hall," Associated Press, August 31, 2000.

Chapter 26

1. "Drew Brees Ties NFL Mark with 7 TDs," ESPN.com News Services, November 1, 2015.
2. Gary Myers, *Brady versus Manning: The Untold Story of the Rivalry That Transformed the NFL* (New York: Crown Archetype, 2015), 239.
3. Tom Chiarella, "Just Throw the Damn Ball, Tom Brady," *Esquire*, August 6, 2008.
4. Mark Leibovich, "Tom Brady Cannot Stop," *New York Times Magazine*, January 26, 2015.
5. Lew Freedman, *Peyton Manning: A Biography* (Santa Barbara, CA: Greenwood Press / ABC-CLIO, 2009), 8.
6. Ibid., 92.
7. Ibid., 89.
8. Ibid., 110.

Chapter 27

1. "Baugh at Home on the Range," United Press International, January 10, 1955.
2. Dave Brady, "Sammy Baugh: He's Content to Remain on His Ranch," *Washington Post*, October 15, 1978.
3. Ibid.
4. Hal Bock, "Baugh Thinks Washington Tried to Lose '40 Title Game," Associated Press, November 28, 1999.
5. Ibid.
6. Ibid.
7. Ibid.
8. "Samuel Adrian Baugh, Football's First Great Passer" (missing publication and exact date, 1973), Pro Football Hall of Fame Library Archives.
9. John McLain, "Legendary Texan Baugh Is Final Link to Football's Hall of Fame Pioneers," *Houston Chronicle* (date missing), in Pro Football Hall of Fame Library Archives.
10. Ibid.
11. Ibid.
12. Ibid.
13. Dennis Tuttle, "Still Slingin'," *Sporting News*, November 7, 1994.
14. Ibid.
15. Ibid.

BIBLIOGRAPHY

Books

Barr, Michael. *Remembering Bulldog Turner.* Lubbock: Texas Tech University Press, 2013.

Boss, David, Jim Campbell, Seymour Siwoff, Rick Smith, and Bennett Wiebusch. *The NFL's Official Encyclopedic History of Professional Football.* New York: Macmillan, 1977.

Cameron, Steve. *Brett Favre: Huck Finn Grows Up.* Indianapolis: Masters Press, 1997.

Canning, Whit. *Sam Baugh: The Best There Ever Was.* Indianapolis: Masters Press, 1997.

Cochems, Eddie (with editor Walter Camp). *How to Play Football.* Spalding Football Guide. New York: American Sports Publishing, 1907.

Cochran, Mike, and John Lumpkin. *West Texas: A Portrait of Its People and Their Raw and Wondrous Land.* Lubbock: Texas Tech University Press, 1999.

Dent, Jim. *Monster of the Midway.* New York: Thomas Dunne Books, 2003.

Dunnavant, Keith. *Montana: The Biography of Football's Joe Cool.* New York: Thomas Dunne Books, 2015.

Freedman, Lew. *Peyton Manning: A Biography.* Santa Barbara, CA: Greenwood Press / ABC-CLIO, 2009.

Gelman, Steve. *Pro Football Heroes.* New York: Scholastic Book Services, 1968.

Goodman, Murray, and Leonard Lewin. *My Greatest Day in Football.* New York: A. S. Barnes and Company, 1948.

Gotteher, Barry. *The Giants of New York: The History of Professional Football's Most Fabulous Dynasty.* New York: G. P. Putnam's, 1963.

Graham, Duey. *OttoMatic: Otto Graham.* Wayne, MI: Immortal Investments Publishing, 2004.

Greenberg, Murray. *Passing Game: Benny Friedman and the Transformation of Football.* Philadelphia: Public Affairs Books, 2008.

Herndon, Booton. *Football's Greatest Quarterbacks.* New York: Bartholomew House, 1961.

Holley, Joe. *Slingin' Sam.* Austin: University of Texas Press, 2012.

Horrigan, Joe, and John Thorn. *The Pro Football Hall of Fame 50th Anniversary Book: Where Greatness Lives.* New York: Grand Central Publishing, 2012.

Luckman, Sid. *Luckman at Quarterback: Football as a Sport and a Career.* Chicago: Ziff Publishing Company, 1949.

———. *Passing for Touchdowns.* Chicago: Ziff, 1948.

Maggio, Frank P. *Notre Dame and the Game That Changed Football.* New York: Carroll & Graf, 2007.

McCambridge, Michael. *America's Game: The Epic Story of How Pro Football Captured a Nation.* New York: Random House, 2004.

McCann, Richard P. *The Life Story of Sammy Baugh.* St. Louis: C. C. Spink & Son, 1949.

Myers, Gary. *Brady versus Manning: The Untold Story of the Rivalry That Transformed the NFL.* New York: Crown Archetype, 2015.

Namath, Joe Willie, and Dick Schaap. *I Can't Wait until Tomorrow . . . 'Cause I Get Better Looking Every Day.* New York: Random House, 1969.

Nelson, David. *The Anatomy of a Game: Football, the Rules, and the Men Who Made the Game.* Newark: University of Delaware Press, 1994.

Rea, Mark. *The Diehard Fan's Guide to Buckeye Football.* Washington, DC: Regnery Publishing, 2009.

Ryczek, William J. *Crash of the Titans: The Early Years of the New York Jets and the AFL.* Jefferson, NC: McFarland and Company, 2009.

Sahadi, Lou. *Johnny Unitas: America's Quarterback.* Chicago: Triumph Books, 2004.

Sullivan, George. *Pro Football Greats: Pass to Win.* Champaign, IL: Garrard, 1968.

Tittle, Y. A., and Don Smith. *I Pass!* New York: Franklin Watts, 1964.

Zimmerman, David. *Curly Lambeau: The Man behind the Mystique.* Hales Corners, WI: Eagle Books, 2013.

Magazines and Periodicals

All Sports News

Esquire

National Football League game programs

New York Times Magazine

Pro Football Hall of Fame *Fifth Down* newsletter

Quarterback Magazine

Sports Collectors Digest
Sportfolio
Sporting News
Texas Christian University game program

Newspapers

Benecia (CA) *Herald*
Chicago Daily News
Chicago Tribune
Dallas Morning News
Fort Worth Star-Telegram
Houston Chronicle
Los Angeles Times
Lowell (MA) *Sun*
Milwaukee Journal
Milwaukee Journal-Sentinel
New York Times
Racine (WI) *Journal Times*
St. Louis Post-Dispatch
Washington Herald
Washington Post
Washington Star
Washington Times

Websites

bigblueinteractive.com
espn.com
no2minutewarning.com
packers.com
pophistorydig.com
profootballhof.com

Wire Services

Associated Press
North American Newspaper Alliance
United Press International

Other

Pro Football Hall of Fame Research Library, undated material.
St. Louis University Public Relations Office.

Index

References to illustrations are indicated in **bold** uppercase letters

ABOUT THE AUTHOR

Lew Freedman is the author of numerous books about sports and Alaska. A veteran journalist, he has worked on the staffs of the *Chicago Tribune*, *Philadelphia Inquirer*, and *Anchorage Daily News* and currently is a columnist, feature writer, and sports reporter for the *Cody Enterprise* in Wyoming. Freedman was inducted into the US Basketball Writers Hall of Fame in 2018.

His previous book for the Texas Tech University Press is *Becoming Iron Men: The Story of the 1963 Loyola Ramblers*, the story of the Loyola University of Chicago men's basketball team capturing the 1963 NCAA title in the face of adversity.

Among his books on football, Freedman has written *73-0! Bears over Redskins, The NFL's Greatest Massacre*, and *The Rise of the Seminoles*, the story of Florida State University football's ascension under Coach Bobby Bowden.